'Race is the elephant in the room in all
brave enough to acknowledge it. Martin
just brave, it is fearless. The elephant is fi.
    Shadd Maruna, *Director of Institute of Criminology & Criminal Justice,*
Queen's University Belfast, Northern Ireland, UK.

'Martin Glynn's challenging new book is an important and novel contribution
to debates about desistance – but it is also more than that. Rather than
focusing on how ethnicity affects desistance, he draws on Critical Race
Theory – and on the accounts of "Black British" and "African American"
men he interviewed – to examine how racism and racialisation influenced the
men's life chances and pathways through crime and justice. In seeking to
develop a "black criminology of desistance", Martin Glynn's analysis enjoins
and compels us also to engage with the racialised politics of crime and justice
– and of criminology itself.'
    Fergus McNeill, *Professor of Criminology & Social Work,*
University of Glasgow, Scotland, UK.

'In the book Black Men, Invisibility and Crime, Martin Glynn has produced
an innovative and crucially important monograph that provides keen insights
into desistance among Black men.
    Drawing on Critical Race Theory, Martin skilfully explores the contours of
desistance specific to the condition and experience of Black men. His fresh
comparative perspective provides readers with an examination of the
analogous and divergent desistance concerns among Black men in Britain
and America. Martin is clearly an important scholar on the rise whose
thoughts on re-entry and desistance in the Black community need to be heard
by the discipline and the larger criminal justice community in the UK and the
USA.'
    Shaun Gabbidon, *Professor of Criminal Justice,*
Penn State Harrisburg, USA.

Black men, invisibility and desistance from crime

Past studies have suggested that offenders desist from crime due to a range of factors, such as familial pressures, faith-based interventions or financial incentives. To date, little has been written about the relationship between desistance and racialisation. This book seeks to bring much needed attention to this under-researched area of criminological inquiry.

Martin Glynn builds on recent empirical research in the UK and the USA and uses Critical Race Theory as a framework for developing a fresh perspective about black men's desistance. This book posits that the voices and collective narrative of black men offers a unique opportunity to refine current understandings of desistance. It also demonstrates how new insights can be gained by studying the ways in which elements of the desistance trajectory are racialised.

This book will be of interest both to criminologists and sociologists engaged with race, racialisation, ethnicity, and criminal justice.

Martin Glynn is Research Assistant at the University of Wolverhampton and completed his PhD at Birmingham City University, where he is also a visiting lecturer. His research interests include desistance, race/racialisation and crime, critical race theory, ethnodrama, masculinities and crime, and crime and social determinants of health.

International Series on Desistance and Rehabilitation

The *International Series on Desistance and Rehabilitation* aims to provide a forum for critical debate and discussion surrounding the topics of why people stop offending and how they can be more effectively reintegrated into the communities and societies from which they came. The books published in the series will be international in outlook, but tightly focused on the unique, specific contexts and processes associated with desistance, rehabilitation and reform. Each book in the series will stand as an attempt to advance knowledge or theorising about the topics at hand, rather than being merely an extended report of specific a research project. As such, it is anticipated that some of the books included in the series will be primarily theoretical, whilst others will be more tightly focused on the sorts of initiatives which could be employed to encourage desistance. It is not our intention that books published in the series be limited to the contemporary period, as good studies of desistance, rehabilitation and reform undertaken by historians of crime are also welcome. In terms of authorship, we would welcome excellent PhD work, as well as contributions from more established academics and research teams. Most books are expected to be monographs, but edited collections are also encouraged.

General Editor
Stephen Farrall, University of Sheffield

Editorial Board
Ros Burnett, University of Oxford
Thomas LeBel, University of Wisconsin-Milwaukee, USA
Mark Halsey, Flinders University, Australia
Fergus McNeill, Glasgow University
Shadd Maruna, Queens University Belfast
Gwen Robinson, Sheffield University
Barry Godfrey, University of Liverpool

4. Offender rehabilitation and therapeutic communities
Enabling change the TC way
Alisa Stevens

5. Desistance transitions and the impact of probation
Sam King

6. Black men, invisibility and desistance from crime
Towards a critical race theory of desistance
Martin Glynn

Black men, invisibility and desistance from crime

Towards a critical race theory of desistance

Martin Glynn

Routledge
Taylor & Francis Group

LONDON AND NEW YORK

First published 2014
by Routledge
2 Park Square, Milton Park, Abingdon, Oxfordshire OX14 4RN

and by Routledge
711 Third Avenue, New York, NY 10017

First issued in paperback 2015

Routledge is an imprint of the Taylor & Francis Group, an informa business

© 2014 Martin Glynn

The right of Martin Glynn to be identified as author of this work has been asserted by him in accordance with sections 77 and 78 of the Copyright, Designs and Patents Act 1988.

All rights reserved. No part of this book may be reprinted or reproduced or utilised in any form or by any electronic, mechanical, or other means, now known or hereafter invented, including photocopying and recording, or in any information storage or retrieval system, without permission in writing from the publishers.

Trademark notice: Product or corporate names may be trademarks or registered trademarks, and are used only for identification and explanation without intent to infringe.

British Library Cataloguing in Publication Data
A catalogue record for this book is available from the British Library

Library of Congress Cataloging in Publication Data
Glynn, Martin.
  Black men, invisibility and crime : towards a critical race theory of desistance / Martin Glynn.
    p. cm. – (International series on desistance and rehabilitation)
  Includes bibliographical references and index.
  1. Recidivism–Prevention–Great Britain. 2. Blacks–Race identity–Great Britain. 3. Race discrimination–Great Britain. 4. Recidivism–Prevention–United States. 5. African Americans–Race identity–United States. 6. Race discrimination–United States. I. Title.
  HV6049.G59 2013
  364.3–dc23
                    2013023822

ISBN13: 978-1-138-93367-5 (pbk)
ISBN13: 978-0-415-71535-5 (hbk)

Typeset in Times New Roman
by Taylor & Francis Books

Contents

Foreword

Martin Glynn's book – based on fieldwork conducted in both the UK and the USA and in both prison and community contexts – is an attempt to understand the processes through which black men living in these countries desist from crime. In this respect it builds on the works previously published in the series by Adam Calverley (on ethnicities and desistance) and Alisa Stevens (on therapeutic communities). Martin Glynn's approach is different, however, developing as he does his understanding of desistance via critical theories of race. His aim is to produce what he terms a 'black criminology of desistance' and in so doing he advance considerably the research undertaken thus far on desistance. This is an important study of desistance and one which is ground-breaking in lots of ways. This is a book which really gets to the heart of the dilemmas facing many black men as they try to leave behind prolonged engagement with crime, gangs and prisons. The data gathered is rich and makes for a stimulating read for both those interested in ethnic identities and those interested in desistance. This book is a 'must have' for those working in this field.

Stephen Farrall,
Sheffield,
June 2013

Acknowledgements

Routledge for enabling this salmon to swim upstream.

Professor David Wilson for supervision, guidance, mentoring, pastoral support; and friendship; Professor Joyce Canaan for enabling me to understand what to do, being a friend, and walking me through the darkness; Professor Michael Brookes for believing in me when I stopped believing in myself; Dr Matt Badcock for support and guidance on ethics; Barbara McCalla for typing and support; Professors Shadd Maruna, Fergus McNeil, and Stephen Farrall for their insights, encouragement, and belief in me; Dr Vinette Cross who guided me throughout my academic 'rite of passage' as a colleague, friend, and learning mentor; Anne Peaker (R.I.P.) who gave me my start in this work; Dianne Curry who continues to support me when I forget myself; Dr Peter Bennett for recognising that I can make a difference; Richard Shuker for persevering with my ideas; Dr Michelle Newberry, her colleagues and prison officers who supported me throughout; the prisoners of HMP Grendon, who gave their time, energy, and commitment to a stranger; the Lab crew; Victoria, Emma, John, Adam, Charlotte, and Louise, lecturers and colleagues at the Centre for Applied Criminology (Birmingham City University); the people of Baltimore; all the participants who became diary entries; to all my critics, haters, and blockers, thanks for giving me a reason to prove you all wrong.

To my Jamaican and Welsh family, my mother Jill Glynn who supported me in whatever I did; to my step-father Ted Glynn who gave me my love of books and music, my father, Astley Roy Moore, you missed so much, but in the end I became someone in spite of you not being there, Jennifer 'Jenso' for being there every step of the way, my children, Melanie, Sherene, and Adika; my grandchildren, Jeniece, Jahmal, Samuel, Kayla and Lily Rose for having to endure their father/grandfather's absence, my brothers and sisters; Anne, Wendy, and my brother Malcolm, who like mum have always loved me unconditionally; Pauline Bailey and Pauline Carty for joining and guiding me part way through the journey, tight bredrins: Andrew, Lisa, Craig, Ray, Cipher, Robin, Carver, Kenny Mackay, Dr. Kenny Monroe Paul, James, Moqapi, Curtis, Ivora, Tunde, Mpume, Junior, Andrew 'L', Jo, Melissa, Jamal, Jackie, Jazz, Pamela, Flo, Sonia, Shona, Dionne, Peggy, Tanayah, Pat, Vicky, Natalie, and Garry for 'havin' my back' throughout, the communities of

Nottingham and Birmingham who gave me the drive; transatlantic cousins: Ted, Phil, Linda, Sharan, Gary, and Mary, not forgetting my Jamaican family: Judith, Taitu, Uncle 'P', Uncle Larry, Flo, Neil, my aunties, and nuff others who welcomed me back to my father's homeland. Rest in peace Mum (Jill), Dad (Astley), Step Dad (Ted), sister Alison, my twin brother, Neville, Carlene, Devone, and Jean.

1   Introduction

This book, *Black Men, Invisibility, and Desistance from Crime: Towards a Critical Race Theory of Desistance* has been three decades in the making, culminating in the completion of my doctorate in February 2013. In the intervening years I have worked tirelessly in prisons, communities, combined with numerous other settings and locations trying to gain insights, knowledge, and understandings into 'race' and the 'racialisation of crime' with specific reference to black men. The term 'black' therefore in this book is used to identify peoples of 'African descent' and locates itself within a frame of reference used by many of the research participants both here in the UK and the USA to define themselves as a way of representing a 'unity of experience' in relation to racism, white privilege, and oppression among people whose skin is not white.

Historically and politically, the use of terms to describe 'racialised identities' has been an extremely contentious issue, related to the language and associated meanings that attempt to describe those racialised identities, inasmuch as the term 'black' is not static but changes over time both within and between groups (Serrant-Green, 2002). It is therefore important that any terms used to identify individuals in this book are defined at the outset and placed in a context relevant to the tone and shape of the book.

My countless encounters with black men in the community and prison have also set the backdrop for my relationship with the study of desistance and extending its boundaries. Having spent nearly three decades engaging black men in a dialogue about their offending, I felt there was an even greater need, and a more urgent 'call', to investigate those factors that either enhance or hinder the cessation of their offending behaviour (referred to as desistance) in this under-researched area of criminology. Desistance is increasingly conceptualised as a theoretical construct used to explain how offenders orient themselves away from committing crimes. Previous studies have suggested that successful desistance occurs due to one or several factors: a 'rite of passage' (Maruna, 2007); a 'current status' (Farrington, 1986); a decision (Cusson and Pinsonneault, 1986); 'ageing out' or maturing away from criminal activity (Gottfredson and Hirschi, 1990); personal and social circumstances (Healy, 2010), space- and place-specific factors (Flynn, 2010), or ethnicity (Calverley,

2013). The list is not exhaustive, highlighting that the desistance project is ongoing and still developing.

To desist, a returning prisoner must be equipped with the necessary tools to successfully 'reintegrate' back into the community, contributing to its overall development by being reformed as a consequence of experiencing positive rehabilitative processes. On concluding their prison sentence, the offender will then be released and 're-enter' the community, hopefully prepared for a life free from crime, and ultimately 'desist'. However, my doctoral research revealed that this is certainly not the case for many men returning back to the community that they left behind after being sent to prison. And for black men, there are significant barriers to overcome, based on how they engage and encounter the racialisation of the social structure post-release.

It is right therefore to assume that the privileging and promotion of the stories of black men's experiences of both 're-entry' and the movement towards their desistance provided me with a unique opportunity to expand the current thinking in a 'racialised' area of criminology that is both under-researched and under-theorised. In reality, the visible absence of available academic information and data when looking at, investigating, or theorising black men's own understandings of their desistance not only weakens contemporary debates on 'race and crime', but criminology as a whole. Indeed, my observations and participation within prison rehabilitation programmes targeted at black men over three decades has led me to believe that seldom have black men's insights, understandings, and 'lived' experiences within the UK and the US criminal justice systems, been taken into consideration in the study of both re-entry and desistance as a whole.

This state of affairs led me to believe that any future investigation into black men's desistance must give voice to the 'minority perspective' (Phillips and Bowling, 2003). This 'minority perspective' should not only acknowledge and validate the stories that black men themselves tell of their own understandings and insights into their desistance, but it must also enable them to 'narrate' and 'interpret' their own reality by bringing coherence to their 'real-life' stories, creating a 'counter-narrative' that would challenge and contest what many academics claim about their criminality, with reference to their desistance trajectories (McAdams, 1988). The research started by posing several key questions:

1 What impact does the racialisation of crime/criminal justice systems have on the desistance process for black men?
2 How do black men construct their own insights and understandings of their desistance in relation to being both black and male in a white society that renders them subordinate?
3 What are the factors that contribute to black men's commitment to accept or negate notions of their desistance?

The research used an 'interpretivist perspective'. That is, it focused on the meanings that black men gave to their lived experiences in relation to the racialisation of crime and criminal justice systems and its impact on their desistance trajectories. The study involved 11 black men from the community from Birmingham in the UK, 10 prisoners, located in HMP Grendon's Therapeutic Community (TC), and 9 black men from the city of Baltimore in the USA. Semi-structured interviews and 'urban ethnography' were the methods used to gather the data (Anderson, 1999). The theoretical framework employed throughout was Critical Race Theory (CRT) that has been widely applied to law (Delgado and Stefancic, 2005); education (Ladson-Billings and Tate, 1995); and more recently sport (Hylton, 2005).

CRT became the foundation from which a 'counter-narrative' was developed to privilege the racialised voices of black men in relation to their insights and understandings of the desistance process. The research also examined 'prison' as a possible may site where the trajectory towards desistance possibly may begin. This assumption was motivated by the few prison studies that alluded to the possibility of 'transformation' and 'change' while in prison.

Wacquant (2002a) argues that researchers conducting research in prison should worry less about interpretation and start producing research that moves away from 'state-centred' approaches to 'social inequality', and should focus more on the effects of penal policies and institutions. The research therefore also provided a focus from which to engage black men in a dialogue on the role of prisons which would hopefully add to this limited literature by focusing the lens of 'racialisation' on the desistance trajectory.

An example of how prison becomes a site for the trajectory towards desistance in a racialised context is in the conversion of Malcolm 'X'. The journey of Malcolm 'X' from prisoner to human right activist occurred during his time in prison. Haley (1965) highlights how the desistance of Malcolm 'X' was rooted in a 'faith-based' conversion as a consequence of his desire to create a replacement 'self', one not shaped by 'white expectations', or notions of 'black subordination'. Likewise, I will argue that some black men construct insights and understandings of the desistance trajectory while incarcerated, by occupying a liminal space, where transformation is part of a sustained period of 'ontological reflection', where the psychological 'masks' they wear are removed and replaced with a more positive self-image (Turner, 1969). The African-American poet Paul Dunbar emphasises that if this 'ontological reflection' does not take place for black men, the result will mean having to 'wear the mask' when he writes:

we wear the mask that grins and lies;
it hides our cheeks and shades our eyes,
this debt we pay to human guile;
with torn and bleeding hearts we smile.
(Dunbar, 1892: 167)

Dunbar's verse highlights a deep psychic challenge of 'wear(ing) the mask' that some black men face in a society where they feel that their sense of being and their abilities are undermined by racialised constructs, that in turn places restrictions on them becoming 'the authors of their own lives' (McAdams, 1988). Dunbar's image of 'torn and bleeding hearts' further suggests that, in spite of the pain and burden of an oppressive history of slavery, colonialism, and racism, black men are forced to put on a brave face, and don a 'mask' in order to survive their oppression and subsequent subordination in a predominantly white society.

Echoing Dunbar's sentiments, the need to 'remove the mask' and reframe the context in which black men's own insights and understandings of their desistance are defined in some criminological theorising is important here. The need for black men to reveal their 'own truths' and to tell their own stories becomes significant if they are to transcend their 'racial subordination'. Denzin (2003) argues that for 'subordinated voices' to be heard, they must be helped to speak. It is therefore wholly appropriate that there is recognition of how the worldview of black men is distorted as they encounter racial injustices that are embedded in social networks, as the basis for creating a platform for those voices to be both heard and understood. This worldview is also shaped by negative beliefs that emerge from their lived experiences of 'racial subordination' (West, 2004). Robinson (2005) notes that the rules, resources, and language of society constrain black men by restricting access at all levels of their lives. West (2004) further declares that any discourse centring on how black men construct their lives must start with the flaws within society itself, not with the problems of black men, but, in particular, those of white society.

To date, much of what black men themselves understand of their insights into crime and criminal justice systems remains invisible in the current criminological literature. However, a key contribution that begins to unpack some of the complexities surrounding desistance has been the examination of 'masculinities and crime' (Connell and Messerschmidt, 2005). That is, these studies have shown that often men commit crimes as a consequence of not having previously been able to realise their masculinities through legitimate means. It could be argued that as a consequence of the racialisation of criminal justice systems, black men face additional pressures, barriers, and stress surrounding their desistance based on the impact of white oppression on their masculinities and subsequent aspirations.

The problem here is in the lack of available data that is conspicuously absent and, as I have discovered, what does exist has at times been rendered 'invisible'. I have also discovered that even when the literature on desistance has alluded to a racialised context, it still generally failed to account for black men's own understandings and insights. The inability of this literature to examine how the racialising of criminal justice systems privileges some groups over others was also extremely troubling. The irony of this situation is that there is an abundance of data that is readily available on racial disparities/disproportionality, and unsurprisingly, the over-representation of black men in the criminal justice system in England and Wales, which raises another question. Namely, if data does exist, why are they not being accessed, analysed, and included in wider criminological debates? A deeper analysis of this situation also highlighted that the lens being used to examine racialisation for black men may also be flawed. I come to this view in part through personal experiences of black men in prison insofar as I have black friends who have been incarcerated.

Some of these men have, through particular experiences while in prison, developed strategies for moving towards their desistance. Others, however, did not. Moving beyond the confines of constructs of the 'race' locates this research within a frame of reference that focuses attention on 'racial disparities'. 'Racial disparities' denote a difference in outcomes, indicating that discrimination is present in areas such as policing, sentencing, etc. (Walker *et al.*, 2004). Where does this unequal treatment spring from and how does black men's oppression shape their worldview? And how does this worldview enhance or inhibit the trajectory towards their desistance?

Fryer (1984) suggests that any attempt to understand black men's worldview must take into consideration the history of oppression (slavery, colonialism, racism, etc.), as this history demonstrates how racial disparities have been generated, maintained, and sustained. The Bromley Briefings (2011) provide a statistical snapshot that further highlights the 'racial disparities' in relation to black men in the criminal justice system in England and Wales:

- On 30 June 2010 just less than 26 per cent of the prison population, 21,878 prisoners, was from a minority ethnic group. This is slightly less than in 2009, but represents an increase on that recorded for 2005 (25 per cent). This compares to one in 10 of the general population.
- Of the British national prison population, 11 per cent are black and 5 per cent are Asian. For black Britons, this is significantly higher than the 2.8 per cent of the general population they represent.
- Overall, black prisoners account for the largest number of minority ethnic prisoners (53 per cent) in the UK penal system.
- At the end of June 2010, 32 per cent of minority ethnic prisoners were foreign nationals, a higher percentage of those in Black and Minority Ethnic (BME) groups were sentenced to immediate custody for indictable offences than in the white group in 2010 (white 23 per cent, black 27 per cent, Asian 29 per cent, and Other 42 per cent).
- In 2010, the highest average custodial sentence length (ACSL) for those given determinate sentences for indictable offences was recorded for the black ethnic group, at 20.8 months, followed by the Asian and Other groups with averages of 19.9 months and 19.7 months respectively.
- There is now greater disproportionality in the number of black people in prisons in the UK than in the United States. The US prison population is commonly thought to be the most disproportionate with regard to the incarceration of black men (Alexander, 2010).

The above statistics highlight the importance of engaging black men in a dialogue that will shed some light on their own understandings and insights into these disparities, in relation to their over-representation in the criminal justice system, as well as indicating what resources are available to them to support their trajectory towards desistance. As stated previously, both personal and professional observations of and direct participation in prison rehabilitation programmes targeted at black men over the past 25 years have shown that seldom, if ever, have the racialised experiences in the prison system been considered (Glynn, 2005). These observations have prompted yet another question. How does the development of a 'racialised criminological perspective' that begins from an appreciation of racism in society create the scope to respond to these concerns?

The consideration of the development of 'black criminology' becomes important here (Russell, 2002). Russell highlights how an independent sub-field, similar to that of feminist criminology, might open up so-called 'mainstream criminology' in order to look critically at black men's relationship to the criminal justice system. It could also consider how black men are located in a system which acts and operates within a racialised context. Russell's position also suggests that it is the 'ivory tower,' not the 'ebony tower', that still dominates much criminological theorising.

White (2008) seeks to improve the understanding of the ways in which the 'narrative of racialisation' is constructed by examining how the limited access to power in society, according to white men's privilege, may result in criminal activity becoming a choice for some black men. It could therefore be argued that the ability to desist from criminal activity for some black men could be increased, if they gained more of a foothold in the social structure in a way that would enable them to transcend their unfair treatment and ultimate subordination. This book therefore seeks to reveal those accounts that have largely gone unnoticed by scholars and the public to date. As stated previously, the need for a racialised analytical lens with which to give voice to black men's stories in relation to the racialisation of crime/criminal justice systems and its impacts on the desistance process is important here. The analytical lens used was Critical Race Theory (CRT). Delgado and Stefancic (2005) cite several tenets that locate CRT as an analytical framework:

1   Racism is ordinary, not exceptional, and it is the usual way that society does business. Its ordinariness makes racism hard to recognise and much less address.
2   The social construction of race, and the related idea of differential racialisation, hold that race and races are products of social thought.
3   Not objective, inherent, or fixed, races correspond to no simple biological or genetic reality; rather, they are categories that society invents for particular purposes, usually ignoble ones.
4   Building on this insight, differential racialisation calls attention to the ways in which the dominant society racialises different minority groups in different ways at different times in response to shifting needs, such as the labour market, with the system of laws following suit.

Valdes *et al.* (2002) too acknowledges that CRT 'resists the subordinating messages of the dominant culture by challenging stereotypes and presenting and representing people of colour as complex and heterogeneous' (2002: 244). Valdes further suggests that CRT not only can enable the subordinated persons (black men) to narrate, to interpret events in opposition to the dominant narratives (of white men), but also recognises the complexity of the issues being addressed. The narrative potential of CRT therefore lies in 'its ability to re-story the past and to then re-imagine the future' much the same as black feminism has done (ibid.: 246). CRT offers new insights with which to explore and explain the understanding processes of the racialisation of crime/criminal justice systems and its impacts on the desistance process, for black men. CRT's use of storytelling as its analytical framing provided a unique creative opportunity to look at the role of narrative in desistance, a position previously not explored in this context.

CRT operates with two distinct storytelling paradigms. 'Majoritarian stories' told by privileged white people, and 'counter-stories' told by subordinated black people (Solorzano and Yosso, 2002). Hill-Collins (2000) sees the internalised oppression for black women as a journey that leads towards a need for self-definition. She further suggests that black women can gain a richer self-definition if they strive to tell their own stories as free from the oppressive gaze of white women. It could be similarly argued that the black men's understandings and insights of their desistance are more effectively told if efforts are made to delink this telling from white oppression. McAdams (1988) provides a further context that demonstrates that beginning the process of desistance requires black ex-offenders to make sense of their lives in the form of a 'life story' or 'self-narrative'. McAdams advocates the interrogation of one's own story and creating a space to rework it by the development of a 'counter-story'.

hooks (1991) highlights that black men's 'counter-stories', when they do contest white men's accounts of maintaining their privileged position, are seen as posing a threat by challenging their subordinate status. She further states: 'Often when the "radical voice" speaks about domination, we are speaking to those who dominate' (ibid.: 80). hooks' assertion suggests it may be a better proposition for black men themselves to 'name their own reality' and to further consider how they can encourage and institutionalise 'outsider within' ways of seeing, to overcome the struggle to transcend their 'subordinate status' (Hill-Collins, 2000: 29). 'Subordinate status' invariably means that some white men will have privilege over black men (Connell and Messerschmidt, 2005). However, the problem may lie less in whether black men are subordinated, but more in the way data and evidence is gathered, analysed, and understood in relation to black men and supporting.

Halsey (2008) sees a future-orientated vision that becomes the basis of a narrative of change that releases hope, without which, in my opinion, desistance is hardly feasible. This has highlighted how many black men face a dilemma in relation to their desistance that rests on the uncertainty about whether to pursue a new future (desistance), or to stay on the familiar road of re-offending after re-entry. A returning black prisoner who has been to prison, is seen very differently, based on the continuing onslaught of racialised processes that continue to blight their lives way beyond release. Maruna (2010) sees that reintegration of prisoners back into the community requires well-orchestrated rituals. He further states: 'I argue that ex-prisoner reintegration, as it currently practiced, is one such failing ritual that should be re-examined' (ibid.: 21).

My research suggests that Maruna's comments have some merit, and highlights one of the over-riding problems that face black men's desistance, namely the rituals associated with re-entry for some black men are empty, and in turn create more barriers blocking the trajectory towards their desistance. This emptiness is based on a series of systemic failures (structure) that restricts how the individual (agency) can actualise their journey through engaging with their flawed rituals. My research has demonstrated how the barriers that black men face, need to be overcome both in and out of prison, and there needs to be a revision of expectations. This is combined with envisioning new models for black men's desistance that will alleviate the negative impact that racialised criminal justice processes have had on their lives. It could be argued that without a relevant and appropriate lens for looking at black men's desistance, which applies the same standards, values, judgements, and insights to that of white men, then criminology will fail to account for the role that 'race' plays in thwarting black men's desire to be free from criminal involvement and investment.

More importantly, my research has provided unique access into a world where few criminologists have ventured, as it revealed a world that lay hidden in the wider studies on desistance. The issue here is me operating as an 'insider researcher', which will be discussed later in the book. By insider, I mean I share the same cultural background, am exposed to similar racialising experiences in my personal and professional life, combined with having a shared history of oppression. It is my view that there is a greater need to call on the services of researchers operating from an 'insider' perspective to provide some balance to the over-representation of the 'outsider' perspectives that do little to change the understandings and insights of the racialisation of crime and criminal justice systems. What has emerged from the research is that the study of desistance is far from complete, and, more importantly, requires deeper probing into how the role of the subordination of black men by white men is a key indicator, and a significant barrier in their desires towards their desistance goals and aspirations.

However, a few recurring questions have continued to occupy my thoughts throughout; firstly why do some black men in prison and those returning to the community continue to accept this subordination, while others do not? It is reasonable to think that a history of racial subordination should clearly make many black men more vigilant and defiant in the face of continuing and sustainable pressure coming from the forces designed to keep them down. One explanation could be that when black men are rendered powerless in a system that privileges one group over the other, black men do not have a sense of equal justice. Those who are denied a voice might speak without fear of recrimination, while others will break unjust laws.

Secondly how then do black men who have been to prison and want to return to a crime-free life maintain the balance between challenging the status quo, while at the same time not being sucked into the very machinery that grinds their energy down, forcing them back into crime and ultimately back to prison? The inability of those black men who suffer racial disparities in the criminal justice system to successfully operate independently of street-level bureaucrats, policy-makers, and strategic agencies is also problematic and requires a new approach that provides those men with a platform that has power. Central to this proposition is in the way the narrative of oppressed people is produced and produces change. The dominant narrative that restricts and renders counter-narratives invisible would suggest that there needs to be a reframing of what constitutes a counter-narrative in the first place. Art, music, theatre, poetry, dance, all give rise to the exploration of subordinated people's experiences, but have limited impact on contesting the very power structure that continues to reign supreme.

Without a clear, precise, and focused approach to challenging power within society, black men will merely replicate a reactionary approach to their oppression. If black men are to seek transformation as way of transcending their subordination, then they must seek transformative spaces where the interrogation of the obstacles and barriers to their freedom is given voice, complete with the development of an action plan designed to push their counter-narrative into a strategy for meaningful and productive change. This strategy must not replicate a structure that has kept them down, but instead must create a more equitable and empowering way to function and live in a society that still privileges different groups over each other.

In the course of my study, the helplessness of many black men became obvious. Watching them break down as they had their hopes and dreams destroyed was painful. It was clear that many black men are crippled by the pain that them held in captive a system that fuelled and maintained that pain, indefinitely. The racialisation of the criminal justice system has left little room for personal growth, as those very definitions have created a powerless and subordinate group who languish in the prison system and in turn at the bottom of society. If these men are taken away from their families, the community, and in turn, society, then desistance as a construct for black men may have to be reframed. It is for this reason that the fight to validate the narratives of subordinated black men must continue.

The structure of the book

Chapter 1 sets the backdrop and context for this book, detailing its genesis and my journey as the author. Chapter 2 looks at racialisation and criminalisation in relation to the complexities of black men and their insights and understandings into their desistance trajectories. Privileging the voices of black men offers a unique opportunity to expand the understandings of desistance, whilst acknowledging that the attention paid to race and processes of racialisation in desistance is scant and is both under-researched and under-theorised. It is also important to give a platform for black men to articulate their own understandings of desistance and to both contest and challenge any previously made assumptions about black men in relation to their desistance. Chapter 3 lays out the methods used, the analytical framework, the participants, and other considerations undertaken while conducting the research.

Chapter 4 looks at the development of a black criminology of desistance. Choosing to do research on black men's desistance with black men was about giving voice to their insights and understandings, alongside transcending what Du Bois (1938) refers to as 'carwash sociology'. 'Carwash sociology' refers to those researchers who undertake research from a physical or symbolic distance far from the subjects of the research inquiry. Therefore, looking critically at the researchers' position becomes an important consideration in the research journey. The chapter therefore explores the conflict, contradictions, and experiences of 'black on black' research. Chapter 5 looks at black men from the community in Birmingham in the UK in relation to factors that have enhanced or hindered notions of their desistance.

The community participants were drawn from the faith communities, community organisations, and criminal justice agencies, and were classified as individuals who had terminated their offending and represented a wide spectrum of offending behaviour: robbery, gangs, drugs, etc. Chapter 6 focuses on a UK prison-based Therapeutic Community (TC) and looks at the role of therapeutic intervention and assesses its impact in relation to the trajectory towards desistance. HMP Grendon was chosen as the site for this particular strand of the research inquiry to investigate and compare how the experience of TC in relation to desistance differed from that of the wider prison estate. Chapter 7 focuses on a comparative element of the study that examined how African-American men in the city of Baltimore in Maryland in the USA experienced and articulated their insights and understandings of desistance. The research took place during August and September 2010, as part of a Winston Churchill International Travel Fellowship.

Chapter 8 presents 'a theoretical framework of masculinities in relation to black men's desistance'. This framework asserts the position that an element of successful desistance for black men is bound up in making successful masculine 'transitions'. I further argue that these transitions are situated and contextualised within the worldview of black men that is as a result of the negative experiences they have faced within the criminal justice system. The data confirm that black men in this study understand that the criminal justice system treats them less fairly. This framework also hypothesises that black men who do not build strong social and cultural bonds after being released from prison, struggle with making positive transitions within their 'life course', that in turn has a negative impact on their ability to desist. A case study of Ibrahim is presented here.

Chapter 9 argues that future research into black men and desistance should develop counter-discourses through storytelling, narratives, chronicles, bio-graphies, etc., that draw on the real lived experiences of black men in relation to desistance. It further argues for the necessity of conceptualising black men's desistance beyond the current 'colour-blind' criminological lenses, and explores how critical theoretical methodologies such as Critical Race Theory (CRT) are necessary to privilege the voice of black men. It concludes by citing CRT as a theoretical lens and pedagogical orientation that helps us better comprehend the issues associated with black men and desistance, that would also challenge the dominant narrative that has denied black men's voices by operating through a lens that is both 'colour-blind' and privileged in favour of white men. Chapter 10 looks at possible new directions for the ongoing study of black men and the desistance project, and assesses the implications for desistance as a whole.

This chapter concludes by highlighting how my doctoral research grew out of a paucity of research information on the racialisation of crime/the criminal justice systems and its impact on the desistance process for black men. It further concludes the need to critically examine how black men's 'subordinated voices' can be helped to speak using their stories and to better understand how they have ceased to engage in activity considered 'criminal'. In doing so, the accounts described in this book centring on the construction and articulation of a 'counter-narrative' may enable others to understand how 'differential racialisation' reveals ways in which the dominant society creates the conditions that restrict the trajectory towards their desistance for black men. It is intended that scholars who are looking at other areas where power and subordination need to be contested and challenged will find an ally in the fight for social justice that is denied to many by the dominant few.

2 Racialisation and criminalisation

Introduction

Garner (2009) argues that the concept of 'racialisation' is based on the idea that the object of study should not be 'race' itself, but the process by which 'race' becomes meaningful in a particular context. 'Racialisation' therefore draws attention to the process of making 'race' relevant to a particular situation or context, and thus requires an examination of the precise circumstances in which this occurs. In this chapter, I explore the context of racialisation in relation to the criminalisation of black men. Webster (2007) argues that black offenders, who end up in the criminal justice system and prison, are disproportionately represented, compared to their numbers in the population.

He further argues that black men are disproportionately victimised, in part because they tend to live in poorer urban areas. Patel and Tyrer (2011) express the view that when race enters the 'othering' process, particularly within the context of crime and deviancy, it is important to consider the roots of racially charged concepts that disproportionally targets minority groups such as black men. Similarly, Gabbidon and Taylor-Greene (2009) argue that the disenfranchisement of black men involved in crime is ideologically driven as a way of bolstering the carceral estate.

Lewis *et al.* (2006) also put forward the proposition that some black men may experience the criminal justice system differently as a consequence of 'disadvantageous treatment' based on the racialisation of the probation services that can disable some black men's re-entry back into the community, invariably impacting on the trajectory towards their desistance. Hallett (2006) sees that these social injustices tend to follow clear racial, class, and gendered patterns that emphasise the political power of identity categories themselves. Hallett's premise sees 'whiteness' as a category associated with access to power, and 'blackness' associated with powerless and imprisonment. It is within these binaries a power game is played out, subordinating black men in the process. Tonry (2011) proposes that these 'racial disparities' are unjustifiable and are more about the maintenance of political dominance over blacks. He concludes by arguing that the visualisation of black people through the media, film, and television has created a culture that views black people as criminals and as being predisposed to anti-social behaviour.

Russell-Brown (2009), like Tonry, suggests that criminology is flawed in the way it looks at race, as it focuses too much on 'black criminality' in relation to 'white criminality', that it falls prey to media persuasion, and ultimately perpetuates the dominance of whiteness by using a 'colour-blind' lens when viewing the criminal justice system. Alexander (2010) argues strongly that we have not eradicated racial disadvantage, but have merely redesigned it. Mauer (2010) also strongly expresses the view that the responsibility for alleviating these disparities falls not only on criminal justice agencies, but on society as a whole, and needs to be addressed appropriately through both policy and practice at all levels of government. Hill-Collins (2005) sees black men as being situated near the bottom of a social hierarchy, revealing that they are seen differently and treated unequally.

Connell and Messerschmidt (2003) also express the view that racialised masculinities in relation to the study of crime as a whole are significantly under-theorised, and state more needs to be done to create a more equitable lens with which to view the complexities surrounding the issues facing black men. Marable (1993) also suggests that inequality for black men involved in crime is based on black male stereotypes that white society imposes via institutions, and says the wider social structure generates the type of inequality that produces subordination for black men within the criminal justice system. It could be argued that if racism underscores the plight of black men within the criminal justice system, then legitimate pathways towards desisting from criminal activity for black men will be blocked. Alexander (2010), like Marable, notes that white men in power generally ignore the role played by slavery and colonialism in the over-representation of black men in prison. They both contend that criminal justice systems adopt a 'colour-blind' position that renders black men subordinate. It could be that this subordination is played down and rendered 'invisible' in the wider understanding of black men and crime that pushes some black men into nihilistic patterns of behaviour (West, 1993).

Frazier (1957) considers that the gaining and sustaining of employment form one way to counter the impact of the subordinate position that black men find themselves in, and would give some respite from the oppressive racialised forces within society. Frazier, echoing Du Bois (1938), sees the so-called 'American Dream' as being beyond the reach of many black men, based on the devastating impact of slavery, combined with the failed attempts of America to include those citizens it has historically and systematically excluded. This, he argues, leads to a propensity for black men to be involved in criminal activity, based on the racialisation of the social structure.

Sampson and Wilson (1995) further view the 'social isolation' and the 'ecological concentration' of disadvantaged sections of the community as leading to structural barriers and cultural adaptations that undermine social organisation and ultimately the control of crime. Again, West (1993) feels that white society should focus less on seeing black men as the problem, but more on the failure of white society to treat black men fairly. West's view highlights a painful reality, namely, black men have to contend with additional stress in achieving an equal status in society. Marriot (2000) argues that the picture of black men as aggressive and hedonistic embeds itself in the consciousness of society and constructs racialised typographies of black men as 'criminal'. hooks (2004) challenges Marriot's assumptions and contextualises how black men historically have defined their own sense of identity as a consequence of 'confronting the hardships of life without allowing their spirits to be ravaged' (ibid.: 147). The evidence thus far would suggest that the racialisation and criminalisation of black men have implications when looking at black men's desistance. To support this assumption requires an understanding of theories that underpin the understandings of 'desistance' itself.

Desistance

Maruna and Immarigeon (2004) approach the term 'desistance' in relation to understanding 'why and how former offenders avoid continued involvement in criminal behaviour'. They further declare that desistance has been defined and modelled in criminological research as the termination point at which offending ceases (ibid.: 43). Maruna and Farrall (2004) do acknowledge that 'as desistance research grows and matures into a fully fledged programme of research, new areas of exploration will emerge from research that will influence future criminal justice policies'.

Giordano *et al.* (2002) see that changing the way offenders think may assist them in conquering the barriers imposed upon them by a racist criminal justice system. So, too, do Cusson and Pinsonneault (1986), who suggest that the decision to give up crime is generally triggered by a shock of some sort, a delayed deterrence process. They make a link between the fears of punishment as a core factor in the desire to go straight. However, with the racialisation of criminal justice systems it is hard to envisage how black men can undergo such a transformation while incarcerated. Carlsson (2012) expresses the view that processes of individual change in offending and desistance from crime are complex, and 'often involving multiple, and context-specific processes' (ibid.: 2). He further argues that two concepts are often seen as central to understanding life course dynamics: 'trajectories' and 'transitions' (Elder, 1985).

A trajectory, he points out, is a pathway over the 'life span' and is marked by transitions. Transitions, as Carlsson suggests, explore those events, stages and processes where changes in the trajectories towards desistance occur, and he concludes by suggesting that the concept of turning points in qualitative inquiry lies in its ability to help us explore, analyse and understand these life course processes in (greater) depth. Similarly, Siennick and Osgood (2008: 163) argue for a deeper analysis when looking at desistance, as they feel that individuals who feel the constraints of conventional role restrictions are the same individuals who tend to show high rates of offending. Likewise, Serin and Lloyd (2009) argue that there are two elements necessary for desistance to take place: a history of multiple criminal acts, and the subsequent cessation of all criminal behaviour. Thus, desistance is directly tied to the psychological mechanisms that drive changes in criminal behaviour patterns. Maruna (2001) further provides many powerful testimonies from ex-offenders in a way that addresses how they reform and rebuild their lives.

The emphasis on narrative, redemptive rituals, and having a sense of purpose, reaffirms that desistance theory and practice can be located within notions of a 'rite of passage' (Van Gennep, 1960). Maruna (2007) builds on van Gennep's work with a position that highlights that the reincorporation of social rituals associated with desistance and re-entry should engage men through processes of holistic transformation. Reno (2002) also cites 'redemptive change' as something that can be achieved by offenders atoning for their past indiscretions by finding spiritual purpose and servitude as a basis of desistance. Reno's position addresses the issue of how the pressure of modern living can act as a tipping point in relation to developing new core values rooted within a spiritual context. Wilson (2003) sees the need for participants to be acknowledged and respected as individuals in their own right as a way of building offender resilience that can assist in building the cognitive resources required for successful desistance.

Bottoms *et al.* (2004) view the progression from conformity to criminality and the progression from criminality to conformity (desistance) as false. Their view takes the position that for many people the progression towards desistance is faltering, hesitant and oscillating. They also feel that the ex-offenders' overall movement towards desistance may be thwarted by the pressures of daily living, concluding with the understanding that desistance cannot be considered outside the social context in which it occurs. Maruna and Roy (2006), however, conclude that the process of 'knifing off' where individuals can change their lives by severing links with places, people, and their past can be actualised. In light of the systemic imposition placed on black men, whose social mobility is not guaranteed, based on the lived reality of racism, I would suggest 'knifing off' is problematic and requires further investigation.

McAdams (1988) suggests that 'storytelling' may provide a framework that reveals 'desistance' as a 'narrative journey'. Agnew builds on McAdam's idea by proposing that the key events leading up to a crime, or series of related crimes, are what is referred to as 'storylines' (2006: 120). He expresses the view that 'storylines may help us better understand why background, situational factors and variables affect crime'. He states that 'storylines begin with some event that is out of the ordinary, and this event temporarily alters the individual's characteristics, interactions, and/or settings in ways that increase the likelihood of crime' (ibid.: 119). Rather than being a linear progression to the state of non-offending, however, the process of desistance has been likened to a zigzag path and to a drifting in and out of offending (Matza, 1964).

Maruna (2007) also highlights that desistance also requires that ex-offenders develop a coherent pro-social identity for themselves and feels that there should be recognition of the salience of involvement in 'generative activities' as critical to this process. He specifies the varieties of civic participation that can contribute to such an identity and their associated subjective meanings for desisters. They show how role transitions across socio-economic, familial and civic domains relate to identity shifts over the life course. However, Uggen *et al.* (2004) emphasise the reduced citizenship status and the enduring stigma experienced by offenders, resulting in 'the reduced rights and capacities of ex-offenders to attain full citizenship'. These status deficits undermine commitment to conformity and create new obstacles to desistance and the assumption of pro-social roles. Healy (2010) argues that the majority of offenders eventually terminate their criminal careers, but feels little is known about the processes underlying it.

Healy further provides a phenomenological account of the psychosocial processes involved in desistance and focuses on a number of key questions: what prompts prolific offenders to periodically cease their criminal activity? Are there different factors involved in the onset and maintenance of desistance? What impact, if any, does desistance have on the minds and lives of ex-offenders? And, finally, can probation supervision support individual efforts to change? Flynn (2010) similarly examines the extent to which criminal desistance is affected by personal and social circumstances that are 'space'- and 'place'-specific. Grounded in criminological spatial analysis, as well as more general social scientific investigations of the role of space and place in contemporary social, economic and cultural life, it examines why large numbers of prisoners in the United States and the United Kingdom appear to be drawn from, and after release return to, certain urban neighbourhoods. In doing so, Flynn assesses the effect of this unique 'life course' experience on the pathways and choices open to ex-prisoners who attempt to give up crime. Important as these perspectives are, a deeper examination of the process and how it is impacted by processes of racialisation are important here.

Racialisation and desistance

In spite of the significant body of literature on desistance, Farrall and Calverley (2006) acknowledge that there are few studies in the area of desistance and ethnicity but do acknowledge that some studies have attempted to rectify this situation. So too Laub and Sampson (2001), who also acknowledge that pathways towards desistance may differ according to race, but concede that the absence of available data inhibits a more representative view.

It could be argued that without a clear understanding of the role that racialisation plays in the cessation of criminal activity for black men, the contemporary understandings and insights of the desistance project are both flawed and incomplete. Calverley (2013) focuses on ethnicity in relation to engagement in offending and raises the question of whether or not processes associated with desistance vary by ethnicity. Using data obtained from in-depth qualitative interviews, Calverley investigates the processes associated with desistance from crime among offenders drawn from some of the principal minority ethnic groups in the United Kingdom. By exploring how structural (families, friends, peer groups, employment, social capital) and cultural (religion, values, recognition) ethnic differences affect the environment in which their desistance took place, Calverley concludes that ethnicity and cultural contexts are important facets of understanding desistance. He further suggests a need for a research agenda and justice policy that are sensitive to desisters' structural location, and for a wider culture that promotes and supports desisters' efforts.

Russell (2002) expresses the view that criminology has failed to cultivate a cohesive, continuous, and recognised body of research on what is termed 'black criminology'. Inasmuch as the theoretical framework of the discipline is limited by its failure to develop this sub-field, policy recommendations proposed to and adopted by the criminal justice system are limited. Russell's view underpins the need for developing relevant contemporary 'minority perspectives' in criminology when looking at black men in significant criminal justice issues (Phillips and Bowling, 2003). In criminological theorising much is written about why black men commit crime and its relation to high rates of incarceration of black men both in the UK and the USA.

However, little is known about black men and their desistance. Devlin and Turney (2001), even when they attempt to explain why criminals 'go straight' and cite a diverse range of factors enabling offenders to 'go straight', see the absence of a racialised context in their analysis as requiring further questioning and probing. Grover (2008), on the other hand, does investigate the complex relationship between crime and equality with a special reference to ethnicity. However, an over-emphasis on poverty, unemployment, social mobility and barriers towards cessation from crime, without probing the role that racialisation plays in the claims being made, creates a somewhat confusing picture. Although Grover does express the view that black men struggle to desist from involvement in crime and disorder, the analysis does not root itself within a sound socio-historical context, which in turn limits the impact of the overall perspective put forward.

Weaver and McNeill (2010), however, do acknowledge that the dialogues on desistance, identity, and diversity are underdeveloped, with a telling view on the way the current discourse frames notions of desistance, when they state:

> When we look more closely at the evidence around gender differences, ethnic differences, and the significance of religion, we find clear evidence that the common elements of the process can be differently experienced and constituted depending on the socio-structural, cultural, and spiritual position that people occupy and move through and how they negotiate their personal and social lives.
>
> (ibid.: 55)

Weaver and McNeill's acknowledgement has implications for how racialisation is located within the study of desistance.

Hughes (1998), on the other hand, cites several factors that have governed desistance for African-American youth: having children, fear of incarceration, reflection, and social modelling. An important facet of this study was the acknowledgement that the investment in building young people's 'social' and 'human' capital can determine the outcome of the future stability of the inner cities where many young black men reside. Hughes further acknowledges the impact of racism on the lives of young black men as a factor that pushes them towards criminal lifestyles. Hughes's view suggests that developing a resilient approach to transcending racism and its impacts could also play a significant role in desisting from criminal behaviour for some black men. Kanazawa and Still (2000) see the gendered nature of desistance and locate the problems for black men ceasing engagement in criminal activity as predominantly about being 'black' and 'male.'

Maybe theorising around black men's desistance should follow black feminist thought by grounding assumptions on the gendered and racialised nature of crime. It may also be important to bring together the intersection of race, class, and gender as a way of developing a broader context in the understanding of being black and male in relation to offending, with specific reference to that of desistance. Liebling and Maruna (2005) present an important set of views designed to challenge the lack of coherent and balanced literature on desistance, but the omission of a clear racialised perspective makes their view problematic. The acknowledgement that prison and its effects can seriously hinder or enhance processes associated with desistance is a powerful argument in principle, but the over-representation of black men in the UK prison system would suggest that the prison experience for black men may require further investigation to begin to understand the journey from incarceration re-integration, and ultimately desistance.

Glynn (2007) suggests that much 'gang-related crime' operates as defiant posture, combined with filling a ritual void in the lives of urban black youth, who seek ways of demonstrating their masculinity and toughness. This position has significant implications in understanding black men's desistance. Namely, if the bonds established through families, community, and society, in turn, are breaking down because of a racialised systemic oppression, then the trajectories for black men's desistance are well out of the control of black men themselves. The problem may then lie in the way in which we gather the data. Duneier (1992) sees some white researchers as failing to understand black men on account of possessing an inadequate insight into the world and context of their subjects. Duneier sees social analysts who fail to take into account the devastating impact of racism on black men as being misguided.

Bowling and Phillips (2002) similarly holds the view that criminology should take a greater role in addressing, answering, and investigating those processes, theories, and insights that will assist black men's desistance. It may be that criminology needs to acknowledge those sub-fields that are situated outside of the so-called mainstream criminology landscape. Unnever and Gabbidon (2011) locate their theory of African-American offending within a historical lens, rooted within notions of a worldview and self-concept shaped by a history of racial oppression. In doing so, they have contested the views of neo-liberal criminologists, who are still clinging to views of black men and crime, operating through a colour-blind lens that renders a 'black-led' frame invisible.

Their work provides a contemporary platform from which to develop a critical dialogue on the issue of the racialisation of crime and criminal justice systems and its impact on the desistance process. Brown (2002) further argues that an increase in the number of black criminologists might hasten the development of useful theories to explain black over-involvement in crime and, more importantly, desistance. Cruse (1967) also argues strongly that it is incumbent on both black and white intellectuals researching black life not to forget that 'the black experience is unique and the irrevocable imperative of cultural self-definition demands that it be treated as such' (1967: 5). Here Bhui (2009) reminds us of the constraints of taking such a position, and states that the difficulty of defining and measuring illustrates the ambiguities and interpretive problems that are inherent in trying to understand the relevance of race issues in the criminal justice process.

Gabbidon (2007) points out that there is no singular theory that explains racial disparities in race and crime, and sees that the study of the role of race and ethnicity needs to be pushed to the forefront of criminology. Gabbidon builds on his argument by expressing the view that scholars need to produce original qualitative and quantitative research that examines this important question. Bhui (2009) further highlights that since the turn of the century a body of work by black scholars has examined race and crime in a social, economic, and political context. Spalek (2008) however, argues that the concept of racialisation directs our attention away from the question 'What is the relationship between race and crime?' As race is socially constructed, it seems to be a stronger proposition to expand racialisation, which involves an intersection of class and gender.

Again, where are the voices of black men considered in determining how they are contextualised in relation to their own understanding and insights into their desistance? Webster alludes to a racialised position in relation to black men's desistance and states, 'It is necessary to place racialised criminal justice processes in their social and economic context, and note the roles that the criminal justice system plays in a complex and continuum of social control institutions and practices' (2007: 200). Interesting as Webster's point is, there is a failure to acknowledge the voice of black men as a way of understanding how those same processes work to uphold white privilege.

Barak *et al.* (2001) point out that criminology stands to benefit from the integration of criminological perspectives, as traditionally race, class, and gender have been seen as separate variables in relation to the study of crime. According to Barak, an integrated theoretical perspective 'incorporates an appreciation of differences in the patterns of crime attributed to socialisation, opportunities, and bias in the context that everyone's life is framed by inequalities of race, class, and gender' (ibid.: 251). In addition to the unique theoretical contributions that this framework can make to understandings of black men's desistance, the intersectional approach offers a broader context when looking at black criminality in a manner that goes beyond white hegemonic assumptions. Franklin (2004) contends that the lens through which we view black men ignores the intersectional oppressions that black men face when living in a white society, and therefore a realistic picture of black men cannot be built. Hughes (1998) does attempt to locate black men's desistance in a wider context, using an intersectional reference point that sees black men integrating back into a society that had previously excluded them, based on racialised, classed, and gendered divisions within society.

So too Sampson and Wilson (1995), who tie their theory of race, crime, and urban inequality to the lived reality of inner city communities. They comment on the fact that black men who are segregated by race and class within the confines of the inner city have significant restrictions placed on them, making it difficult to actualise strong social bonds, and are then forced back onto the street corners as a way of validating their manhood (see also Clark, 1965). Therefore, in the concluding section, it is important to examine a race-centred approach that might realign the lens through which desistance is viewed. This provides scope for at least seeing black men's desistance through a more appropriate lens from which to draw stronger conclusions than currently exists. McAdams (1988), for one, suggests that stories represent critical scenes and turning points in our lives, and that the 'life story' is a joint product of person and environment.

He states: 'The life story suggests developing a sense of who I am, what I am going to do in the future, and what do I need to do in order to generate a legacy' (ibid.: 19). McAdams' view presents a plausible argument that suggests storytelling or 'self-narrative' may provide criminology with a framework that identifies desistance as a journey best told by the individual making the trip. Therefore, it could be argued that the understanding of the destination to be arrived at must be understood in terms of the journey travelled. Could understanding what went before bring clarity to the journey towards black men's desistance? A theoretical framework that could offer new insights when looking at the racialised nature of desistance is Critical Race Theory (CRT).

Desistance and Critical Race Theory

Critical Race Theory (CRT) has been widely associated with law, education, and more recently sport, and uses storytelling as the basis of its theorising as a means of privileging the voices of those who are oppressed and subordinated by white privilege and supremacy. Stories within a CRT framework are split into two categories: 'majoritarian' stories and 'counter-stories' (Solorzano and Yosso, 2002). Majoritarian stories, as the term suggests, privilege the collective narrative of those who have the power to subordinate (white people), while counter-stories operate as an oppositional narrative told through the voices of those subordinated (black people). So why are the 'stories' associated with insights into the desistance process so important? McAdams (1988) suggests that if we can understand people in terms of their life stories, then we can make sense of the past and this can orient us towards a new future.

McAdams contends that we can systematically analyse our stories that represent critical scenarios and turning points in our lives in relation to the social structure. His position is further evidence that stories are significant in understanding the role of racialisation of crime and criminal justice systems and its impact on the desistance process. As the research here principally was centred on the gathering of black men's stories, CRT was ideally suited in this case, given CRT's use of storytelling to challenge the maintenance of white privilege. Using the 'counter-stories' of black men provided insights into those factors that have assisted or hindered black men's ability to desist from criminal activity, by enabling them to 'name their own reality'.

As Fine and Weis argue 'the stories we tell, and those we don't derive from our position within social and economic hierarchies' (1998: 442). Fine and Weis provide a conduit through which black men not only can tell their story but also can address those who oppress them within those same social and economic hierarchies. Delgado and Stefancic see the lack of acknowledgement of these 'counter-stories' as a process in which society presents a pile of explanatory scripts, plots, narratives, and understandings that enable us to make sense of or construct the social world (2000: 229). They further develop a position that argues that black people must understand and articulate their counter-stories that will enable them to shape and determine who they are, what they see, how they select, reject, interpret, and order their subsequent reality (ibid.: 229).

So too hooks (2004: 25) argues that by ordering subsequent reality, there may be opportunities for black men to create a new narrative that situates itself according to their own dreams, hopes, and desires. Bowling and Phillips (2002), however, express the view that the narrative of racism, when it occurs in the criminal justice system, can best be explained by examining 'the prejudices, stereotyping and discriminatory acts of individual criminal justice practitioners, the cultures of criminal justice organisations, or institutional racism'. Bowling and Phillips further argue that some criminologists feel that the question of 'ethnicity and crime is unanswerable' due to the methodological and conceptual problems inherent in defining and measuring crime (ibid.: 243). Likewise, Brown (2002) sees 'race and crime' as something 'where researchers consistently point fingers, and cover their eyes' (2002: 1). CRT can therefore hold a mirror up to a society to render 'colour-blindness' null and void, and allow a reframing of black men's stories in relation to the racialisation of crime and criminal justice systems and its impact on desistance.

CRT sees colour-blind approaches to race as suppressing personal stories of those affected in the pursuit of neutral and unbiased scientific inquiry. West (2004) sees this colour-blindness as part of an ongoing liberal/conservative discussion that conceals the most basic issue now facing black people. West primarily is asking a question about speaking to the issue of colour-blindness that leads to a profound sense of psychological depression, personal worthlessness, and social despair that is so widespread (ibid.: 10). West further argues that the rendering of stories of many black men is driven by the need to protect the liberal/conservative position. The need for CRT then is embellished in the understanding that when black men do speak, they are constantly pushed to the margins of society and in doing so are not seen and remain invisible in the consciousness of society.

Dixson (2006) reinforces their position and says the voices of people of colour are required for a wider analysis of the racism within the criminal justice system. Dixson further states that experience revealed through the stories of people of colour must be subjected to a deeper analysis using a CRT lens and claims, 'The point we strive to make with this meta proposition is not that class and gender are insignificant, but that "race matters" and blackness matters in more detailed ways' (ibid.: 38). A challenge comes from Hallett, who acknowledges that Critical Race Theorists 'have been discontented with the overreliance on the belated enforcement of minority's civil rights, arguing that deeper and more fundamental changes are necessary for equality to be achieved' (2006: 27). He further states that 'to be ultimately effective critically minded activists must anchor their work in the public sphere' (ibid.: 10). But if that public sphere happens to be controlled and run on a foundation of white privilege, then Hallett's view will surely run aground.

Valdes *et al.* (2002: 244) argue that academics and activists must enable the subordinated person to narrate, to interpret events in opposition to the dominant narratives, and to reinvent one's self by bringing coherence to one's life stories, see also (McAdams, 1988). The narrative potential of CRT therefore, lies in its ability to free us to move backward and forward in time, to re-story the past and to re-imagine the future. In saying that, the fear of academic retribution is a real threat to using CRT in the academy, when the lens may be turned inward and focus attention on the academy itself. Delgado and Stefancic (2000) feel that understanding the impact of racism through a CRT lens can find the way out of a trap of unjustified exclusion when it is time to reallocate power. They extend their position by recognising the role of 'whiteness' in furthering the wider discourse on racialised identities.

Whiteness, as Franklin (2004) argues, places black men at risk of not actualising a true sense of authenticity. Wilson (2009) also argues that denial of access to the social structure based on attributes of white men's power contributes directly to racial group outcomes such as differences in 'social acts' and 'social processes'. By social acts, Wilson means when individuals or groups exercise power over others, whereas social processes refer to the machinery of society that exists to promote ongoing relations between members of the larger group. Examples are laws, policing, and institutional practices that operate from a position of 'white privilege'. He further argues that there are also cultural forces at work, where he views that national views and beliefs about black men drive a sense of 'moral panic' that fuels the collective experiences in these settings. Traditionally, racism is ideologically driven and has placed black men in a subordinate role in relation to white men.

Hill-Collins (2000) argues that there is always choice and the power to act, no matter how bleak the situation may appear to be. She further argues that the domain of white male power manipulates ideological leanings and acts as a link between social institutions and the level of everyday social interaction. The relevance of the previous statements lies less in the traditional understandings of desistance and more in finding a way to let other voices that have been silenced speak for themselves on this matter. In this case, we are talking about black men. The Combahee River Collective Statement (Smith *et al.*, 1978) like-wise argues that the subordination of black women in society has something to offer in terms of explaining the subordination of black men. They see racialisa-tion as a pervasive factor that does not allow black women to look more deeply into their own experiences and from that experience be able to share and grow consciousness. They further argue for the need to build a politics that will change their lives, end their oppression, and contest notions of whiteness.

Dwyer and Jones (2000) locate whiteness in contemporary terms that can enrich our understanding of a wide range of social practices and argue that racial identities can also be differentiated (2000: 17). Akom (2008) also sees 'whiteness studies' as an outgrowth of critical racial studies and sees the need to get beyond the way we see CRT, by broadening discourse centring on race to include an intersection of other forms of oppression. As such, Akom challenges traditional claims of objectivity, meritocracy, colour-blindness, and neutrality and illustrates that traditional research methods often mask the self-interest, power, and privilege of dominant groups (see also Solorzano and Yosso, 2002). Akom (2008) also acknowledges that 'critical reflexivity' should consider how various formulations of whiteness are situated in relation to contemporary formulations of black people's identity formation, politics, and knowledge construction. He further posits the view that researchers should examine how cultural practices are employed by white people, as they reconstitute, support, and maintain forms of white supremacy.

Trainor (2002) sees the deconstruction of whiteness as a political construct that has more currency than CRT's focus on people of colour. He states: 'We may first have to find ways, paradoxically, to embrace discourses that we might have once "preferred not to honor, even with our gaze"' (ibid.: 647). In con-clusion, intersectionality may offer a new possibility for gaining new insights and understandings of black men's desistance by recognising the limitations of race, class, and gender as independent variables. The use of CRT as a method of gathering the narratives of those most affected by discriminatory practice could also offer fresh insights that are required if desistance is to be part of the criminal justice lexicon in operational terms.

Ironically, since the turn of the twenty-first century, a body of work by black scholars have examined race and crime in a social, economic, and political context. Unfortunately most of these works have not filtered into mainstream criminology and are often omitted from textbooks and classroom discussions.

It could be argued that if the development of feminist criminology is any indication, the growth of black criminology will create its own sub-divisions. As stated previously, there could be some value in having a black criminology working alongside feminist criminology to rectify this situation. Webster (2007: 200) also alludes to the relationship between race and class, as a position that transcends only the notion of race.

Webster's view places strong emphasis on the systemic response to processes of racialisation within criminal justice processes. However, who is best placed to articulate that position? It would suggest that CRT may be best placed to create a theoretical context, articulated by those who are on the receiving end of racist treatment and action. As CRT uses counter-stories to explain and explore racist treatment and acts, the story of assimilation to one of black liberation must be a goal that validates the stories of black men in relation to their insights on desistance. The key elements in narrative are the story and its telling. The story is the abstract sequence of events. Telling is the way in which the story is manifested, the statement in a particular medium such as a novel, myth, lecture, film, conversation, or whatever. It is the action, the act of narrating, and the communicative process that produce the story in discourse.

If black men's stories are given meaning, they may enable us to see that present as part of a set of relationships involving a constituted past and a future. This storytelling position may be a vital tool for criminologists to use in much the same way as anthropologists understand, tell, and retell the nature of animal and human behaviour. One of the key tenets in CRT is the understanding that racism is normal and creates a society that is 'colour-blind'. Swann, in his report on black pupils' under-achievement (HMSO, 1985), found a widespread colour-blind attitude, premised on the basis that in the teaching profession it was firmly accepted that to recognise differences between people of various ethnic origins is divisive and can in fact constitute a major obstacle to creating a harmonious multi-racial society. A straightforward rejection of people with a different skin colour is the same since both types of attitude seek to deny the validity of an important aspect of a person's identity.

Swann's view highlights that there is a need to find a way to connect the real lived experience of those most affected by racism, so that any hint of colour-blindness removes the possibility of the sustainability of the majoritarian story (Solorzano and Yosso, 2002). Critical Race Theorists argue that traditional approaches to race suppress personal narratives of those affected in the pursuit of neutral and unbiased scientific inquiry. West writes:

> The liberal/conservative discussion conceals the most basic issue now facing black America: the nihilistic threat to its very existence. This threat is not simply a matter of relative economic deprivation and political powerlessness. It is primarily a question of speaking to a profound sense of psychological depression, personal worthlessness, and social despair so widespread in black America.
>
> (2004: 10)

West's assertion suggests that the narrative of many black men is driven by a need to protect the liberal/conservative position and encourage nihilism, almost guaranteeing that the narrative space black men do occupy is enabled by a system that supports and encourages notions of hyper-masculinity, and then criminalises it for asserting that position. However, Delgado and Stefancic (2000: 228) recognise that racial change is slow, then, because the story of race is part of the dominant narrative that we use to interpret experience. The narrative teaches that race matters, that people are different, with the differences lying always in a predictable direction. It is important then to reaffirm the importance of narrative in CRT, and its importance to society as a whole, when they state:

> We subscribe to a stock of explanatory scripts, plots, narratives, and understandings that enable us to make sense of, to construct, our social world. Because we then live in that world, it begins to shape and deter-mine us, who we are, what we see, how we select, reject, interpret, and order subsequent reality.
>
> (ibid.: 229)

By ordering subsequent reality, there may be opportunities for black men to create a new narrative that situates itself according to their own dreams, hopes, and desires (hooks, 2004). Powerful as it may appear, the normalising of racism means that any views that oppose or denounce the majoritarian narrative may be ignored or have no audience to witness its telling. It may also be the case that the privileged position of many white people in society may distort the narrative that will ultimately impede the cause of racial reform when elite groups use the supposed existence of the market place of ideas to justify their own position. Delgado and Stefancic (2000) further argue that even when minorities do speak, they have little credibility. They conclude with a cautionary piece of advice to scholars such as myself who take up the mantle of CRT.

They feel that because of the way the dominant narrative works, we should prepare for the near certainty that these suggestions will be criticised as unprincipled, unfair to innocent whites, and wrong. Understanding how the dialectic works, and how the scripts and the counter-scripts work their dismal paralysis, may perhaps inspire us to continue even though the path is long and the night is dark. It could be argued that CRT merely provides a new and different lens and way of systematising the search for knowledge of the con-fines of race, as well as trying to go beyond the ordinariness of racist acts and treatment. The experience revealed through the stories of people of colour must be subjected to a deeper analysis using a CRT lens. However, CRT is not without its critics. Darder and Torres (2004) argue that there is a need for a critical theory of racism, and that we need to move away from notions of race in the realms of racialisation.

They are critical of CRT that does not address the issue of class, when they argue quite strongly that much of the literature on subordinate cultural populations, with its emphasis on issues such as racial inequality, racial segregation, or racial identity, has used the construct of race as a central category of analysis for interpreting the social conditions of inequality and marginalisation. Yet, they continue, in much of the work on African-American populations, an analysis of class and a critique of capitalism are conspicuously absent (ibid.: 247). They also see the lack of a class analysis as a serious shortcoming and flaw of CRT. They feel that understanding racism should be viewed through an 'understanding of racialised inequality, whilst simultaneously encompassing the multiple social expressions of racism' (ibid.: 260). Similar to Darder *et al.*, Schneider (2003) is critical of storytelling and feels that critical race theory teaches manipulation of emotions and plays out the issue of race. Schneider feels that constructed narratives by black men are better placed within notions of class and identity that would better highlight the oppressive structures in society.

Davis (1998) challenges Schneider's view by arguing that issues of race have undermined the ability to create a popular critical discourse to contest the ideological trickery that posits the imprisonment of black men as key to public safety. The Combahee River Collective Statement (Smith *et al.*, 1978) also argues that race and not class is something that can be contested in competing for the understanding of the position of black people in society. They see racial politics and racism as pervasive factors in our lives that do not allow most black women to look more deeply into their own experiences and, from that sharing and growing consciousness, to build a politics that will change their lives and invariably end their oppression. The Collective's position talks about 'naming our own reality' as opposed to working to end somebody else's oppression. They conclude by stating: 'We struggle together with black men against racism, while we also struggle with black men about sexism' (ibid.: 4). The intersection between gender and race adds weight to CRT as a way of not watering down 'race' as an ideological and political position.

Dwyer and Jones (2000: 211) counter this position as they feel that locating whiteness in contemporary terms can enrich our understanding of a wide range of social practices, and they argue that racial identities are also differentiated, in that subjects never occupy a single system of difference. They further state: 'Considerations of racialisation are a fundamental aspect of geographical understanding. in much the same way that more and more geographers have recognised that no human geography is complete without a consideration for gender' (ibid.: 218). In my own interpretation, I have used CRT to include an intersection of other forms of oppression such as class, gender, religion, nationality, etc., by illustrating how these elements interlock, thus creating a wider system of oppression.

Akom (2008) views the intercentricity of racialised oppression as challenging traditional claims of objectivity, meritocracy, colour-blindness, and neutrality, and claims that traditional research methods often mask self-interest, power, and the privilege of dominant groups. Akom also feels that critical reflexivity should consider how various formulations of whiteness are situated in relation to contemporary formulations of black people's identity formation, politics, and knowledge construction. Akom further holds the view that researchers should examine how cultural practices and discursive strategies are employed by white people, as well as people of colour, as they struggle to reconstitute, support, and maintain forms of white supremacy. Reconstitution of whiteness, as well as how white supremacy is resisted, have been the central focus of third-wave studies.

If stories hold the key to collective memory, define meaning and purpose, and assist in the development of communities themselves, then what does this mean for the study of black men's desistance? Personal stories are a core element of processes that mark significant changes as part of an individual's life cycle. The social labelling of black men can at times be a barrier to meaningful and productive communication, as those narrow definitions deal with a set of ideas that seldom provide the opportunity for a common and shared value system. This fractures the possibility of reconciliation and unity among those kept in prison institutions. Unless those institutionalised communities can reclaim a sense of 'self', redefined in terms of 'dreams', 'desires', and 'sense of purpose', the result will be a narrative associated with the apocalyptic science fiction genre. Akbar states:

> The self is a kind of community. It has within it the specialists which one finds within any community. These specialists perform certain functions for the benefit of the whole community. The road to inner peace is the same road to outer peace. Such peace is acquired by the harmonious cooperation of these members under a leadership of a common good.
>
> (1991: 15)

When one analyses the contemporary life journeys of many black men living on the margins of society, they can be seen as negative, oppressive, despairing, with no way forward.

However, if we see those difficult stages of their lives as part of a 'heroic' journey (as depicted throughout mythology and folklore), they may begin a process of personal reframing, where the obstacles they face are seen merely as barriers to becoming stronger and more self-determined individuals. By sharing and promoting successful personal narratives, it should be possible to celebrate and strategically plan a re-birth. This provides a template to go from coping to survival, from survival to desistance. By reclaiming a new identity and consciousness, those individuals who remain within closed institutions like prisons can learn how to live meaningful and productive lives again.

Rodriguez (2008) argues that we have to confront whiteness and privilege, both inside and outside of our classrooms. She further argues that transformative spaces will require pain, struggle, and an uncomfortable space (ibid.: 503). Rodriguez offers a perspective on the way people of colour have been marginalised and oppressed in a race-obsessed society that privileges white over black, and sees whiteness as something that must be faced. The competing views here not only create some kind of 'theoretical confusion', but also reveal that with all the competing ideas being expressed, seldom are the views of those being talked about considered. It may be that a CRT of black men's stories is an expression of how the racialisation of criminal justice systems affects and impacts the other variables of class, gender, culture, faith, etc.

So let us further seek how this understanding shapes new understandings and directions for the study of desistance as a whole. This chapter has given an overview of racialisation of crime and criminal justice systems in relation to black men's desistance. Chapter 3 begins to look at the actual journey of the research itself.

3 Approaching black men's desistance

An offender, whilst serving a sentence, must be equipped with the necessary tools to successfully re-enter and 'reintegrate' back into the community. It is then hoped that they will rebuild their lives and contribute to the continuing development of the community by being 'reformed', as a consequence of experiencing positive rehabilitative processes. They will then hopefully be prepared for a life free from crime, and to ultimately 'desist'. However, my research has revealed that for many black men returning to the community from prison, this is not the case. It is right, therefore, to assume that by privileging the voices of black men's experiences of both 're-entry' and their journey towards desistance, a unique opportunity to understand how the racialisation of criminal justice policy has presented itself in either enhancing or hindering this possibility.

Indeed, my observations and participation in prison rehabilitation programmes targeted at black men over three decades have led me to believe that seldom have the insights, understandings, and 'lived' experiences of the black men who come into contact within the criminal justice system been taken into consideration when contributing to the broader dialogue on the study of both re-entry and desistance. Approaching black men's desistance confronted me with a range of searching questions about the ability to objectify a research journey, where I shared much of the same socio-historical context and positioning as those I was researching. The research therefore started with several key questions:

- What impact does the racialisation of crime/criminal justice systems have on the desistance process for black men?
- How do black men construct their own insights and understandings of their desistance in relation to being both black and male in a white society that renders them subordinate?
- What are the factors that contribute to black men's commitment to accept or negate notions of their desistance?

These questions also prompted me to consider what was the most appropriate and relevant approach that would do justice to the subjects of the inquiry, as well as ensuring I could locate myself as an 'insider researcher'.

The research

The research operated from an 'interpretivist perspective'. That is, it focused on the meanings that black men gave to their lived experiences in relation to the racialisation of crime and criminal justice systems and its impact on the desistance process (McAdams, 1988).

The study involved 11 black men from the community from Birmingham in the UK, 10 prisoners, located in HMP Grendon's Therapeutic Community (TC), and 9 black men from the city of Baltimore in the USA. Semi-structured interviews and urban ethnography were the methods used to gather the data (Anderson, 1999). Critical Race Theory (CRT) was the key theoretical framework applied in the research. Others have used it in different spheres: law (Delgado and Stefancic, 2005); education (Ladson-Billings and Tate, 1995); and sport (Hylton, 2005). It was then possible to make CRT into the basis to develop a 'counter-narrative' to privilege the racialised voices of black men.

Prison was also examined as a site where the trajectory towards desistance possibly begins as a place where possible 'transformation' and 'change' might occur. According to Wacquant (2002a), those who conduct research in prison should focus their attention less on interpretation and pay more attention to research on the effects of penal policies and institutions. This would be a move from 'state-centred' approaches to one of 'social equality'. As Wacquant's position argues, I felt the importance of taking this approach was to create a platform for those silent and invisible 'voices' who needed to tell their stories as a way of contesting and challenging some of the mythology that surrounds one of the most incarcerated prison populations on the planet. To do so, my own positioning became important right from the outset.

Methodology

Milner (2007) argues that researchers should be actively engaged, thoughtful, and forthright regarding tensions that can surface when conducting research where issues of race and culture are concerned. Social science research is complex and diverse, where its goals and its basic assumptions vary significantly. In any research inquiry, linking philosophical traditions or schools of thought helps clarify a researcher's theoretical frameworks (Cohen *et al.*, 2000). The framework for any research includes beliefs about the nature of reality (ontology), the theory of knowledge (epistemology), and how that knowledge may be gained (methodology). Ontology and epistemology influence the type of research methodology chosen, and this in turn guides the choice of research design and instruments used. The ontology informs the methodology about the nature of reality and what social science is supposed to study, whereas the epistemology informs the methodology about the nature of knowledge or where knowledge is to be sought. Methodology is a research strategy that translates the ontological and epistemological concerns into research activity.

The ontological concern in this case raised something that I discovered was seldom asked of my research participants who had encountered other researchers. That concern was, 'What is it to be black, male, and an offender, in a society that renders your difference subordinate?' Freire (1970) expresses the view that the oppressed are better prepared than other people to understand the oppressed. He further expresses the view that oppressed peoples, in order to surmount the situation of their oppression, must critically recognise its causes, so that through transforming action they can create a new situation, one that makes possible the pursuit of a fuller humanity (ibid.: 29).

Hence the research started from an interpretivist perspective. An interpretivist perspective accepts that the social world is constructed through meaning, and that those meanings in this case are rooted within a raced, classed, and gendered context (Zamudo *et al.*, 2011). It was then decided to conduct the research in three different sites:

- the community in Birmingham;
- HMP Grendon's Therapeutic Community (TC);
- the community in Baltimore.

The objective here was to push the conventional boundaries of understanding in relation to desistance. I wanted to explore some of the more searching and far-reaching issues concerning the complex nature of desistance trajectories themselves, not just in terms of point of cessation, but other possible influences in relation to black men's desistance, with a specific emphasis on the racialised processes that both inform and govern it. I was mindful of the pursuit in some quarters to create a template by which we can measure desistance or present it as a uniform set of principles.

However, if the ability to desist is impacted by social processes that are racialised, then the possible outcomes are a bit too complex to present in such a simplistic way. It was also important that as I was undertaking doctoral research, the contribution to knowledge was uppermost in my mind. The choice of research sites became important here on account of moving beyond the traditional confines of research that is less about finding something new, and more about reaffirming things we already know.

The community in Birmingham was chosen as it has a significant population of black men within the community who had at some stage been incarcerated in the local prison, HMP Birmingham. The relevance here was engaging with men who both lived and went to prison in the local community. Choosing HMP Grendon was critical for slightly different reasons. First, to discover if desistance began while incarcerated, and, second, to discover what role, if any, a prison-based TC would have on the trajectory towards the cessation of offending. Likewise, conducting research in inner-city Baltimore provided both a comparative element to the research, alongside the deployment of 'urban ethnography' as the method for gathering the data (Anderson, 1999). It is important at this stage to clarify my own position in the research, especially for those using a qualitative methodology that involves 'reflexivity' (Creswell, 1994). As previously mentioned, I positioned myself as the 'insider' researcher alongside being an 'outsider' to the research domain (Bonner and Tolhurst, 2002).

The 'insider–outsider perspective'

Generally, 'insider researchers' are those who choose to study a group to which they belong, while 'outsider researchers' do not belong to the group under study. Bonner and Tolhurst (2002) outlined three key advantages of being an 'insider' in the research domain:

1   a significant understanding of a group's culture;
2   the ability to interact naturally with the group and its members;
3   a previously established, and therefore greater, relational intimacy with the group.

In addition, as an 'insider researcher' I was confronted with methodological and ethical issues that do not necessarily apply to 'outsider researchers'.

Taking on the role of the researcher often acts as a barrier that separates the 'insider' from those in the setting they are researching. A further difficulty encountered when operating as the 'insider researcher' relates to some of the ethical considerations. Ethical issues continuously arise, and need to be dealt with on an individual and daily basis. Although ethical principles of privacy, confidentiality, and informed consent do guide the research, there is often an uneasy tension as to how these principles play out in community and prison-based applied research (Gerrish, 1997). The 'insider' positioning views the research process and products as 'co-constructions' between the researcher and the participants in the research; it regards the research participants or respondents as active 'informants' to the research; and attempts to give 'voice' to the informants within the research domain (Denzin and Lincoln, 2000). As such, these perspectives allow the researcher to conduct research 'with' rather than 'on' their group, which contrasts starkly with 'outsider researcher' perspectives.

In embodying an insider role, undertaking this approach to research creates particular challenges that require careful consideration and appropriate responses. It was impossible to avoid complete impartiality, but the ethical considerations ensured that there were no improper actions, or the possibility of 'going native'. Being immersed in the world of the research subjects was required in order to access the data, and in doing so generate new insights in an area that is under-researched, under-theorised, and misunderstood. Therefore, a range of safeguards needed to be put in place to reduce the amount of subjectivity that would lead to the contamination of the research process.

This manifested in the use of a reflexive aspect of the research methods. Reflexivity became an important tool in understanding my own levels of subjectivity in relation to the research as a whole, which will be discussed later in this chapter. This next section deals with the selection of participants.

The study sample: the participants

Birmingham

This strand of the study involved 11 black men from the community. Participants reflected a diverse range of offending behaviours, as well as representing several geographical locations from across the city of Birmingham (Table 3.1).

HMP Grendon

Participants from HMP Grendon reflected a diverse range of offending behaviours, as well as representing several geographical locations from the UK, Africa and the Caribbean. HMP Grendon's research committee guided the research process throughout. Participants were then drawn from the widest cross-section of HMP Grendon's prisoner community, and which resulted in 4 men from G wing, 4 men from D wing, and 3 men from C wing (Table 3.2).

Baltimore

This strand of the research focused on black men in the city of Baltimore. The objective was to undertake a comparative analysis in relation to factors that enhanced or hindered notions of desistance. The US strand of the research was undertaken in Baltimore during August/September 2010, as part of a Winston Churchill International Travel Fellowship. The participants were as shown in Table 3.3.

Positions of the participants

All of the participants in the study occupied a variety of different positions within the desistance paradigm, ranging from those who had ceased offending

Table 3.1

Name	Age	Status
Leroy	35	Former gang member
Henry	28	Former gang member
Marvin	40	Former gang member
Robert	41	Former gang member
Jay	25	Former gang member
Paul	32	Former gang member
David	32	Current gang member
Kieran	27	Current gang member
Chris	31	Former gang member
Noel	29	Former gang member
Stefan	26	Former gang member

Source: Information was gained during preliminary interviews with participants. Establishing their current status was based on building a level of trust prior, during, and on completion of the research process.

Table 3.2

Name	Age	Status
Peter	42	Attempted murder
Nathan	43	GBH
Donavan	49	Robbery
Stewart	45	Firearms offences
Everton	35	Aggravated burglary
Yusef	28	Murder
Pablo	51	Rape
Linton	31	Attempted murder
Simon	41	Attempted murder
Winston	22	Murder

Source: Information was supplied by HMP Grendon.

Table 3.3

Name	Age	Status
Neville	67	Served 16 years
Al	58	Served 15 years
Jason	50	Served 10 years
Brian	30	Former drug dealer
Ishmael	25	Former gang member
Rahim	19	Current gang member
Tyrone	40	Former gang enforcer
Byron	60	Former drug dealer
Barry	35	Current gang member

Source: Information was supplied by the participants themselves.

for a short period of time (primary desistance) to those who had had a significant period of time away from their last offence (secondary desistance).

Equally as important were the incarcerated men who, in spite of not being free to commit more crimes, were important in understanding the psychological aspects of determining 'desistance readiness' prior to release. Once selected, an important next step was in the way access was granted in all three sites. Once again there were some complications regarding uniformity of access.

Access

The community in Birmingham

The objective here was to look at the role of the community in relation to the factors that enhanced or hindered the understanding and insights of the racialisation of crime and criminal justice systems and its impact on the desistance process. Thus, key community informants and gate keepers were contacted in order to recruit participants. They were drawn from the faith communities, community organisations, and criminal justice agencies. All of the participants were then given relevant information about the research prior to taking part in the research. This aspect of the research took the form of initial meetings via phone calls, leading to more structured meetings that worked out the detail of the research being undertaken in conjunction with the participants themselves. The selection of participants was made by compiling a short list of appropriate candidates, followed by a sifting process. Successful participants were then informed about the specific nature of the research in detail, before meeting up and signing a 'release form' where they were informed they could withdraw at any stage of the research.

Many of those from the community revealed how they had previously experienced difficulties with other research inquiries and had ongoing issues of trust or confidentiality, so personal safety became a key consideration in terms of where the interviews took place and how they were conducted. Key community contacts assisted in locating the subjects for the inquiry and established an initial dialogue. A series of meetings with each participant, prior to the interviews was arranged to clarify any details and establish clear boundaries. Once clarity had been established and the initial trust had been built, each participant then read and signed a release form that clearly stated the aims, objectives, and expectations of the research. In the later section of this chapter there is a reflexive account of the researcher's position designed to highlight some of the challenges faced when trying to gain access to the research participants.

HMP Grendon

HMP Grendon is the only prison in the country that operates wholly as a therapeutic community (TC) (Genders and Player, 2010). HMP Grendon was chosen to be part of the research for several reasons:

- Prisons are socially divided and hierarchically structured, whereas the TC is organised to minimise social divisions.
- Prisons operate with a rigid set of rules, whereas a TC is self-regulating.
- Prisons depersonalise the individual, TCs promote the development of personal identity.

It was the contrast in differences between traditional prisons and a TC that was the main reason for HMP Grendon's inclusion in the research. Operating within the TC in HMP Grendon, the research process was subject to the prison's ethics committee. So too, while conducting the research, prison officers were on hand to ensure the timings were adhered to, as well as assisting in the management of the schedule of the research itself. This strand of the research focused on black men in a prison-based therapeutic community (TC). The aim was to look at the role of therapeutic intervention in prison in relation to the racialisation of crime and criminal justice systems and its impact on the desistance process and compare how the experience of TC in relation to desistance differed from that of the community. After lengthy negotiations with the prison, three days were allocated to conduct the field research.

All participants were informed of the nature of the research, and were advised that at any stage of the research they could withdraw. Each participant was interviewed separately, and issues pertaining to confidentiality were also discussed and agreed. It was also agreed that prison officers would not be present during the interviews as it was felt they would be an inhibiting factor for those taking part. However, prison officers were consulted prior to conducting the research, as it was important that their views were also considered as part of the process. In all cases, prison officers were supportive of my requests and cooperated throughout. It was also intended to investigate the role of the TC in enabling black men to reflect on those understandings and insights of the racialisation of crime and criminal justice systems and its impact on the desistance process differently from the prison estate as a whole. The interviews were coordinated in conjunction with the prison to ensure that they did not breach prison security.

Moving from a paradigm of 'researching on', to one of 'researching with' prisoners laid a stronger foundation on which to build trust between researcher and interviewees (Freire, 1970). Meeting the prisoners for the first time required a small amount of negotiation in terms of establishing the scope and boundaries of the research. Once that was complete, each individual read and signed a release form that clearly stated the aims, objectives, and expectations of the research.

Baltimore

A significant amount of liaison took place via email with Johns Hopkins University in Baltimore, Maryland, and key community contacts in Baltimore. Both the university and the community contacts assisted in locating the subjects for the inquiry and brokered the initial connection. On arrival in Baltimore, a series of individual and group meetings with potential participants was set up, creating a connection, clarifying any concerns about the research, concluding by establishing clear boundaries.

A process of selection was then undertaken with colleagues at Johns Hopkins and key community informants, in relation to suitability for participation. Each individual participant then read and signed a release form that clearly stated the aims, objectives, and expectations of the research. Du Bois (1938) points out that 'car wash sociologists' operating from an ivory tower vantage point, who do not venture into black communities, cannot fully understand black men's social reality. He further argues that one must study black men at first hand. Operating from a racialised context does remove some of the barriers between me and the subjects of the inquiry, but more importantly as explained previously, recognises the importance of not 'going native'.

So though I was operating from the 'insider' perspective in relation to my racial identity, my position as a criminologist and researcher also placed me in an 'outsider' position in relation to the subjects of the inquiry. Overall, the building of trust was paramount, especially as many of those involved in the research had experienced previous negative experiences with researchers, both black and white. It was also important to assert the role of being an 'insider researcher' to access a section of the community that is seldom accessed. To adopt this position was not easy, but necessary in order to conduct research that was both challenging and controversial. A look at the tensions in relation to being an outsider–insider researcher is important here.

Reflexivity

The reflexive part of the research focused on how my own racial identity impacted on my ability to remain objective. It also acted as an analytical tool to assess if my 'insider' position in the research would hinder my objectification throughout the research journey. As stated previously, total impartiality was impossible, but operating as 'the insider' gave me a unique insight into the world of the subjects of the inquiry. There were obvious risks involved throughout the journey but careful planning and consistent supervisory support not only minimised those risks, but also ensured an academic focus was kept throughout. Reflexivity demands that the researcher relinquish a certain level of control within the research process, as a way of enabling the voices of the participants to be heard, for as Duneier (2006) argues, participants in research should 'become authors of their own lives' and in doing so should experience some dignity within the research process.

This is a view echoed by Becker who states, 'We focus too much on questions whose answers show that the supposed deviant is morally in the right and the ordinary citizen morally in the wrong' (1967: 240). It was therefore wholly appropriate for black men who have been rendered invisible in many research studies not only to voice to their understanding of desistance, but also to give an offender/reformed offender perspective. Therefore, the reflexive aspect of the research acted as a barometer designed to identify the ongoing conflict between the objective and subjective aspects of the research itself. Frequently the view has been expressed that occupying a 'space' where the individual does not have to defend their cultural perspectives, 'linguistic codes' or expressions of 'blackness', becomes a liberating factor within the interview process. Eight key elements were identified in my process as an interviewer. These elements were predicated on the notion that as I was operating in an 'insider position', my own sense of identification as a black man would be important here. Those eight elements were:

- *Connectivity* – My understanding of black/street vernacular enabled me to gain access to both the cultural and linguistic aspects of those black men being interviewed.
- *Perception* – My 'rite of passage' was rooted in the perception that those whom I interviewed had of my politics, knowledge of black history, culture,

and blackness. In doing so, I gained a level of credibility that encouraged and increased the motivation to be interviewed.

- *Mediation* – Based on my ability to gain credibility, the exchange of ideas felt less of a scientific process and one where the individuals being interviewed 'told their stories' in a relaxed and non-threatening way.
- *Negotiation* – Throughout the interviews there was a sense of ongoing negotiation. Once again, the credibility I had gained made negotiation that much easier. There were revelations that at times were private, painful, and awkward. Accommodating those who were interviewed was central to the process and exchange between interviewer and interviewee.
- *Exchange* – At times, those interviewed wanted to ask me questions. This tended to take place either before the interview started or directly after. The process research was respected but for many of those interviewed, it was the first time they had been interviewed by a black person. As their curiosity was aroused, they felt comfortable enough to ask me questions also.
- *Discharge* – At times, their views came out in a range of emotive ways. When telling their stories, some powerful things were expressed that occasionally resulted in a few tears, angry outbursts, or long silences.
- *Revelation* – When telling their truths, they became very vulnerable, which at times was hard to deal with, as I had to remain in interview mode. Keeping myself together was also an important part of reassuring them that it was a safe space to let out the deep feelings and strong emotions that came to the surface.
- *Closure* – In the debriefing that followed each interview, it was important to bring closure to the interview. Sometimes a small prayer was said, a hug was given, or a few moments spent in silent contemplation.

Each of the eight elements will invariably involve some aspect of value judgement rooted in a context that will reveal aspects of the researcher's social, cultural, and political understandings.

However, access to communities who have traditionally been marginalised or who feel subordinate will require a flexible approach that validates the difficulties that can be encountered when undergoing a positive experience. This position also highlights the importance of ethical considerations when involved in doing this type of research. Establishing the ethical codes provided important boundaries for both the researcher and those involved as participants. The ethics also locates itself within the type of methods chosen to conduct the research. In this case, qualitative research was used. Unlike statistical research, the protection of the participants from being harmed, combined with trying to ensure the researcher acts in the best interest of the research, is always a topic for discussion. Broadly speaking, two types of research methodologies dominate debates in criminological inquiry: quantitative and qualitative methods.

Both methods require different approaches to acquire data. Therefore, the choice of the methodology used should be guided by the research questions and hypotheses that are being examined or developed. Quantitative methods are rooted in the scientific method derived from the physical and natural sciences. These methods are objective and formal (Creswell, 1994). Using quantitative methods, values are removed from the research process (Babbie, 2002). One of the strengths of quantitative research is the transparency that comes from the methods that are used to arrive at the findings. Quantitative methods capture and use numbers (ibid.). Qualitative methods, on the other hand, try to develop theories rather than test them. They use the language of the subject to provide the understanding and not the number of the subjects. Qualitative methods also allow the researcher to become part of the study by shortening the distance between him or herself and the research subject.

One of the biggest conflicts between the two methods is that of reliability. Reliability is the consistency of a result over time (ibid.). A quantitative method is more likely to generate results that are consistent over time; they are reliable, as a result of the controlled environment and the standardisation that may arise from the standardisation in testing. Bryman (1988) argues that sometimes quantitative and qualitative may appear at odds with each other, when the data deriving from the two types of research appear to clash. Chilisa (2012), on the other hand, argues that all research methodologies should centre on the concerns and worldviews of the research subjects so that they understand themselves through their own assumptions and perspectives. Mills (1959) too states that whatever methodology is used, the researcher should be a good craftsman. In doing so, Mills argues that researchers should avoid any rigid set of procedures and seek to develop and to use the sociological imagination. Mills feels that the conventions of research methods can limit envisioning ways of knowing and seeing that will contest conventional wisdom. Likewise, Goffman (1959) argues that in the period when the individual is in the immediate presence of the others, few events may occur which directly provide the others with the conclusive information they will need if they are to direct their own activity wisely.

Denzin (2010) argues that mixed methods are important inasmuch as they help the researcher to confront and work through the epistemological, methodological and ethical stance toward critical inquiry when each generation must offer its responses to current and past criticisms. Agnew (2011) maintains it is difficult to accurately measure this reality, particularly since individual reports of it are biased for several reasons. Some progress, however, has been made in developing 'reduced bias' measures of this reality by using a mixed methods approach. Trahan (2011) argues that quantitative findings can give precision to qualitative data.

However, in light of the absence of available qualitative data to incorporate into a mixed methods approach to the study, it was decided to privilege the voices of a small number of black men, as a way of laying the groundwork for further and larger studies that would involve quantitative methods of inquiry. Again, in qualitative research, conducting interviews is the vehicle by which data are gathered. Working with participants deemed 'high risk' or 'hard to access' requires significant skill and management if the data is to be gathered correctly in preparation for the analysis.

The interviews

Semi-structured interviews were used throughout to collect the life histories on a range of themes, such as: childhood memories; involvement in crime; masculinities; and the racialisation of crime and criminal justice systems. In all three sites, interviews were then conducted over a period of weeks, subject to the availability of the participants. In saying that, interviews in HMP Grendon were conducted within a set time frame according to the rules laid down by the prison itself. As the interviews were about gathering the stories from the participants, this situation did not have any bearing on the outcomes, but did reveal a discontinuity in relation to researching in three different sites and differing time spans. All those interviewed would be classified as individuals who had terminated their offending and they represented a wide spectrum of offending behaviour: robbery, gangs, drugs, etc. The rights of the research participants were constantly being re-negotiated and brokered throughout the research process as it was vital that community participants had some level of control in the research process.

Each participant was interviewed separately at a venue of their choice (except HMP Grendon) and issues pertaining to confidentiality were also discussed and agreed. Each interview lasted approximately one hour. The use of a micro recorder at times became problematic. This was on account of previous experiences of being recorded when coming into contact with the criminal justice system. Care and sensitivity had to be observed at all times. All the identities of participants in the research were kept hidden in the text, but for ease of reference they have been identified by the use of pseudonyms, as some participants felt uncomfortable with being identified.

Special permission needed to be granted in HMP Grendon to allow me to bring a recorder into the prison, which at times presented problems. Namely, the equipment including batteries would have to be checked each day. If, for any reason, the amount of batteries or ancillary equipment differed, additional restrictions would be placed on the interview process. In itself, this was not a problem, but if failure to gain access to the participants because of equipment failure had occurred, it would have severely hampered the overall process. Central to all of the interviews was the creation of a 'safe space' where participants felt free to share their experiences away from the observation of others. What was especially noticeable was how there was a uniform expression of trepidation on the part of most of the participants. In probing further, I discovered how many times throughout their engagement with the criminal justice system they had been interviewed in one form or another. Most had been conducted in an adversarial way, which means that some of the resistance I encountered emerged not from my own desire to interview them, but from the legacy of previous negative encounters. Hence safety became critical in gaining and building trust that in turn led to my being granted access by my participants. In essence, I had to prove that my intentions were honourable.

Safe space

Creating a 'safe space' for black men to talk freely about their understandings of the racialisation of crime and criminal justice systems and its impact on desistance was designed to make the process open and transparent. Spence (2010) sees this 'safe space' as serving an important function where black men do not have to defend their racial existence or humanity (ibid.: 68). As stated previously, many of those interviewed expressed reservations about working with 'insensitive researchers', based on numerous experiences of being 'researched on'. They also expressed the importance of having an 'insider researcher' who came from a similar background to their own.

Gunarathum (2003) argues that the race of the interviewer and the space where the interview takes place can have a significant impact on the levels of openness and honesty of the research process. Of note, unlike prison, the community is a place full of distractions. There was never a perfect place to interview, as well the nature of participants who at times would turn up late, express doubts, or struggle with their confidence throughout. Overall, the participants expressed appreciation with the approach taken. It was also very evident that black men who have been to prison and have re-entered the community needed a similar 'safe space' to voice and share their experiences, free from judgement and suspicion. During the research process the participants who were being interviewed expressed a desire for the researcher to be sensitive to their racial and cultural identity. The term used by both community participants and the prisoners to describe this type of interaction was 'keepin' it real'.

Keepin' it real

Not only did 'keepin' it real' create and build trust, but also it validated these black men's sense of worth and boosted their self-esteem. In spite of the relative safety of HMP Grendon, the occupation of space free from racialised judgements was an important consideration for all those who took part in the research. In general, the prisoners and reformed offenders who took part in the research expressed the view that their lived experience in prison was rooted in a lack of trust in the system, where most people (prison officers, ancillary staff, and criminal justice professionals) 'didn't keep it real'. They further argued that trust was something conspicuously absent within the prison regime and post-release services, based on the lack of acknowledgement of their cultural identity. The lack of culturally competent services for black men in the research has implications for desistance as a whole (Brookes *et al.*, 2012). A critical point of reflection was how the interviews started and concluded. It was important that the participants felt the way things were conducted met their own aspirations regarding how research with them was to be conducted.

Briefing and debriefing

All interviews started with a 'briefing' session and concluded with a 'debriefing session'. Both sessions were invaluable in raising and addressing any additional concerns. Participants further expressed the view that they had little space to address common issues, for fear of being seen as deviant and subversive, and they welcomed the approach taken. Many participants in the research expressed the view that the negation of race, ethnicity and culture while incarcerated had brought out a range of adverse responses while being locked up. Being acknowledged as 'just men' throughout the research process, not tied to issues of their 'racial and cultural' identities was seen as important by all participants, as they felt 'humanised' by the process.

Similarly, many participants expressed their frustration at being labelled a 'black ex-offender' and felt this description was a continuing barrier to the journey towards desistance, on account of not being treated fairly in areas such as education, training, or employment. They stated that in previous encounters with researchers there had been no briefing and debriefing sessions, where arising distress was considered, that may have been triggered as a consequence of other issues in the process. In the debriefing a significant issue recurred, namely, that of analysis of the gathered testimonies. Giving reassurance that their testimonies would not be adapted, watered down, or manipulated meant using an approach that did justice to those concerns. In this case it was decided to use an adapted form of 'grounded theory' as the instrument for the initial analysis.

Grounded theory

All the interviews were transcribed and analysed using an adapted form of grounded theory (Charmaz, 2006; Strauss and Corbin, 2007). Grounded theory means theory is derived from data, systematically gathered and analysed through the research process. In this method, data collection, analysis, and eventual theory stand in close relationship to one another (Strauss and Corbin, 1998: 13). The key components of grounded theory are:

1   Build rather than test theory.
2   Provide researchers with analytic tools for handling masses of raw data.
3   Help analysts to consider alternative meanings of phenomena.
4   Be systematic and creative simultaneously.
5   Identify, develop, and relate the concepts that are the building blocks of theory.

Once the data had been gathered, they were coded. Saldana (2009) states a code in qualitative inquiry is a word or short phrase that symbolically assigns a summative, salient, essence-capturing, or evocative attribute to the language of the data. Although there was software available to make the job easier, the route chosen was to do it the old-fashioned way. This involved hours of pains-taking work where categories were grouped and regrouped. The act of coding required me to use my own researcher's analytic lens, where the interpretation depended on what type of filter covered the lens. There was also a significant amount of preliminary jotting and the emergence of many analytic memos as additional thoughts and feelings sprang to mind. The cumulative impact of this approach generated so many code categories that emerged in Birmingham and Baltimore, that I decided to use 'theoretical sampling' to complete the 'data gathering' that would strengthen the previous grounded theorising.

Using theoretical sampling, a new set of questions emerged. It is important to state here that the theoretical sampling process cannot be planned before start-ing the analysis, and specific sampling decisions were made during the research process. Though statistical sampling aims to obtain accurate evidence on dis-tributions, theoretical sampling aims to discover new categories and their properties to allow a theory to emerge. When categories are saturated, the theoretical sampling process is completed (Strauss and Corbin, 1998). The logic of theoretical sampling emerges from the idea that the researcher develops a theory about a substantive area through the sampling process (Locke, 2001). Eventually, the data gathering and analysis were complete, but, as stated previously, there were some challenges along the way which placed some level of strain and limitations on the overall study itself. Something else emerged as the inquiry developed regarding things that went 'unsaid' but were visibly noticeable. Serrant-Green (2010) refers to those moments as 'silences'.

Hearing silences

What made a significant impact in the development stages of the research were the countless encounters with participants who expressed the view that they had spent many years 'suffering in silence' regarding their own views, thoughts, and visions on their own desistance. This led me to investigate things further and begin to interrogate notions of black men's silences. In assessing the situation, I discovered that notions of invisibility, colour-blindness, and white privilege, at times force black men to construct a 'code of silence' as a way of protecting themselves from the harm that may arise from the agents of their oppression. In researching further, I found a framework which I am suggesting could be useful for other researchers wanting to enable black men to transcend their 'silences'. In doing so we may learn valuable insights into a world that at times is not seen or heard, as a consequence of black men's silences. Serrant-Green (ibid.) developed 'silences' to unite the theoretical and philosophical approaches that underpin the experiences of the researcher and participants, as applied in a sexual health and 'ethnicity' context.

This approach provides a useful basis for a theoretical framework to research sensitive issues of marginalised populations. Silences reflect the unsaid or unshared aspects of how beliefs, values and experiences of (or about) some groups affect their health and life chances. They also expose issues which shape, influence and inform both individual and group understandings of health and health behaviour. How, then, could the 'silences' framework be located within a criminological context, with specific reference to black men's own understandings of the racialisation of criminal justice systems with reference to their desistance?

Freire (1970) argues those who suffer the effects of oppression can better understand the necessity of liberation within the oppressive prison environments and difficult communities. Like Freire, a committed criminologist must be someone who acknowledges that liberation from oppressive forces must be the key goal when researching with communities who themselves are oppressed and require support in transforming pain and suffering into healing and transformation. It is my contention that black men are both the 'experts' and 'knowers' of their own experiences but their oppression and exposure to racialised criminal justice processes render their voices 'silent'. Some of the blame here must be placed at the feet of researchers themselves, whose responsibility is to give marginalised voices a platform from which to speak. Du Bois (1938) refers to those researchers who do not venture into inner-city communities as 'car wash sociologists'.

Katz (1988), equally as condemning, similarly criticises those social scientists who can 'graciously transport themselves' to worlds they have never been to before by making claims from the 'safe vantage point' of the 'ivory tower'. Denzin (2010) too directs attention to the need to transcend the confines of the 'ivory tower' and demands qualitative researchers heed the 'call to arms' for all of those who believe in the inter-connection between 'critical inquiry' and 'social justice'. Young (2011) argues that all too often criminology finds some kind of satisfaction by using research as part of an 'othering process' that is designed to reveal deep insights and understandings of people's lives, based on the objectivity of the researcher conducting research where they 'jump in' to communities, and then 'jump out' once they have found what they are looking for. It is against this backdrop that this section on 'silences' is framed.

How can accessing 'silences' reveal something new about the racialised experiences of black men within the criminal justice system, and further shape a new worldview and ultimately their motivation towards desistance as an agency choice? 'Silences' can form the backdrop through which we can view the systemic way black men have been stigmatised and over-represented, i.e. disproportionally represented, within criminal justice systems. The term 'silences' in this context is used to reflect elements of the research process where voices, experiences, insights, and understandings of the social world are rendered absent or invisible (Serrant-Green, 2010). In simple terms, 'silences' reflect viewpoints and information that are not openly said, heard or evidenced in the available (mainstream or easily accessible) bodies of literature related to a specific subject. 'Silences' derive from anti-essentialist viewpoints which accept that reality is neither objective, nor fixed; rather, the social world is constructed and determined by human beings in a particular society at a particular point in time (Williams and May, 1996).

'Silences', therefore, in my case, value black men's interpretations of events and their experiences as a key part of what they believe to be their truths. An important point arising out of this is that ultimately 'silences' are situated in the subjective experiences of black men and the social and personal contexts in which their experiences occur. It is often in the recounting of human experience and insight into research studies that the recognition of black men's 'silences' makes a unique and original contribution to the evidence base where previously it has been rendered invisible. Researchers like myself should be encouraged to address issues and increase the validity of their research by enabling the participants to support the study from research question formulation through to analysis and decisions about dissemination, where possible.

As we seek to expand our understanding of the broad range of factors impacting on black men and desistance, research is increasingly called upon to explore issues which have a degree of sensitivity in particular communities at a point in time. In addition, exposing how those experiences may be differently experienced may call on researchers to seek out the views of seldom heard or marginalised groups in a society. This requires researchers to be able to utilise an approach to conducting studies which centralises the sensitive or marginalised nature of the research in order to appraise criminal justice policies in the light of these hidden perspectives. Inevitably there are problems inherent in any research study. My study was no different in this case and had to account for possible flaws and limitations.

Limitations of the study

In relation to the research, there were significant challenges that emerged in relation to both epistemological and ontological concerns. Those concerns were:

1 How did participants understand being black, male, and in relation to the racialisation of the criminal justice system? How would they apply that understanding to provide a true account of those insights?
2 How would I, as an 'insider researcher', position myself in relationship to the epistemological concerns?
3 How much would my own reflexivity reveal ontological flaws within the process?
4 How were the standards of 'reliability' and 'validity' adhered to in relation to the study of the racialisation of crime and criminal justice systems and its impact on the desistance process?

The reliability of the research was relative to the scope of the study. In the context of the aims of the research, the qualitative relationship between researcher/researched, in this case, provided a reasonable level of reliability, based on the subject matter, and methods used. However, as was stated previously, the research can not claim anything more substantive until a wider project is undertaken. If validity is rooted in notions of a 'truth', then the findings of the research were quite valid. To pathologise the truth by proclaiming that a single version of events is 'real' and 'valid' is a flawed argument. The research quite clearly did not represent a huge constituency, but the collective 'counter-narrative' did present a bundle of 'self-truths', which in themselves are important.

However, to make any significant valid claims to the study of the racialisation of crime and criminal justice systems and its impact on the desistance process, the research would have to be wide-ranging, include more participants, and adopt methods and methodologies that would create a stronger validity in its findings. The next stage was to look at the framework for looking at the racialisation of crime and criminal justice systems and its impact on the desistance process. After much deliberation and additional research, it was considered important to identify an approach that would validate the desire to give voice to black men, within a racialised criminal justice context. The instrument that was chosen was Critical Race Theory (CRT).

Critical Race Theory (CRT)

This study used CRT to better understand notions of the racialisation of crime and criminal justice systems and its impact on the desistance process. At the same time it used CRT as the basis of an analytical approach to processes of racialisation and gender. It was planned that CRT would be used as a way of enabling the naming of 'one's own reality' so as to legitimise and validate black men's understandings of the racialisation of crime and criminal justice systems and its impact on the desistance process. CRT would provide a 'counter-narrative' designed to challenge and contest the privileged position of white academics who have rendered a black perspective in these areas invisible. McAdams (1988) maintains that abstinence from criminal activity requires ex-offenders to make sense of their lives in the form of 'life story' or 'self-narrative', and sees the use of 'narrative' as a tool for both understanding and theorising the understanding and insights into racialisation of crime and criminal justice systems and its impact on the desistance process.

As stated previously, grounded theorising provided a crucial framework from which to build a Critical Race Theory (CRT) in the form of a 'counter-narrative' (Solorzano and Yosso, 2002). The results of developing a 'counter-narrative' of black men's desistance will be discussed later in this thesis. Constant reflection on the process as a whole meant there were a range of issues that arose as by-products of the research and associated processes.

Matters arising

Researching black men in the community required me to become absorbed in the lives of the subjects of the research. As such, temporary relationships were formed between the researcher and the researched. This was at times difficult, but there was a successful exchange of ideas.

As the participants from the community had encountered few researchers coming from a similar racialised background, there were some additional obstacles to overcome. Hence the importance of meeting, sifting, and selecting appropriate participants. My own sense of identity was what appeared to underlie issues centring on the complex relationship between researcher and subject. Recognising and establishing my own relationship and position in relation to the participants is a process common to any researcher, regardless of their racial identity. Researching with and within a community who historically have been marginalised and placed in a subordinate position by previous negative encounters with other researchers, it was understood beforehand that resistance might emerge as a consequence of those previous encounters.

As stated previously, the 'insider' position was quickly limited by the participant's empathetic recognition of my role as a researcher and was a role that they did not want to breach. Working in TC differed from working in the 'mainstream' prison estate and created a strange paradox. On the one hand, the researcher engages in a process of investigation and undertakes interviews, while at the same time the prison regime observes the researcher at all times in the name of security. Access to participants was made easier by HMP Grendon's coordination and support. Being in a controlled environment meant being constantly aware and vigilant in relation to prison security. Prison interviewing in HMP Grendon was very stressful at times, as there was little in the way of emotional support before, during, and after. Overall, there was a strong sense of satisfaction in the approach taken, though there were at times smaller gaps in terms of the emotional distance between the participants and myself.

Often, the harrowing nature of the stories caused me to question my own position in their lives. Baltimore was at times challenging, frightening, and in some cases very harrowing. Not being from Baltimore, or being an African American, all had some level of impact in terms of gaining access, trust, and more importantly, credibility. On a street level, interactions were not in a controlled environment, while the opposite was true when working in HMP Grendon. Similarly, working on a street level on the streets of Baltimore meant that I as the researcher was scrutinised and viewed with suspicion and caution on several occassions. Although there was a level of reactive resistance, overall those who assisted in the brokerage, in relation to participants, enabled me to gain credibility quite quickly. There were occasions I was subjected to a series of tests, rituals, and ordeals to see if I was fit for purpose to conduct interviews in the community.

Like any piece of work on a street level, there is an element of personal risk. Using semi-structured interviews combined with a shortened version of urban ethnography were not only suitable methods, but necessary to access the participants who at times were living in precarious situations. It is also true that other forms of research might bring a different sensibility to the so-called mainstream research agenda, but the approach taken was both relevant and appropriate in light of the circumstances. As stated previously, there were many ethical dilemmas that needed to be addressed. Interestingly, it was when I was faced with dangerous situations that the 'ethical considerations' were called upon and tested by the participants themselves. Declaring my intentions when viewed with suspicion became a powerful way to share and validate my ethical standpoint. Working with black men in Baltimore was not a joyride, as it was often painful, unrewarding, and scary. Much rested on my temperament, attitudes, and 'street knowledge'. Being a so-called 'good researcher' counted for nothing if there was little or no understanding of black men's social reality.

Being black was also not a prerequisite. It is the type of black person I am that mattered. Handling participants in difficult circumstances, and having a sense of honest commitment to representing the issues you are there to represent, were at the core of gaining credibility in Baltimore's most dangerous neighbourhoods. However, prison and community outreach can depend on factors that are outside of the control and scope of the researcher. Using a semi-structured interview approach may have limited the amount of emotional attachment to the process but empathy with the situation of the participants was hard to escape. As the interviewees journeyed through the research, they were interested in my own views on the subject.

Familiarity with black men has its pros and cons. However important empathy may be, it can cause some level of distraction. How much that influenced the outcomes cannot be directly measured. It is a factor that could influence not what was said, but how some of the guys felt. In an area where there is little precedent regarding interviewing black men, there is no doubt things can be done to improve or strengthen the methods used. It is evident that black men need a space to voice and share their experiences. Sensitivity must be the key element in relation to the ethical considerations when accessing these testimonies. At all times, openness and transparency are the values that inform the core component of the research, if it is to be successful. The findings highlight some significant and key meanings that will bring some new understandings to understanding the racialisation of crime and criminal justice systems and its impact on the desistance process. This chapter highlighted why the research operated from an interpretivist perspective and explained why it used CRT as the basis for the analytical approach used.

It also revealed some critical methodological issues pertaining to the researcher's reflexive account of his own journey contained within the research. Milner (2007) argues that researchers should be actively engaged, thoughtful, and forthright regarding tensions that can surface when conducting research where issues of race and culture are concerned. The aim of interpretative analysis is to explore in detail how participants make sense of their personal and social world. The approach involves detailed examination of their world; to explore personal experience and is concerned with personal perception. At the same time, it also emphasises that the research exercise is a dynamic process with an active role for the researcher in that process. Essentially, the researcher is trying to get close to the participant's world from an 'insider's perspective'. This perspective, as I have argued, depends on, and is complicated by, my own conceptions, perceptions, and levels of subjectivity.

In essence, the participants are trying to make sense of their world, while at the same time the researcher is trying to make sense of the participants trying to make sense of their world. In Chapter 4, I attempt to account for some of my concerns by presenting a 'reflexive' account of my 'insider researcher' status. The aim here to locate my own thoughts and feelings throughout the different aspects of the process. It is not to try and justify my own level of subjectivity, but to reveal the difficulties of achieving objectivity, thus evidencing my claims that objectivity in this type of research is not possible. What is possible is the researcher's account for any level of subjectivity that occurs during the research.

4 Developing a black criminology of desistance

The 'urban' criminologist

Russell (2002) calls for the development of a 'black criminology' as a viable sub-field of criminology, while Phillips and Bowling (2003) further argue the need to develop 'minority perspectives' in criminology. These authors highlight the ongoing dialogue in relation to the context and location of the role of how to ensure that black contribution to criminology is not rendered invisible. The concept of 'invisibility' was put forward by African-American novelist, Ralph Ellison, where he states:

> I am an invisible man. No, I am not a spook like those who 'haunted' Edgar Allan Poe; nor am I one of your Hollywood movie ectoplasms. I am a man of substance, of flesh and bone, fibre and liquids – and I might even be said to possess a mind. I am invisible; understand, simply because people refuse to see me.
>
> (1947: 7)

This chapter therefore explores the conflicts, contradictions, and difficulties faced by my own sense of racialised identity in relation to being a black male criminologist researching other black men. While the struggle to validate the 'insider researcher's' position continues to throw up challenges, it is still apparent that the generation, maintenance, and sustainability of academic 'subordination' in relation to being a black researcher with research participants who also black is problematic.

By using an auto-ethnographic analysis, this chapter confronts the issues of researcher 'invisibility' and 'racialisation' that provides a 'counter-narrative' to both legitimise and represent the real, lived experience of a black 'on-road' criminologist who also comes from an innercity 'on road' background. A set of question emerge; who conducts research inquiries with participants who come from communities deemed 'high risk', 'hard to reach', 'hard to identify', or 'hard to access'? Who is qualified to access those same communities and demonstrate both 'sensitivity' and 'credibility' regarding those research participants' ontological and epistemological realities? What does a criminologist do when faced with an emerging situation that is 'spontaneous' and 'instant', requiring an 'improvised' approach when the data emerges 'in the moment'? What happens when such encounters are captured at a site where the events that took place are frenzied and chaotic?

Who then decides whether these encounters are valid forms of data from the 'social world' of participants who are disconnected from the gated confines of the academy? And who has the right to adjudicate on the gathered data in relation to issues of 'reliability' and 'validity' by imposing inappropriate measurements that dismiss and discount the 'gatherer' of such data, when the researcher is accused of acting more like a journalist than a criminologist? What happens if the context and circumstances regarding access to research constituents and the spaces they inhabit require a deep knowledge of the 'code of the streets' (Anderson, 1999)? Sanelowski argues that qualitative research is 'an array of attitudes towards strategies for conducting inquiry that are aimed at discovering how human beings experience, interpret, and produce the social world' (2004: 893). Similarly, Goffman sees that many crucial facts lie beyond the time and place of interaction or lie concealed within it (1959: 13).

How then in those same communities where there are important things to learn, understand, and gain understanding from, do criminologists use their abilities, not only to gather and analyse data, but to also use the outcome for the purposes of 'social justice'? Berger and Luckmann (1966) see reality as being socially constructed and state that the sociology of knowledge must analyse the process in which it occurs (1966: 13). Their position would suggest that at times criminologists must place themselves in the world of their participants in order to observe and engage in their socially constructed worlds, even if that world is chaotic, messy, and dangerous. Failure to do so will render the concerns of those communities who are in need of change and transformation invisible.

It is my contention that residents of inner-city communities who are exposed to extreme levels of poverty, crime, and violence in context are both the 'experts' and 'knowers' of their experiences. They also offer all criminologists an opportunity to engage in a dialogue on those same understandings, thoughts, feelings, insights, and experiences through the telling of their own stories and, more importantly in their words. This auto-ethnographic account therefore categorises my work as an 'urban' or 'on road' criminologist designed to highlight the important contribution of the communities I engage with, as playing a key role that informs the understanding of the social conditions that both shapes and affects their lives. This account also speaks to those excluded, marginalised, and neglected 'on road' criminologists who, like me, feel our voices should be heard, by exercising our right to contest the views of those who 'talk cricket from the boundary, but seldom face a fast bowler from the crease'.

Du Bois (1978) calls those researchers who do not venture into inner-city communities 'car wash sociologists'. Katz (1988) similarly is critical of those social scientists who can 'graciously transport themselves' to unknown places they have never visited by making claims from the 'safe vantage point' of the 'ivory tower'. The 'ebony tower' position may be relevant here. The 'ebony tower' starts from a position that acknowledges position that the limitations of the criminologist can be strengthened by a community's engagement and involvement with the formulation, undertaking, and dissemination of research inquiries that will have an impact on their lives. An example is Rich (2000) when recounting the stories of young black men who had experienced trauma as a consequence of street violence states, 'Without any access to their voices, we could easily formulate solutions that are out of sync with the reality of their lives and that would be ineffective and downright destructive' (2009: xv).

Rich clearly makes a point, namely, that the world we inhabit is at times messy, dangerous, and chaotic, requiring some extraordinary measures to access these stories as and when they arise. In relation to crime, violence, and social disorganisation in some of the UK's volatile inner cities, events can flare up instantly: shootings, robbery, fights, and civil unrest. For some criminologists, the newly formed hypothesis and accessing the resources to undertake an inquiry will emerge post-event, when there is sufficient distance and reflection to warrant such an investigation. However, the need to make sense of the chaos in the eye of the storm is also an important consideration in relation to insights that can be gained 'in the moment' the event occurs. Denzin (2010) too directs attention to the need to transcend the confines of the 'ivory tower' and demands qualitative researchers heed the 'call to arms' for all of those who believe in the inter-connection between 'critical inquiry' and 'social justice'.

Matthews (2009) puts forward a proposition that the development of a more coherent 'realist' approach to criminological research must transcend and replace the existing forms of what he refers to as 'so what criminology.' Green (2010) also calls for new frameworks to be developed when researching 'sensitive issues' or 'marginalised perspectives' from populations who have been 'over-pathologised' within the so-called mainstream research domain. So how do 'on road' criminologists working with 'high risk' and 'difficult' populations manage to position their research in relation to 'social justice', as well as continuing to contribute to the knowledge base? A new set of question emerge What happens when you are refused a research grant? When you have no tenure? Or the 'insider perspective' you hold is labelled as too subjective, too militant, or challenges the orthodoxy?

What do you do when you yourself are at times stigmatised on account of coming from the same community and have the same cultural background as your research participants? How do you manage the range of mixed emotions that emerge when you are constantly being told that conducting research in communities you're connected to is too risky, in spite of having 30 years' experience and a PhD? In my experience, when words like 'urban' or 'inner city' are pushed in front of the word 'research', it pinpoints not just the kind of research you're engaged in, but also the location where it takes place. In the UK, naming your operating context becomes important in criminology, especially when you're dealing with the dark world of drug dealers, gangsters, ex-offenders, victims of crime, and numerous other cohorts who languish at the tail end of society. In the UK, the vernacular used to name what I am doing is not coined by me, nor the academy, but the community itself. The demarcation here is not about whether you are a criminologist, but more about the kind of criminologist you need to be if you want access to the stories of those in challenging inner-city communities.

'On road criminologist'

So I have now been bestowed with the title of an 'on road' criminologist. Essentially, operating as an 'on road' criminologist means gaining acceptance, approval, and permission from sections of the community who occupy the world of the 'streets' (on road). It means having unprecedented access to those whom some criminologists cannot or will not access. Other criminologists through fear will avoid entering a world where the 'code of the streets' is what every criminologist needs to know and understand. The key to gaining access to the lives of my constituency comes through my own 'lived experiences', which, like theirs, has also been fraught with danger and fear, though in my case not because of a criminal lifestyle. Another contributory factor is the way as an 'on road' criminologist I inhabit the world from which my constituents come. I am not talking about holding focus groups in comfy constructed spaces, or handing out questionnaires in the safety of a classroom, or sitting in the comfort of an office, tape recording someone who has signed up to your research. I'm talking about dialogue that takes place in shopping centres, barber shops, bookies, car parks, street corners, and other locations within the confines of the inner cities.

Those I frequently come into contact with are gang members, ex-gang members, others maybe released from prison, or a mother wanting insights into her son's challenging behaviour, or faith leaders who need to find ways of welcoming ex-offenders back into the congregation. In essence, you are 'on tap' constantly, when the community sees you as someone they can go to, as well as wanting your insights into the pressing problems of the day. 'On road' research requires me to use my powers of persuasion, reasoned argument, and negotiation where I have to be open and transparent at all times. I also have to continually deliver on promises made. Failure to do so will lose respect, with serious consequences.

There are times when the people I talk to are angry and exhibit the kind of distress that for many would be frightening. Unless there is a finite understanding of the 'code of the streets', it is easy to be on the receiving end of aggression, based on the consequences of having a lack of understanding of 'street runnins'. In all areas of research, criminologists should operate in a 'sensitive' and 'mindful' way. What makes 'on road' research both compelling and challenging is that the culture of the streets is not uniform and requires constant revision. For me however, 'on road' criminological research is a vital component in the way we understand the changing nature of our inner cities. Like traditional forms of qualitative research and ethnography the boundaries, rules, ethics, etc., of 'on road' research differs in relation to the context in which it takes place. As much so-called 'mainstream criminological research' is predicated on well-planned, resourced, committee-approached, university-backed, theoretically driven, work, as an 'on road' criminologist, I am both the 'observer' and 'chronicler' of the events taking place, which extends the scope of how we undertake this type of work.

For my own sanity, I have also had to learn how to emotionally detach myself from this type of work when the events have passed, and, more importantly, not take it home. As an 'on road' criminologist, it is difficult to observe, and delve into the lives of others when your own reality is at times inter-connected with theirs. The dominant conservative criminological paradigms that at times are oppressive, disempowering and controlling can marginalise an 'on road' criminologist, like myself when notions of your 'blackness', 'politics', and academic credentials, feel more like an excuse for others to flee from, as opposed to engaging with them openly. Undertaking criminological research with those who live in the same community, who share a common cultural heritage with you, can and does create its own pressure, as working on your objectivity is testing at the best of times.

However, every researcher researching their passion will experience that difficulty. It is the management and handling of the difficulties that count. Many of the subjects of my inquiries have a story to tell. Stories of pain, hurt, loss, and trauma push you on all levels to ensure you do not let your personal feelings get in the way. With traditional forms of qualitative research, the ethics of not 'going native' are clearly important, so as not to breach the boundaries between the researcher and the subjects of the inquiry. When you are researching 'on road', you can become so embroiled in someone's story that you can get seriously physically hurt, as well as destroy your credibility in the community. When the community suffers pain, oppression, or trauma, it demands that an 'on road' criminologist is first and foremost a good listener, a talent combined with integrity, and an impartial position on the arising issues. You have not only been invited to listen to the concerns being raised, but you have to act as the voice of reasoned objectivity.

In essence, the 'on road' code places you as a researcher in a position where you are truly made accountable for your ethical position. However, there are times when I have felt attached to the experiences of those who look like me, and you can feel yourself 'going native'. If that happens, then it is time to pull back, reframe, and, reposition yourself. A key aspect of being a successful 'on road' researcher is in socio-cultural identification, especially in relation to the perception and articulation of your 'blackness'. 'Blackness', as a short-hand for 'black consciousness', centres on the understanding of the history of black oppression and subordination, combined with acquiring the psychic tools and ability to transcend its impacts. By using tactics of 'colour-blindness', operating within a 'white privileged' position, any notion of my 'blackness' is seen at times as lacking in objectivity, when researching the black community. So how does an 'on road' criminologist's expression of their 'blackness' improve or reduce the possibility of academic validation, when one is constantly having to confront 'whiteness' in both the research environment and the academy, that at times is oppressive and debilitating?

So, what is the role of an 'on road' criminologist who is black, British, urban, and politicised? I see my role first and foremost as a criminologist who sees the need to contest and challenge the way the racialisation of crime and criminal justice systems impacts black men and the wider community, while at the same time operating as an 'insider researcher'. For black men in UK and the USA, a range of socio-historical experiences can be influential: slavery, colonisation, race riots, etc., that indirectly or directly informs the worldview that both they and I possess. It is therefore my duty to investigate black men in ways that are sensitive to the socio-historical context from which they have emerged. How then do I negotiate and balance my own interests and research agendas with those of my research participants?

It is my experience that some black men demand that the person research-ing them possess a high level of politicised and cultural 'blackness' as a benchmark for gaining access to their hearts and minds. In my own experi-ence, it is also apparent that some white criminologists I have met when researching black people never account for their subjective 'whiteness' or demonstrate any understanding of notions of their participants' 'blackness'. Again in my experience, some white criminologists can play the 'identity politics' card, where using white privilege gives them the power to abstain from addressing their own bias. This is one reason 'reflexivity' becomes an important tool for examining our own subjectivities in relation to how our personal values may influence the research outcomes.

If any researcher focuses purely on the research outcomes, without under-standing the 'by-products' that emerge from any interactions, then important insights might not be gained and in effect may be lost and be deleted from any findings. It could also be argued that a researcher who possesses notions of blackness with black men has more to offer subjects of inquiry who have traditionally felt powerless and subordinate to white researchers. I would also argue that black men generating and creating their own agency involves con-fronting what white society presents as both obstacles and aspirations. In doing so, it is hoped that they will further interrogate their own cultural contexts and examine how to transcend society's limited expectations of them. So what does a white criminologist do if they do not pick up or see the relevance of social, historical, and cultural factors of black men's construction of their social reality? The context for my racialised positionality is also framed as a 'counter-narrative' that at times has to speak in opposition to the so-called 'majoritarian narrative', of so-called white privilege, or colour blindness within academia.

It is therefore wholly appropriate for me as a black man to engage with my own sense of racial and cultural knowledge, the community I come from, and the subject of the inquiries without the imposition of oppressive whiteness. In my experience seldom is there a questioning of white men researching white men, but the continual battle I undergo in having to justify my desire to research those who look like me takes up energy I could better spend just doing my work. As stated previously, reflexivity demands that the researcher relinquish a certain level of control within the research process, as a way of enabling the voices of the participants to be heard, for as Duneier (2006) argues, participants in research should 'become authors of their own lives' and in doing so should experience some dignity within the research process.

I am arguing for the acknowledgement that some aspects of the research encounters are not uniform; do not take place in safe environments, and at times struggle with notions of objectivity. A history of racial subordination should clearly make an 'on road' criminologist more vigilant and defiant in the face of continuing and sustainable pressure from forces designed to keep them down. One explanation could be that black researchers, qualified as we are, are also rendered powerless in an academic system that privileges one group over another, which does not provide us with a sense of equal justice in terms of validating both our research and the methods we employ. How then do 'urban' researchers maintain the balance between challenging the status quo, while at the same time not being sucked into the very machinery that grinds one's energy down?

The inability of the 'on road' criminologist who suffers racial disparities in the criminal justice research domain to successfully operate independent of street-level bureaucrats, policy-makers, and strategic agencies, is also problematic and may require a new approach that determines its own destiny. Central to this proposition is the way the narrative of the 'on road' criminologist is produced and produces change. The dominant narrative that restricts and renders my 'counter-narrative' invisible needs to cease. Regardless of the exclusion zone that surrounds the loneliness of the long-distance, 'on road' criminologist, we continue to strive and struggle for validation, not just in the eyes of those who oppress us, but also in the eyes of those who see the abilities of the 'on road' researcher as part of a remedy leading towards transformation and liberation.

Without a clear, precise, and focused approach to challenging power within our society, we will merely replicate our own oppression. If I am to seek transformation as a way of transcending my academic subordination, then I must seek transformative spaces where the interrogation of the obstacles and barriers to my right to speak is given voice, complete with the development of an action plan designed to push my counter-narrative into a strategy for academic justice. 'On road' criminologists like me will continue to challenge the dominant social and cultural assumptions regarding the researcher's ability to 'name my own reality'. Maybe a union of African-American and black British criminologists is what is required to enable independent approaches and visions within the discipline to grow and become relevant to this area of the inner city where I reside. Chapter 5 looks at the role of the community in relation to factors that enhance or hinder notions of black men's desistance. These findings concretely counter 'colour-blind' criminological claims and give rise to a narrative that is not smooth, uniform, or free from contradiction when it comes to gaining insights about and understandings of black men's desistance.

5 Black men and the barriers towards desistance

These findings have given voice to those who are attempting to make sense of how the internalisation of their experiences of racialised criminal justice systems impacts on their aspirations to desist. The findings will also highlight how the impact of those racialised social processes is partly responsible for pushing them further towards criminal lifestyles which ultimately place restrictions on the way they can desist from criminal behaviour.

The participants

This strand of the study involved 11 black men from the community, drawn from across the West Midlands region. Several of the participants identified themselves as current gang members who are continuing to engage in criminal activity.

Emergent themes

Using an adapted form of grounded theory (Glaser and Strauss 1967; Strauss and Corbin, 1998; Charmaz, 2006) the following themes emerged from the interviews:

- lack of fathering
- fatherhood
- hyper-masculinity
- gangs
- on road
- the system
- towards desistance.

Lack of fathering

'Father absence', as the interviewees saw it, was about the impact of growing up without a father in their lives. Many cited this absence as being directly linked to the problems they have encountered; their poor opinions of themselves; and a reason for their involvement in gangs and criminal activity. Many felt they grew up in communities where they felt marginalised, undervalued and frustrated at their lack of social status by not having a father. Without proper guidance and support, their worldview became distorted, leading them into both anti-social behaviour and criminal activity. The responsibility ultimately fell on their mothers, who struggled with bringing sons to manhood, as articulated by Leroy:

> Growing up as a boy in a so-called ghetto it was hard for mum. Dad left when I was 4. I'm the first child so it was up to me to kind of be the man of the house. I felt like I had a lot on my shoulders.
>
> (Leroy)

Leroy highlights how the absence of his father became the catalyst for him having to grow up too soon, bypassing his childhood. Leroy's mission to 'be the man of the house' at such a young age thwarts a significant positive transition in his life course. Similarly, Henry sees his father's absence at a young age as partly responsible for pushing some young people to see crime, not as a personalised goal, but as a way of providing for himself where his mother has failed to provide for him. It involves a sense of taking on a role that became vacant as a consequence of his father's absence. He states:

> At the age of 8, I first found myself in the police system for shoplifting. I then started stealing to buy all the good things that all the other kids had, like the latest trainers and other stuff, coz my mum never had the money to buy all the latest gear.
>
> (Henry)

By citing his motivation for involvement in crime as a consequence of not having the means of acquiring the good 'stuff' that other children had, Henry attempts to displace his actions. It could be argued that if his father had been around, this situation would not have arisen. However, by taking on the role of a father figure before experiencing the benefits of having a childhood, Henry reveals how arrested development can occur as a consequence of a father's absence. Another aspect of the impact of a lack of fathering is highlighted by Marvin, whose father had a history of imprisonment:

> My dad was always in and out of prison. I had to lie to people at school saying my dad's gone on holiday because I was too ashamed to say he was in jail.
>
> (Marvin)

It could be that Marvin's feelings of shame were the start of his journey towards involvement in crime from a young age, as he felt the void that was created pushed him into criminality. He also cites this absence as partly responsible for his inability to make good choices in his life. He states: 'Maybe if my father was around, wasn't in prison, or stayed in touch I might have made some different choices in my life.' The lack of developing a strong social bond with his father did have consequences later in his life, in Marvin's opinion. Similarly, Robert reflects on having to make choices that would have been best supported by his father, if he had been part of the household:

> I had to face the reality of the issue of my lack of fathering and how I would deal with it. You had to do what you had to do. Dad wasn't there, so you had to step up and get what you could, when you could. If crime was the way to do, then so be it. My Dad wasn't there; I needed stuff, so I needed to get it.
>
> (Robert)

Robert sees his father's absence as a void that subsequently led him to get involved with anti-social behaviour and criminal activity at a young age to provide for his mother. Jay, on the other hand, goes back a further generation and acknowledges that his father also suffered from father absence:

> My father never knew his father. I never really bonded with him as a child. I had a fearful respect for him, based on his size and status within the family, but never felt close to him. He shared very few of his life experiences with me. He never sat me down for talks about boyhood, manhood, relationships, life goals, and so on. I feel cheated, afraid, excited and dejected. People say, 'It's never too late', but sometimes I think it really is.
>
> (Jay)

Jay is articulating a pattern of handed-down 'father absence' that has left him feeling angry and carrying a burden of loss. Jay clearly articulates the need for a father to show him how to navigate life, as well as giving unconditional love. It is clear that father absence is a symptom of a deeper issue in relation to the establishment of security, guidance, and love that an experience of positive fathering can bring. As Roy (2006) argues, fatherhood improves human agency and gives meaning to men's lives. He further argues that the negative social context in which black fathers operate can result in increased criminality or gang-related activity. A key theme that emerged was the impact that incarceration had on their children, as well as their ability to re-connect to their children as a father.

Fatherhood

Several participants revealed how a mixture of shame and embarrassment was underpinned by their reflections on their inability to provide adequately for their own families. Paul highlights several difficulties in his role as a father, especially being an ex-prisoner, cutting off his past, moving into a pre-dominantly white community, and having a mixed-race son.

> It's not easy bringing up a mixed-race son in a white community. Plus finding employment as a black man is not easy. When you've been to

prison you're not accepted for who you are, so it's hard to achieve your full potential and be a proper father.

(Paul)

Here, Paul identifies the need to move away from his past, and identifies the struggle with trying to gain employment. In acknowledging himself as an ex-offender, Paul sees the raising of a mixed-race son in a white community, combined with the task of shaping his son's identity, clearly impacts on how he sees his ability to be a 'proper father'. Robert also illustrates how notions of the 'prison code' creates a barrier to meaningful communication between fathers serving time and their children:

There was no one to discuss my problems within prison so I didn't discuss stuff about my kids as it is considered a weakness to express what you feel. Even on visits you don't really open up, so you keep stuff you're concerned about to yourself. In prison you have to lock your feelings about being a father deep inside. That's the case for lots of us when we're banged up.

(Robert)

The inability to discuss parenting issues freely and openly is not specific to black men, but Robert highlights how the 'prison code' of being 'tough' and 'desensitised' compounds the problems associated with being a prison parent. Robert also states that even when he had contact with his children while serving time, he tended to keep things to himself. Prison parenting clearly is distressing for both the prison parent and the children left behind, on account of being separated. Henry, on the other hand, has a supportive family network outside of the prison, while serving his sentence and reveals the importance of having a community connection that maintains a positive link with his children:

My mother looked after my son when I was locked up, so I didn't have to rely on anybody for anything. I relied mainly on my family and other relatives. I suppose I was lucky in that respect. If it wasn't for my family, I don't know what I would have done.

(Henry)

Henry highlights how having a supportive extended family provides some respite from the separation a father goes through when incarcerated. Henry has clearly benefited from having such support. Jay, on the other hand, highlights a pro-social aspect of prison parenting seldom acknowledged by serving prisoners:

I made sure they have full knowledge of drugs and gangs, warning them about the consequences. I taught them about the pitfalls I have faced and tell them what education is about and how you can get somewhere in life with the right qualifications. I also don't lie to my kids. I don't tell them everything, but I don't want them to think that I've been a great person, when I haven't. I want them to have a better chance than I did.

(Jay)

Jay's emphasis on educating his children during visits demonstrates how he sees his responsibility as a parent, in spite of being locked up. Jay also uses his own negative experiences of life as guidance to his children. The importance here is in the assumption that incarcerated men as fathers are 'feckless'. Jay is clearly someone who sees his past transgressions as a tool for informing and educating his own children about the right and wrongs of life choices. It could be argued that Jay is doing the most effective parenting he can, in spite of the restrictive circumstances. Likewise, Marvin sees education as a key point of entry in terms of his parenting from prison:

When I was locked up, I let my children know that a good education can lead to a successful life. I pointed out to my children all of those role models who have achieved status through education. I told my children they would be able to access the good things in life with the right education. I also told them that I screwed up my education and it landed me in trouble.

(Marvin)

Marvin also uses his past as a way of reinforcing the importance of education as a positive choice for his children. The importance here is that men like Jay and Marvin do not make excuses for their past behaviour and still see their obligation to their children as a way of signposting them to make better choices than they did. These views would suggest that black men can act as fathers, even when they are physically unavailable to do so. Overall, the men who were interviewed saw sustained communication with their children as a way of both reinforcing their approach to fatherhood, as well as providing a context that gave them a positive motivation towards their desistance. It could be argued that the desire to be a father from a difficult position within a prison can provide both the aspiration and incentive to stay out of trouble. David illustrates this point well:

I had to put my own life on the back burner when it came to my children. I kept the contact and love flowing. I wrote to them and kept constant communication. I know it wasn't the best way to do things, but it was better than nothing. I know certain men inside prison had no contact with their kids. I refused to go that way. Even though I was in prison, I didn't want my kids thinking I didn't care about them.

(David)

David acknowledged the importance of staying in touch not just in terms of contact, but as a demonstration of his love for his children. He also demonstrates that strong parental bonds do not diminish while incarcerated. Kieran, on the other hand, focuses attention on being a black father, who is ensuring that his children are equipped with a strong sense of their 'racial identity'.

> I would tell them that they must know where they are coming from and where they are going. Without it, they will die from ignorance, as there is no balance in this biased world. I told them that black people have lived in the darkness for too long. We need to know what contribution we have made to this world, expose the fraud, and replace it with balance and truth. I don't want white people telling lies to my kids, the way they did to me.
>
> (Kieran)

Kieran sees the significance of trying to ensure his children do not succumb to notions of oppressive 'whiteness', and goes further by urging them to question things they are told. It was very evident that the men in this strand of the research had a strong desire to see their children succeed in spite of the barriers they had faced as prisoners, and still face, as ex-prisoners. However, despite the positive desires they had for their children, the scope of this research does not address the wider issues of being a prison father and the emotional impact this ultimately had on their own children. The next section addresses the issue of the relationship between being a father and an ex-offender who has returned to the 'code of the streets' (Anderson, 1999). The suggestion here is that in some cases black men go from compliant 'prison masculinities' constructed while inside, which is re-converted to 'hyper-masculinities' on re-entering the community on release, based on returning to an unchanged world that remains hostile to all returning prisoners. In many cases 'hyper-masculinity' reconversion was on account of having to revert back to a form of masculinity as a way of regaining the status they had lost when going to prison.

Hyper-masculinity

The construction of an aggressive and militant form of masculine identity is seen as a way of gaining respect and status back on the streets. hooks (2003b) takes the position that black men themselves must take a stronger position on challenging their hyper-masculine status. However, for those black men interviewed, the ability to take a stronger position was constantly undermined by blocked opportunities, racism, and the pressure of being on the streets. In essence, blocked access to the social structure and negative social labelling create the conditions for such a choice. An example is Jay who has a strong sense of remorse for his past, but blames his environment for his involvement in crime:

> You want to know what made me what I am? My environment and most things in it were to blame. I never planned to be bad or end up as a gangster. So I don't have nothin' to lose. They treat me like shit then I'll give it back.
>
> (Jay)

Jay's response reveals a deep sense of anger and retribution. Sampson and Wilson (1995) argue strongly that urban inequality will invariably create militant responses from men like Jay. Indeed, it is hard to see how men like Jay can avoid constructing a hyper-masculine identity if they have no alternative ways of validating their manhood. Chevannes (1999) also argues that the difficulties of cultivating a positive masculine identity for black men like Jay are about countering a past that is continuously thwarted by inner-city deprivation and a failing social infrastructure that render black men subordinate to those structures that privilege white men. In contrast, Chris sees acquiring control of your life as a variable that distinguishes those who are strong and those who are weak. He equates notions of control with being a 'real man'. Chris's view reveals a deeper challenge for black men. Namely, that of cultivating a different identity as a black man living in a white society, as he reveals:

> It's frustrating at times, because you like to be in control. I think every man or somebody that's on the journey to become a man would like to be responsible for their journey, responsible for the decisions that they make, and the things that are not made for them. So I think it can be very frustrating and very stressful at times when someone's not in control. I like to be in control, so no-one can fuck with me. If I have to hurt a man, I will.
>
> (Chris)

How then do black men assume a healthy position in a society that system-atically has relegated them and their aspirations to the margins of society, and create a new template for living? A significant feature in the construction of black hyper-masculinities is the need to be self-sufficient and not dependent on anyone, as illustrated by Robert:

> So throughout me time, I maintained don't do the crime if you are not going to get away with it, and decisions had to be made, so, yes, I had to fend for myself, look after myself especially when you come alongside older criminal heads.
>
> (Robert)

Robert is trapped inside a world of self-imposed isolation where he has to fend for himself. The desire to fend for oneself comes as a consequence of having to adopt a survival mentality, in an environment that is not advantageous to black men returning back to the community from prison. This position could fracture Robert's ability to build stronger and more cohesive social bonds with his family, the community, and in turn society. Robert's sense of social disorganisation could have significant impact on his overall well-being if he operates as a single isolated individual, as opposed to being part of a wider community. Henry illustrates this point in reference to his isolation:

I can't deal with the feelings attached to my emotions, the feelings of abandonment, of being let down, seeing the one you love over a table. So I block it out. Don't think about it. If I think too much I get depressed. And I hate being depressed. It ain't good to be that way. Makes you weak.

(Henry)

Henry's notion of his self-concept highlights how desensitised he has become. It could be further argued that the pressure brought about by not having time to heal, or the headspace to think positively, for black men like Jay, may create the level of internal distress that results in projected anger, rage, and social conflict. Alternatively, Noel counters notions of hyper-masculinity by offering a different solution and cites the acquisition of a faith as a way forward:

I was a bad man, didn't care for no-one, but it didn't get me anywhere. But I found God and that chilled me out. Emotionally, I am a lot stronger, more determined. Through that experience I have a greater bond and deeper understanding of God and the relationship with him, being sincere and truthful towards other people, is what has turned me around.

(Noel)

By developing a new and improved value system, Noel has not only changed his life around, but has reconfigured his masculine identity. Where he was once hyper-masculine, he is now grounded in values that are not aggressive or violent. In effect, by finding God, Noel has become a better person and a responsible member of society. Unlike Noel who sees faith as a way forward, Marvin differently calls for 'services' that should push black men away from being angry and negative:

We need provisions and services that actually reflect what's happening within the community. Within the communities you've got churches, you've got gangs, you've got bad men, you've got decent, upright, self-respecting citizens, you've got academics, you've got professionals, you've got a diverse mix of different people within the services that they're providing, that's what they need.

(Marvin)

Marvin issues a stern warning for failure to address his concerns when he continues:

If you don't provide us with proper things, we're going to kick off, big time. We're tired of watching everyone get things and we get left out. That's why some men behave the way they do. I don't blame them. If you ain't treating me good and give me what I need, then I'm gonna go on the rampage. Standard!

Marvin's pain as a consequence of relative deprivation has implications for all prisoners returning to the community, but is made worse if those services that are on offer are not appropriate or racialised.

Stefan also reveals the impact of limited services available to him:

> The young people out there, they need help, and to me no-one is doing anything. They're just allowing young people to go out there and destroy their lives around drugs and everything that are out there. At the end of the day, all this time while the policy-makers and politicians are sitting down and trying to decide what's best for the young people, they could actually be out there doing something to help. That's my final thoughts.
>
> (Stefan)

Stefan further recognises the limitations on those services in being able to provide the whole solution and places some of his problems firmly at the feet of policy-makers and politicians, with a stark warning at the end of it. Marvin and Stefan articulate the on-going internal struggles to be in control of their lives. Attaining manhood for black men is an active process, where they must continually overcome barriers and opposition in order to maintain a masculine posture that is not rendered subordinate by white men. Kieran returns to his sense of racialised identity, as an explanation and justification for his hyper-masculine identity:

> Being a black man is all about struggle. What you've got to understand is that in this society and in this day and time, a lot of the things that happen to black people are negative. That's why we behave the way we do. Society already sees me as a bad man. So I might as well behave that way. I don't give a fuck.
>
> (Kieran)

Kieran's state of being emerges as a consequence of operating under the oppressive conditions of society, where black men find themselves in situations where they have internalised negative masculine scripts, poor definitions of self, and inadequate coping styles. He continues:

> I come from a smashed-up background, to tell the truth, and if there is one thing that is going to make me feel whole and strong, it is to have someone love me for who I am and that's it. I just need a chance to prove myself but no point being given a chance for someone expecting you to fall. I'd like to be given a chance for someone to really have faith in me, and I'll prove that when you give me that chance, yeah, I'll take it no matter what.

Kieran is part of an angry legion of black men who 'ring fence' space in their communities and will defend the right to occupy it by 'postcode' designation.

However, lingering in the subtext of his argument is a deeper desire to be given a chance and made to feel included and needed. On the flip side, Stefan also declares that for one reason or another he does not want to be accessed or engage with structures he doesn't trust:

> As black men, we have so much pride and we got to be seen as the ones to be the protectors and the gangsta. Yeah, I'm a gangsta. I'm not interested in that rehabilitation shit. It ain't worth it. Even when you get a job or go college, you're still seen as a black man and viewed with nuf suspicion. So if they don't like me, then I don't them. Simple as. You get me?
>
> (Stefan)

Stefan bases his arguments of a self-fulfilling prophecy where he takes on the role he thinks society has prescribed for him. When asked about the term 'hard to reach', used by services who brand black men as big, bad, and dangerous, Stefan was scathing about the term:

> I ain't hard to reach. My bredrins know where I am. The police know where I am. So how the fuck do they tell me I'm hard to reach? They turned me, like me, into this, so it's their fault. To me, badness is a way of life. I enjoy it. It's better than having nothing to do. It's also a way in which I get respect.
>
> (Stefan)

Stefan feels that the definition of 'hard to reach' is too simplistic, and is used as a technique designed to remove any responsibility from those professionals or institutions who use it as a term, almost as a throwaway comment, in meetings and public forums. Stefan also reveals his alternative life values that are a significant reason for his involvement in a gang. It is also apparent the importance Stefan gives to gaining respect 'by any means necessary'. It could be said that Stefan is seduced by being 'bad in a gang', as the alternative is to remain subordinate to a society that has rejected him. Katz (1988) argues people like Stefan embrace the seduction of criminality, as it gives them a sense of purpose and meaning in their lives. Jay reveals how the inability to acquire positive values can have an adverse effect, resulting in more turmoil and even greater challenges to moving towards his eventual desistance:

> People in the community walk around like they're invincible; one of the things that we as black men don't talk about is pain. We talk about how we can deal with pain, what I'd like you to do, just to kind of round up, is just for a few moments to reflect on the times when you haven't been coping, how bad it feels, because this same youth listening, he doesn't know that you've cried or shed tears, or that you banged your fist on the wall, and I think what he wants to know, whether or not this experience

affects you on that emotional level or you just become hard and you just don't feel it.

(Jay)

Jay talks about his pain of incarceration that, despite its claim to promote rehabilitation, still favours the punitive approach. These interviewees at times found solace in the confines of street-based extended family networks such as 'gangs' and 'crews'. The lack of social involvement, the persistence of family breakdowns through father absence, and increasing nihilistic tendencies articulated by some interviewees created an almost religious connection to the streets and to a gang. The next section examines the issue of 'gangs' in relation to this view and its impact on the desistance process.

Gangs

Pinnock (1997) suggests that gangs provide more emotional support than dysfunctional families. He further suggests that racialised criminal justice systems push some black men into joining gang gangs, and in doing so further pushes them away from envisioning a life free from crime, as illustrated by Jay and Marvin:

When you can't get nothin' as a black man in this society, you can roll with da manz dem and feel strong. Trus' me blood, it's a family ting. You feel me? Some of this gang shit is bullshit as I don't like some of these geezers. But I don't like hearing my bredrins gettin' killed. I don't like hearing the other side gets killed either but some of them, fuck knows, ain't got no sense.

(Jay)

You have gang members who have nothing to do with drugs at all; they don't take drugs or sell drugs, so drugs don't have nothing to do with a gang. Obviously there'll be individuals in a gang who might use criminal activities to get their revenue, selling drugs, robbing banks, robbing old women or whatever you want to do to raise money. There will be gangs like that and each gang will have its different mentality of how they raise their money. For me, I see the gang as filling in the gap left by my dad and not having a proper family.

(Marvin)

Jay and Marvin see the gang as part of their lives, combined with the futility of the losses they have encountered by engaging with such a dangerous lifestyle. It could be argued that if the gang becomes part of a normal socialisation for black men, then this position will clearly obstruct any notions of contemplating a desistance trajectory. Gang culture also has historical roots across several generations that in itself highlights that gang affiliation is passed from one life course to another, creating a pattern, where the next generation inherits the previous generation's gang legacy that further places a burden on the possibility of desistance.

As Robert says:

> They live after a reputation of people like me who were like the fore-fathers of badness. The challenge was always the older guys looking on us as the younger crew. People need to understand the history of gang culture in Birmingham, there were three stems of the roots and we were in the middle. I came back as a young man amongst older men and it was the first time that I was really close to older men and hearing their stories and their upbringing, and I suppose I was analysing what they were saying.
>
> (Robert)

Robert's recounting reflects an inner conflict relating to an inter-generational need that becomes sabotaged on account of extended gang histories. Some of the interviewees not only saw the gang as an extension of their families, but as a 'counter-cultural' response to blocked opportunities in society. Jay, Marvin, and Robert had significant social aspirations, but felt they had little or no way of achieving them. Nowhere was this more demonstrated than the way in which the gang provided a way to occupy and dominate the streets, which in street vernacular is referred to as 'on road' or 'code of the streets' (Anderson, 1999). I would define 'on road' as a site where the intersection between black hyper-masculinities and gangs becomes a dangerous cocktail that fuels the way the streets are run. It will further explain how the racialisation of crime and criminal justice systems, not only impacts on the desistance process, but instead poses one of the greatest threats towards black men desisting from criminal activity.

On road

Jay illustrates the 'on road' mindset that revolves around violence and respect:

> I had a couple of fights, coz man's think they try rob me, and shit like that coz I'm from Handsworth and I didn't take anything lightly. I have got rushed a few times but I don't have it. So it escalates and escalates. It's hard escaping this bullshit but some man's don't make it better for themselves.
>
> (Jay)

Jay sees 'road life' as an inescapable reality. For guys like Jay, the world in which he lives is full of fear and violence, which means he acquires 'wisdom', though not the sort that guides you through life, but rather 'street wisdom' designed to assist in navigating life on the streets. Chris has a similar take on road life, but also sees it as a major challenge: 'Road life is hard when you're involved in it. Nuff people are on the road thing for different reasons. Some bout money, some for a rep [name], and some jus' trying to get by.'

Although Chris sees 'road life' as a difficult choice, he also highlights some of the motivations that attract those who do get involved. Robert similarly gives a word of caution to those who are considering this choice: 'To people on the road ting, I would say, are you prepared to go to jail? And if they feel like they ain't got any other options and you can handle jail.' Robert reveals a paradox in relation to being 'on road'. The desire not to go to prison is made all the more difficult knowing that you may have to defend yourself and your territory. Robert also reaffirms the old maxim 'If you can't do the time, don't do the crime.' Marvin, on the other hand, blames the streets for his situation and cites his environment and family breakdown as a causal factor for his affiliation to the streets:

> I grew up in a ghetto area, what I would call inner city. I grew up in a family where I experienced domestic violence by my dad on my mum. So I grew up vex and angry. I used to kick off and then I found my crew. I suppose in some respects I repeated the cycle.
>
> (Marvin)

Marvin clearly attempts to locate his emotional state and subsequent gang affiliation on his parents' conflict, and how he replaced them with a new extended family, the gang. Roy (2006) points out that if we are to engage in a serious discussion about young black men and their activity in gangs, we must interrogate the relationship they have with their own fathers. Roy further sees the inability to look at conflict across the generations as limiting the overall understanding of why young black men join gangs. The important thing here is to acknowledge that joining a gang may be informed by other background factors. Agnew (2006) refers to these background factors as 'storylines'. Storylines, Agnew argues, build a stronger picture of criminality if background factors are taken into consideration. Here, Jay explores those background factors in relation to growing up black and being from the inner city as partly responsible for his connection to the streets:

> Growing up as a black youth in the inner city, I had bredrins from all about, all the inner cities are interlinked, so we all had things covered, and we all used to go around with each other and face the same issues, so when a man was doing his thing, a man was doing it with his crew anyway.
>
> (Jay)

Jay sheds light on the social bonds he has generated while being 'on road'. As stated previously, he has created a new, extended family, which is the converse of a loving family. However, this other family operates with menace.

The important point here is those who engage with the 'code of the streets' and 'on road' also find important personal connections that they may not have experienced with their family or the community. It may not sit comfortably with many of us, but what is clearly evident is the need for young men to experience the love of a family. This is an important consideration when assessing the causal factors of gang formation. Is it the young person's fault for wanting the security of a family he has been denied, or is it the families' fault for not providing the young person with the security he deserves? Leroy illustrates this point as he sees 'on road' as more of a street university, where you learn the rules of survival:

> Where we live is where its drug-infested, prostitutes are about the place, crime was high, no jobs, so what do you expect? What are we going to get involved in? It's not like there's college for us to go to, there's nothing for us to do.
>
> (Leroy)

Leroy offers a sad insight into the social reality that some black men 'on road' face. Namely, the routes to creating a meaningful life are blocked and not available to them. He also highlights that by being 'on road', there is a significant disconnect between being black in prison and the community they return to:

> Ignorance is the main barrier to community involvement in prison and to the integration of ex-offenders into the community. There should be more opportunities for dialogue and rapport with the community, and for skills development by prisoners. How else are we supposed to not go back into the badness?
>
> (Leroy)

Leroy illustrates how a lack of awareness in relation to community sign-posting can thwart the journey towards desistance and encourage further involvement with gangs. By returning to a restricted environment, facing oppressive forces such as gang culture, and being constantly exposed to a crumbling inner-city infrastructure, the level of social disorganisation will only increase the propensity to continuing involvement in gangs (Sampson and Wilson, 1995). Marvin illustrates that by having limited community engagement and weak social bonds, the tools required to navigate the pathways towards desistance will be lacking:

> More contact between the wider community, family members and prisoners within the prison environment could deter others from offending; family ties are broken up by placement in prisons far from home. So I have to depend on the gang for survival.
>
> (Marvin)

Once again, Marvin reveals how when family ties break down, the alternative family kicks in. In this case, that alternative family is his gang, which confirms Pinnock's (1997) notion of a replacement family. However, David sees the need to reconnect to the community as a way of moving towards his desire to desist, and is aware of how the label of 'gang member' is an inhibiting factor:

More opportunities for face-to-face contact between community members and prisoners within the prison. If I saw people from the community, I wouldn't mind, but when you're seen as a gang member, people get frightened and don't want to approach you.

(David)

David's reflection highlights that being a gang member is a complex issue which has no easy solution. Those interviewed presented a range of testimonies and issues that form a narrative that suggests there is a need for further investigation. The cumulative impact of negative experiences faced by black men re-entering the community would suggest that there may be some structural forces at work here. It is questionable whether agency alone, for black men in relation to a social structure that is racist, can guide them successfully towards desistance pathways. This concluding section therefore looks at the role of the system in relation to black men's desistance.

The system

It was evident that the level of frustration with the system, blocked opportunities, and restricted access brought out a range of hostile responses.

Leroy illustrates the difficulties he faced with the cumulative impact of the criminal justice system and talks about his racialised identity as a factor that makes it worse for him:

I feel like I've been kidnapped by the system. I feel held down by the system. The benefit system to the court system, probation system, prison system, all one big system, and I now feel that I will never get out the system. I've come to know this, you cannot beat the system. I also realise as a black man, it's going to be worse for me than it is for white guys.

(Leroy)

Leroy possessed a strong awareness of his situation and located the reality of his existence firmly in the way the racialised aspects of the criminal justice system are unfair. Leroy's sense of helplessness is a clear indicator that creates a significant barrier in his trajectory towards his desistance. Likewise, David expresses a view that locates his reality in a 'liminal' context. By liminal, he feels dislocated from the community and trapped in the prison environment.

I get mad, angry, and frustrated to know that the system is a trap. They say jail is for rehabilitation, so why do people always come back, and how dare they tell us who we can and can't talk to? Where we can and can't go. I am a proud black man, but in prison I am made to feel like I'm rubbish. I get shit from white screws and racist inmates.

(David)

David's story is one of anger and despair and here his racialised identity comes into the frame, where he sees his oppression as having a direct impact on his racial pride. Paul also sees the system as the enemy but chooses to be defiant as a way of managing the situation:

> The system is getting away with liberties. Until we get together and fight the system, we can't make it a better place for our kids to be. As black people we've always had to fight for our rights. This is no different. I can't let white people take away my freedom to be human.
>
> (Paul)

The issue of Paul's racialised identity has also become a rallying cry from which to attack the system directly. Robert, in contrast, suggests that taking on the system is futile and confusing,

> I am a black youth being controlled by the system, told the wrong information, and told no information whatsoever, to keep me muddled up so I can't make any concrete decisions about anything. So what's the point? They win either way. I don't have the energy to fight it. I just play fool to catch wise.
>
> (Robert)

If Robert accepts his subordination as inevitable, it is hard to see how he can plot a pathway towards desistance, as his agency will be dependent on the structure that oppresses him. Jay pushed Robert's point further by seeing the system as wilfully operating to fail him, and drew on the analogy of slavery to illustrate his point:

> This system is set up for us to fail. Come on, you think people who had slaves back in the day ever goin' to see us equal as them? I'm a black man in a white man's system. If they can't get you one way, they will get you another.
>
> (Jay)

Jay's almost fatalistic viewpoint situates his plight in the context of slavery. In short, he feels he is still enslaved. A case of damned if you do, damned if you don't, a point made by both Robert and Jay. Jay also seems resigned to the fact that being enslaved is inevitable, but he gives a warning to those who are oppressing him, much the same way slaves did:

> We're still slaves. Some of us are house slaves, whilst others are in the field plotting to escape. I'm a field slave. I will burn the master's house with him and all the other slaves if I got the chance.
>
> (Jay)

Jay's desire to get retribution on the system suggests that desistance for black men in a white society is impeded, based on the racialisation of crime and criminal justice systems, rooted in both a social and historical context. So is desistance inside a racialised system a realistic consideration for some black men? Chris illustrates this point with a gesture that clearly is fatalistic.

> I think these systems have made me more aware of the impact on black youths. Fuck the system, the government doesn't do anything for us, this is how we're living, get rich or die trying.
>
> (Chris)

Chris clearly had arrived at a point of no return where he saw the options for him are limited, and which have forced him to adopt a reactionary position that could land him back in prison. David, on the other hand, is slightly more reflective and sees the navigation of black men in the system as the need to acquire a raised awareness of the workings of the system itself:

> For me, I think it's all about awareness and going through the system and seeing how these systems affect black men. I'm at a stage of, how do I work with that inside and outside of the system? If not, I'm gonna kick off, but I'm kinda frustrated with the whole damn thing.
>
> (David)

David highlights what Cohen (1985) refers to as 'status frustration' and desires to be compliant. But he also recognises he is frustrated and confused about where his future lies. Robert extends David's position by citing being 'knocked back' as the basis for his exclusion and subsequent offending behaviour.

> The enemy is definitely the system because the system gave me a blow. The system was the one that excluded me, was the one that wouldn't express and give me opportunity to learn in a different way to other folks. I saw all the white kids being treated different from me, and that wasn't fair.
>
> (Robert)

Robert highlights how blocked opportunities lead to anger becoming a central focus, based on the cumulative deficits and negative encounters that he has experienced throughout his life. He also recognised how his racialised identity differentiated his treatment from the white children around him. Kieran, like Robert, noticed how he was treated differently and saw the system as having no respect for black men like him:

> The way I see it, society in general have got no respect for our kind. Anything that we do, no matter if it's good or bad, we still get criticised, you

can't win. Being a black man has its benefits, but when it comes to the system, it's shit. We ain't got a cat in hell's chance of making it through.

(Kieran)

Kieran's 'no way out' scenario seems like a common thread running through all the interviews reported in this chapter, namely, one of helplessness, despair, and blocked opportunities. In this section it was evident that the racialisation of crime and criminal justice systems does impact on the desistance process for black men. The difficulty here is that, in spite of staying out of trouble, the continuing problems associated with re-entry are compounded when housing, family reconnections, access to training/education, and other related restrictions do not help their aspirations to desistance.

Towards desistance

So how, then, does this enhance or impede their desistance? It may be better to see black men as harbouring the desire to desist, or, more importantly, to ask what are the barriers they face. As illustrated by Leroy:

To me, it's all about juggling. Don't get me wrong, I ain't intending to go back to prison, but I've got to do what I've got to do. Some of it might not be legit, but if I keep my head down, then maybe something will turn up.

(Leroy)

'Juggling' refers to a state of being where you have to do anything to survive. Henry, on the other hand, sees building on his skills in prison as a way forward:

There's nothing out there for anyone. But I learnt some new skills in prison, so I'm going back into education. I've got some good people around me. I know the pitfalls, as I've fouled up before. I'm not going to say I ain't going back, but I've got to stay focused. I suppose be more like an athlete. Train myself to do well.

(Henry)

Henry's insistence on being focused is common throughout. Developing a discipline can also be attributed in part to the prison experience where there is a significant amount of structure that converts some people into focused individuals. This point is illustrated by Marvin who sees being an entrepreneur as a possible way forward.

I'm gonna try my hand at business. I don't want no handouts from no-one and I don't really see the system giving me anything. I also know there's a lot of people out there who want me to fail, so I'm going to prove them all wrong. But being a black man who's come out of prison and been in a gang, it's not a good position to be in.

(Marvin)

Marvin still struggles with being able to shake off the negative social labels associated with his past. Robert, on the other hand, sees having a faith as a significant enabling factor towards his desistance:

For me, I've got my faith. I believe in God and no matter what happens, that's the only system I'm accountable to. Being a black man in this society is hard. Going to prison is hard. Living in the inner city is hard. Life's hard. But if you got faith, you can overcome it. Martin Luther King did.

(Robert)

Unlike, Robert, Jay's strategy is a little more patchy, with no real plan. His casual acceptance of 'what will be will be', suggests that he is taking each day at a time, and moving towards a self-fulfilling prophecy of failure:

For me, it's about how 'on road' pans out. I can do all the things to stay out of trouble, but when you've done what I've done, anything can happen. It's beyond my control. So I'll be okay until someone gives me reason to go back to the badness.

(Jay)

Jay, in spite of his confidence about his future, still echoes some level of doubt, almost as a recognition that if all else fails, then you have crime to fall back on. Paul is clearly intent on cutting off those things from his past that may block his progress, but he does recognise that they are all in a similar position as him, isolated with limited opportunities:

Right now, I'm trying to manage my freedom. I'm not sure about the future. I've got some good people around me, but I need to focus. Prison don't prepare you for coming back. So I'm still focused on finding my way back. The problem is my old bredrins are still around. I'm trying to stay away from them, but they just like me.

(Paul)

David, like Paul, recognises the need to think and act smart and expresses the view that he will not go back to prison: 'I'll do whatever I got to do to survive. If I can't get it one way, then I'll get it another. All I know is, I ain't going back to prison. Need to think and act smarter.' However, without clarity about his purpose in life, it is questionable how attainable David's aspiration is. Here, Kieran sees the value of using education to move towards possible desistance:

I wanna continue my studies and get more qualified. In the meantime I'm doing some volunteering, coz I don't have to deal with CRB checks and revealing my past. I'm trying to stay under the radar and keep out of trouble.

(Kieran)

Kieran sees education as the means of negotiating ways of promoting his own agency and is not only going straight, but is actively seeking to find new purpose in his life. Similarly, Chris and Noel have found purpose and have turned their experiences into something meaningful and productive:

All I want to do is help young people not make the same mistakes. Prison has given me a purpose in life. I wanna make sure no more young people turn out like me. It's what gets me up in the morning and keeps me out of trouble.

(Chris)

I'm trying to keep my head clear. I go down the gym, bang some weights, and focus on my music. If I work hard, maybe one day I'll make it. A lot of guys in the US have made it big and they were involved in crime. So if they can do it, so can I.

(Noel)

Whereas Chris's motivation is to serve others, it is contrasted with Noel's who focuses attention on his own personal goals and aspires to be involved in the music industry. It is clearly evident that the stories in this section form the basis of a wider narrative that is constantly being restructured in the light of new events, because stories do not exist in a vacuum but are in effect shaped by lifelong personal, communal, and social narratives.

We all have a basic need for stories, for organising our experiences into tales of important happenings. In stories, our voices echo those of others in the world, and we evidence cultural membership both through our ways of crafting stories and through the very content of these stories. Our stories should not be looked upon as separate from real life, but as forming meaningful connections to that life. Therefore, how might black men construct a new story designed to replace their experiences of oppression with one of internal liberation and a new identity, free from racialised judgements? One that is fashioned through processes designed to bring a new identity and ultimately a commitment to a crime-free life.

Conclusion

This chapter highlighted the complex nature of looking at the experiences of formerly incarcerated black men, who are constantly renegotiating the impacts of a racialised criminal justice system. Their collective narrative indicates a desire to desist, but the evidence is far from conclusive based on the pervasive oppressive nature of the impacts of racialisation on the desistance process for black men. At times, the systemic blockages lead to significant levels of distress and built-up resentment. This is also contrasted by a general desire of black men not to engage with the social structure on a range of levels. The level of anger, frustration, and defiance, coming from some of those interviewed has invariably led many of them to continue to find solace in the confines of their gang, while at the same time trying to seek new ways to stay crime-free. Mauer (1999) argues that without understanding the inequalities faced by black men in relation to incarceration and re-entry, as told in their own words, there can be no real justice. The pressures of expectation placed on black men coming from their families and the wider community on re-entry can be made worse as the racialisation of a 'social structure' can and does block access to meaningful and productive opportunities for black men.

This, in turn, leads to structural barriers that undermine the level of social organisation that is required to enable black men to successfully desist. It is suggested that by reconnecting to the streets on release, some black men use the 'structured action' of criminality to challenge existing social structures that exclude them (Messerschmidt, 1997). This street gang is both hyper-masculine and nihilistic, meaning membership requires black men to possibly lose their lives in exchange for the gains from criminal activity and increased street status. By becoming a full member of the 'on road' community, black men are governed by the 'code of the streets', where respect, toughness, fearlessness, and loyalty, are the benchmarks for measuring the masculine resources they have to possess in order to survive. Black men who subscribe to this way of being justify their decision by saying that the available routes to becoming men are blocked, and therefore crime becomes a way out of their dilemma of accomplishing their duties as men, in spite of the risks involved.

It may also be the case that some black men may also be seduced by the 'code of the streets' and 'on road', where they do draw some pleasure from outwitting the forces of law and order, alongside exercising control over those who try to stop them from doing so (Katz, 1988). Unfortunately, the engagement with the streets is short-lived as many black men are further caught in criminal activity and go back to prison. Adjusting to life outside of prison; meeting old adversaries, combined with encountering numerous obstacles and barriers that emerge from their past life of criminality, make desistance for many black men an awkward choice to pursue. A case of damned if you do or damned if you don't.

Therefore, the ability to successfully negotiate the challenges black men face will determine whether they continue the journey towards desistance or if it will push them to recycle the old patterns of behaviour that will land them back inside. It is also important to understand the role of prison regimes in playing a greater role in equipping black men with the tools required to navigate the hurdle of re-entry back into the community, while they are locked up.

It is clear that many black men would give up their previous identities as lawbreakers if they perceived this identity to be unsatisfying, thus weakening their commitment to it. However, with the obstacles they face, giving up the previous identity feels like a risk many are not prepared to take. To promote a successful, positive return of black men to their home communities, we must first change their value systems while in prison in ways that will increase their appreciation of the challenges facing the communities they have affected, and then connect them to real and meaningful opportunities to make a difference and affect positive change in their lives.

It could be argued that when some black men do propel themselves successfully towards desistance, the maintenance and enforcement of white privilege via the social structure becomes part of the sustainability of the subordination of black men. In essence, black men who threaten the social order that protects the interest of white people must both contest and challenge their subordination at every turn. It is therefore incumbent on all criminal justice agencies to be consistent in reducing the amount of racialised processes that still privilege white men, to the detriment of black men. A further question about what it means to be a black man who has been to prison in a racialised society may be required here, as a form of 're-othering', where new and improved notions of 'self' may assist in countering the negative self-concepts imposed by white society.

Mutua (2008) argues that black men are oppressed by gendered racism, because they are both black and men. Mutua further argues that this gendered racism accounts for representations, stereotypes, and practices directed towards black men. It may be that alternative sites may offer a new vantage point from which to view the issues outlined in this chapter.

It is against this backdrop that Chapter 6 looks at the role of the Therapeutic Community (TC) in prison and to assess what effect, if any, it has in creating a meaningful pathway towards transcending the impact of the racialisation of crime/criminal justice systems on the desistance process.

6 Black men, therapeutic interventions and desistance

This chapter focuses on black men in a prison-based Therapeutic Community (TC). The aim is to look at the role of therapeutic interventions and to assess its impact in relation to the trajectory towards desistance. HMP Grendon was chosen as the site for this particular strand of the research inquiry to investigate what role a therapeutic community in prison plays in relation to the understanding of desistance, and to compare how the experience of being TC in relation to the desistance trajectory differed from that of the community. The study involved 10 prisoners, who reflected a diverse range of offending behaviours, as well as representing several geographical locations in the UK, Africa and the Caribbean. The results in this research have been triangulated with two significant studies dealing with the experiences of incarcerated black men.

Wilkinson and Davidson's study (Wilkinson, 2009) centres on a Black and Minority Ethnic (BME) prisoner in-reach project based at HMP/YOI Doncaster, while Franklin and Franklin (2000) have developed a clinical model of the effects of racism on African-American males. As stated previously, this strand of the study involved 10 black men in HM Grendon. Although the participants in this section of the thesis would not be defined as desisters on account of being incarcerated they have an important contribution to make regarding how prisons become a space that can operationalise their desistance goals and aspirations.

Total institutions

This research project has built on these studies and attempts to broaden their findings by placing the narratives of black men at the heart of the analysis. Goffman (1961) suggested that when prisoners are placed in a 'total institution' such as a prison, the barrier between the inmate and the wider world marks the first attack on notions of self. For Goffman, 'total institutions' create and sustain a particular type of tension between the home world and the institutional world, and they use this persistent tension as strategic leverage in the management of men (ibid.: 23). This assertion has many implications for the penal system generally, and prison therapeutic communities specifically, in being able to meet BME residents' identity needs. Indeed, at Grendon, which opened in 1962, there have been consistently relatively low numbers of BME prisoners (Parker, 1970; Newton, 2000; Newberry, 2010). These low numbers have also been commented upon during recent prison inspections (Home Office, 2004, 2006; Ministry of Justice, 2009).

Possible reasons for the low proportion of BME prisoners were considered in a Grendon Winter Seminar of 2007, with a key feature of the day being the input by BME residents (see Sullivan, 2007). This seminar was convened and opened by the then Governor of the prison. In his presentation, he questioned the ethnocentric nature of therapy, the issues that might arise from this and stated that these would need to be addressed if Grendon was to successfully recruit and support BME prisoners (Bennett, 2007). A paper on culture and psychotherapy was also given by the Head of Psychotherapy (Mandikate, 2007). This research seeks to push further an understanding of why there are few BME prisoners at Grendon. It does this in both a theoretical and a practical way.

This chapter attempts to connect and re-connect the personal stories of BME residents at HMP Grendon to see what contribution they can make to the issue of the racialisation of crime/criminal justice systems and its impact on the desistance process. Maruna and Matravers (2007) place importance on the 'life narrative' as a conduit from which to gain insights that other types of research may negate or ignore. These stories also provide a context to investigate how black men construct their own understanding of desisting from crime (Maruna and Immarigeon 2004). LeBel *et al.* (2008) consider how there is a need to understand the subjective changes such as self-concept, as well as the social changes that may help sustain abstinence from crime. The present study was therefore predicated on the fact that BME residents at HMP Grendon would have something to offer in terms of 'telling and naming' their own stories, in relation to their racialised experiences at the prison. Allowing black men to tell their stories may enable them to create a new and improved self, by bringing coherence to their 'life stories' (McAdams, 1988).

By using these stories the research aims to provide insights into those factors that have assisted, or hindered, black men's ability to positively engage within the TC at HMP Grendon, and in doing so offer some suggestions to the prison as to how they might encourage more BME prisoners to apply to go to the prison, and then succeed while in therapy.

HMP Grendon is a prison run entirely on therapeutic principles and takes long-term prisoners with personality disorders. The prison is divided into separate therapeutic communities, where group therapy sessions take place that are designed to challenge offending behaviour. The primary interest in these interviews was to look critically at the issue associated with black men's understanding of the racialisation of crime/criminal justice systems and its impact on the desistance process, while being located within a TC.

The study sample

The study involved 10 prisoners, all identifying themselves as 'black', who had committed a range of offences, as well as representing several geographical locations from the UK, Africa and the Caribbean. These interviewees came from three wings within the prison. An adapted form of grounded theory (Strauss and Corbin, 1997; Charmaz, 2006) was used to code the data collected from these interviews. All of those interviewed were currently serving 'life sentences' in the categories, 'IPP', 'Determinate', and 'Indeterminate'.

The life sentence

Unlike a prisoner with a determinate sentence who must be released at the end of that sentence, those sentenced to life imprisonment or an indeterminate sentence of Imprisonment for Public Protection (IPP) have no automatic right to be released. This punitive period is announced by the trial judge in open court and is known commonly as the 'tariff' period. No indeterminate sentence prisoner can expect to be released before they have served the tariff period in full. However, release on expiry of the tariff period is not automatic. Release will only take place once this period has been served and the Parole Board is satisfied that the risk of harm the prisoner poses to the public is acceptable. This means that indeterminate sentence prisoners could remain in prison for many more years on preventative grounds after they have served the punitive period of imprisonment set by the trial judge. A release direction can only be made if the Parole Board is satisfied that the risk of harm the offender poses to the public is acceptable.

Themes emerging

The following themes emerged from the interviews and are discussed in more detail below:

- HMP Grendon
- father deficit
- self-concept
- desistance: 'knifing off'

HMP Grendon

It was evident throughout the interview process that prisoners found being at Grendon beneficial in looking at and addressing their offending behaviour, in spite of the difficulties faced. However, there were some contrasting views:

> They want you to do things differently, they want you to challenge people and be challenged but they are not willing to be challenged and challenge themselves. To be honest with you, I wish I never come here, that's how I'm feeling at the moment.
>
> (Peter)

Peter sees his entrance into HMP Grendon as one where he is caught within a 'binary opposition' (Perea, 1997) in the form of an 'us' and 'them' scenario. His sense of regret is rooted less in the reality of being in a TC than in feeling powerless to challenge those in power. Another complaint and fear involved the isolation of being a minority within the prison itself. Prisoners experienced this sense of isolation from their arrival at Grendon and it continued throughout, and which could last as long as two years:

> When I came here, I think I was the only black person on the induction wing, and these things do matter to me. I do pick up on these things and I could tell straight away that the ethos of this place was that they want you to fit in with their middle-class white people – I picked that up straight away.
>
> (Nathan)

Nathan's perception of HMP Grendon being mainly white made him feel powerless as his sense of identity was inadequately recognised. Other prisoners, while acknowledging that HMP Grendon did impact on their cultural identity, felt that the TC experience would afford them the opportunity to look into themselves. Nathan said: 'You've got to think about other people – if you don't think about other people, you're not going to care about yourself and then you're going to create more victims.' Nathan reveals how the TC at HMP Grendon has pushed him to acknowledge his victims. Linton also understands the root of his offending behaviour is linked to an understanding of his personal identity:

> Another reason for being at Grendon is so I can learn a bit about myself, why I do these things, to try and change my thought process and my behaviour to a better way. To stop doing things that make me end up in trouble.
>
> (Linton)

In other cases, the search for 'self' became a difficult exercise of self-discovery and at times also led to other realisations that some prisoners referred to as 'culture stripping'.

As Donovan illustrates: 'When I first came to Grendon I found it a struggle because I was the only West Indian there. I felt lonely and lost. I use Jamaican patois and I've had to change the way I talk.' Donovan's experience of isolation in HMP Grendon caused him to modify his whole demeanour. This in turn led to anxiety and identity questioning, resulting in major bouts of self-doubt that at times brought on depression. However, Everton felt that HMP Grendon provided a welcome opportunity that other prisons did not:

> The good thing with Grendon is that because it's a therapeutic community, you have community members, you have psychologists, who always challenge your practices. In other jails you don't really get challenged. When you come into a therapeutic community, because people are

confident to challenge you, you do get a lot of times when you have to reflect on your behaviour.

(Everton)

Overall, the black men interviewed adapted quite well to entering into a TC and experienced positive outcomes in addressing their offending behaviour.

Father deficit

Various interviewees described the impact of father deficit, though this is also the experience of many white prisoners (Mandikate, 2011, pers. comm.), and how this has created a void within their lives, although this seemed to be seldom addressed as a therapeutic need:

My dad didn't actually think I was his, and he had lots of issues dealing with that so I had problems with people and trust and in relationships. I never got this recognition from my dad and I feel like I got ... from him.

(Nathan)

Nathan, like many black men interviewed, struggled to confidently express his feelings on this issue. However, the impact of this part of his life was clearly visible and could be seen in restless body language, long silences and awkward facial expressions.

Maybe it was the way I was raised – my mum and dad split up when I was 4 and mum was in and out of relationships, and whilst in and out of relationships we were moving around a lot. We never stayed anywhere any longer than, say, five years – I was moving around a lot, so I was never stable in one place.

(Stewart)

As a young black man, Stewart was rootless with no sense of security. He observed and experienced racism, combined with never having had any adequate guidance from a father figure. This lack of stability generated the level of internal distress that pushed Stewart to find solace in the streets. In effect, the streets became Stewart's extended family and that indirectly led him to prison. Anderson (1999), in his 'code of the streets', considers that it is the cumulative impact of poverty, race, and social isolation that pushes many young black men into a subculture of violence and criminality as a way of achieving respect and acquiring 'street manhood'.

When analysing the journey of these black men in prison as fathers and sons, words such as 'absent', 'negative', 'deadbeat', 'useless', recur and manifest themselves in a growing legacy of 'father deficit' that can and does lead to those same young men searching for replacement fathers within the confines of 'gang culture'. Winston illustrates this point:

I grew up in Manchester and my dad was a drug dealer. I lived with my mum but I stayed with my dad every weekend and I looked at my dad as my role model. He lived in Moss Side and for me growing up in that area, it was gangs. I had no brothers or sisters so I found my family in the streets and was out there selling drugs through my dad, so it became like a natural progression for me to go out onto the streets, roll with man and hanging, that was my life. Aged 14/15 I dropped out of school, didn't do any exams, hustling on the corner. I got my first jail sentence when I was 16.

(Winston)

Winston talks about 'rolling with man', a term that describes hanging out with older men, which could be seen as a metaphor for the absence of a father/son relationship. Pinnock (1997) considers that the absence of cohesive and stable families, like the one outlined by Winston, creates an alternative sub-cultural replacement in the form of a gang.

Self-concept

The sense of a 'loss of identity' or notions of 'invisibility' featured heavily in the way black men in HMP Grendon felt disempowered and oppressed. Ellison (1947) cites invisibility as a conscious act by white people designed to render black self-concept obsolete. Franklin (2004) sees this deficit as a form of extreme social exclusion that he refers to as 'the invisibility syndrome' which severely limits black men's self-actualisation.

Black prisoners said they experience a similar invisibility in many areas of the prison regime: food provision (lack of cultural foods), reading material (black literature), staffing (little diversity) and little or no sense of being a culturally diverse community (small numbers of black men).

It's hard, very up and down. You are judged straight away, for your colour and me for my size, for the way you talk, for the way you act. I feel that they don't really understand where I'm coming from and a lot of them don't really care either. If I'm honest, I don't really know who I am. They are trying to make us like them, they're not letting me still be black, they're not letting me still have my culture, and they're trying to take that away from me.

(Yusef)

Yusef sees his current situation in HMP Grendon as having his racial and cultural identity eroded, something over which he has no control. Being in a minority situation is something that white staff and white prisoners may have very little understanding of, or sympathy for. This state of affairs caused many of the interviewees to suppress their cultural and racialised identities, forcing them underground, combined with a built-up resentment and inner tension at the privileged position of white officers rendering those same identities subordinate.

> I've been here for three years and what I am aware of is, this is a majority white male prison or white people prison. There is a minority of black or ethnic inmates here and there is a lack of understanding of us, because there is not enough ethnics or blacks they don't understand me, I've got to lower my lingua, I've got to lower the way I speak, the way I socialise.
>
> (Yusef)

Yusef highlights how the lack of validation of their racialised and cultural identities sets up a level of distrust that can, and does, create barriers to meaningful relationships with officers and other prisoners. Solorzano and Yosso (2002: 31) argue that racism 'distorts and silences the experiences of people of colour'. This situation could explain why black men retreat, stay in the confines of the black community and do not want to defend their racial existence (Spence, 2010):

> You'll get a group of black guys walking on the yard and they're auto-matically labelled as, 'Ah, look at them, they're back into their gang culture behaviour, loud, walking with a bit of a swagger and so forth and so forth.' You get a number of white people walking in their group but it's not an issue, when they do it.
>
> (Peter)

The construction of 'racialised prison masculinities' at times generates stereotypical, negative, assumptions by some prison staff that can restrict the development of a positive self-concept for black men in Grendon.

Desistance: knifing off

The primary interest with this stage of the field research was to discover issues surrounding desistance and how a TC could aid this process. In the interviews themes related to 'knifing off' emerged. 'Knifing off' is about the means by which individuals are thought to change their lives by severing themselves from detrimental environments, undesirable companions, or even the past itself.

Here Pablo expresses his desire not to return to his old ways, based on the acquisition of new skills. However, it is underpinned with a strong sense of self-doubt. On the other hand, Yusef believes that letting go of his past is something that is difficult, based on the embedding of his previous life in his sub-conscious:

> I would like to say 100 per cent that I am not going to go back to crime but you can never say never, and I don't know how things are going to pan out, and you are in control of your own destiny, so how can you say that?

It doesn't sound like sense but within myself I am not 100 per cent convinced but I know I've learnt a lot from being inside. I've gained a lot of self-confidence.

(Pablo)

It's impossible to cut the whole thing off because whatever I've become, I've picked that up from somewhere, whether it's the street knowledge, things that I picked up from home and outside the home, I can't forget everything.

(Yusef)

To successfully 'knife off' the past, one may need to develop a new template for living, where issues of race, ethnicity and culture can be important considerations in the process of re-entry back into the community. Sampson and Wilson (1995) argue that race and urban inequality are significant factors that inhibit notions of 'knifing off' for black men, who invariably have to return back to an unchanged community. Understanding black men's subordination, based on the impact of racism, requires regime delivery at HMP Grendon to be more sensitive towards how black men can be blocked in relation to their trajectory towards living crime-free lives.

Alexander (2010) suggests that the prison experience for many black men may impede the possible journey from incarceration to successful long-term societal reintegration.

That's the struggle I'm going through now, a lot of my old associates have been cut off. They've been killed through beefing on the streets. There's still a lot of people, family members, my dad, cousins, who are still out there and they're part of me, so I would like to get out and totally go in a different direction because I'm sick of that life. If I move out of Manchester and move to London, I'm still going to be in the ghetto, I'm still going to be around certain people because I've never lived around 'normal' people. Everyone I've lived around have been gang bangers, drug dealers, weed smokers, go to the blues, that's my life, so I've never known any different.

(Winston)

Winston describes a life that is full of pain, loss, and trauma. He is clearly at odds with his previous life and has a strong awareness of his current situation, and sees the enormity of the task of being able to let go of his past. Donovan, on other hand, has developed a focused strategy that involves a significant amount of trimming down in his life. The implications here are that he has no way of knowing if cutting his 'brethrens off' will enhance his life, but internally he knows it may be for the better:

In my mind, I have a plan in my head that I just want a quiet life. When I think back to my early days, I'm thinking if I was to cut everything off that I believe in, because I use to believe in my brethrens, my so-called brethrens, I think I would also cut them off from what kind of person I would be.

(Donovan)

Maruna *et al.* (2004) argue for the need to enable offenders to be active participants in their own reformation while Farrall and Bowling (1999) believe that the process of desisting from offending is one that is produced through the interplay between individual choices (agency) and a range of wider social forces (structure). This highlights a potential problem for black men in Grendon. Namely if the ethos within the institution does not provide adequate structural guidance, then black men, by both design and default, may not have sufficient agency to fully desist. Linton reflects on a cognitive desire that he feels is being ignored:

I think I'm preparing myself for all of that. Grendon is talking about the resettlement thing, and the resettlement thing that they're talking about I know it's got to do with accommodation, and all that, but they're not talking about mental resettlement back into the community, for instance.

(Linton)

Linton reveals a deeper psychic need to free himself from his past, but locates his desire to change his life less in the realms of the physical world, and more in the psychological. He clearly feels unprepared to return, as he feels there has been a lack of attention paid to his mental well-being in relation to his re-entry needs.

Psychological functioning

Many black prisoners interviewed reflected on their TC experiences at HMP Grendon, noting that there was little acknowledgement of how they were going to psychologically function when returning back to the community.

This left many feeling that a crucial aspect of their story was missing as it was not talked about or addressed within the TC. McAdams (1988) suggests that stories represent a critical scene and turning points in our lives, and that the 'life story' is a joint product of the person and the environment: 'The life story suggests developing a sense of who I am, what I am going to do in the future, and what do I need to do in order to generate a legacy' (1988: 19). It could be argued that the understanding of the destination arrived at must be viewed in terms of the journey travelled, highlighting that for black men in HMP Grendon, their participation in the TC may in effect be a racialised 'liminal space' (Turner, 1969), where the development of a new and improved sense of racialised identity is part of a wider 'rite of passage' (Van Gennep, 1960; Maruna, 2010). Simon illustrates this point:

My life in the future will have nothing to do with my past. I'm being deported back to Jamaica where I am going to be thrown right back in the deep end and I can't afford to get back inside or go back to the same way of living.

(Simon)

How is Simon, a Jamaican national, being prepared to leave prison, as well as having to return back to a country he has not lived in for many years since being incarcerated? This chapter has been concerned with exploring with a small sample of black men their experiences of the therapeutic process and how this might contribute towards desistance. In doing so, we have tried to establish if anything can be learned to redress the under-representation of BME prisoners. Listening to their life stories, it appears that though black men found being at HMP Grendon beneficial in looking at and addressing their offending behaviour, they nevertheless experience identity difficulties through being minority members of the community.

This leads to feelings of isolation and powerlessness, combined with a sense that their cultural identity is insufficiently recognised. However, it does not prevent them from wanting to challenge their cognitive processes and become better people so that they do not create more victims. Father deficit had created a void within their lives and contributed to their sense of social isolation which, for some was addressed through gang membership. Living in HMP Grendon enabled this to be achieved through more legitimate means as 'there are greater openings for prisoners to be creative, to experience friendship, community, happiness, agency and inner peace' (Brookes, 2010). There is an important need for the prison to address the impact of 'double consciousness', i.e., an 'outsider within' perspective and 'black invisibility', to enable black men to be confident in, and able to satisfactorily express, their black identity and culture in order that a positive self-concept/construct may be achieved. This would then assist their trajectory on their release towards desistance from engaging in criminal activity, by establishing a pattern of life that takes account of their past lifestyle and provides a culturally acceptable alternative. For black men who have been labelled and stereotyped, there is a need for them to create a new template for living. Counter-narratives from black men in HMP Grendon, as Zamudo *et al.* (2011) suggest, would do the following:

- challenge dominant social and cultural assumptions regarding black men's ability to name their own reality;
- utilise interdisciplinary methods of historical and contemporary analysis to articulate the links between societal inequalities, and give voice to the experiences of black men in prison;
- develop counter-discourses through storytelling, narratives, chronicles, biographies, etc., that draw on the real lived experiences of black men in relation to desistance.

A prison regime that does not see, acknowledge, or understand the impact of race and processes of racialisation on black men will only serve to perpetuate the difficulties that some black men experience. The narratives of black men in HMP Grendon lay the foundation not only for improving the regime but also for providing a culturally competent lens with which to do so.

However, a more disturbing feature of those interviews is the negation of the impact of the TC for black men on release. Not only do these men have to deal with the racialisation of criminal justice systems, but the therapeutic experience adds to their dilemma, based on the possibility of returning to communities who may not understand or have any awareness of the changes they have undergone while being incarcerated. This concluding section of the findings looks at how African-American men understand notions of their own desistance in the city of Baltimore in the USA.

7 African-American men and desistance

This chapter focuses on African-American men in the city of Baltimore, Maryland, in the USA. The aim was to do a some analysis of the international community in relation to factors that enhanced or hindered notions of desistance for African-American men. The US strand of the research took place in Baltimore during August/September 2010, as part of a Winston Churchill International Travel Fellowship. This component of the research was comparative in orientation. I chose to use urban ethnography and semi-structured interviews to explore the daily lives of some of the participants to obtain a snapshot of how the city of Baltimore enhanced or inhibited notions of desistance for African-American men. Urban ethnography involves up-close and personal observation listening to people in the context of their everyday lives, and it centres on the analysis of research strategies of the urban landscape (Anderson, 1999). Pryce (1979) feels that an understanding of black men comes not from an intellectual account or the cold analysis of social science statistics but requires the researcher to become more actively involved and to let go of notions of neutrality. This is a position shared by Clark (1965) who moves beyond the 'participant observer' role and becomes more of an 'involved observer' that requires 'participation in rituals and customs, as well as the social competition with the hierarchy in dealing with the problems of the people he is seeking to understand' (ibid.: xvi). Charmaz (2006) also argues that urban ethnographers bring different approaches to their studies, and feels ethnography has a role to play in social action and transformation. Anderson (1999), however, provides a word of caution when he argues that the urban ethnographer's work should be as objective as possible, but knows that to achieve this is not easy, as it requires researchers to try and set aside their own values and assumptions. It was also important to understand how I could develop and analyse the findings using this method. Throughout this process I also questioned how to get behind the daily experiences of African-American men in Baltimore to better understand those issues associated with their desistance trajectories. The study in this chapter asked two basic questions: (1) how do African American men understand notions of the racialisation of crime and criminal justice systems and its impact on the desistance process?; and (2) how do those understandings compare to those of black men in the UK?

The interviewees

All the interviewees agreed to be involved in the research process as they felt it was an opportunity to share their stories, where they felt their voices had been previously been rendered silent in previous encounters with other researchers. It was also apparent that there was a strong sense that, because I was not a native of Baltimore, the research would not be judgemental and would be more objective. In saying that, gaining access was still subject to rigorous community codes and rituals as a way of gaining credibility.

Themes emerging

An adapted form of grounded theory was used to code the data (Charmaz, 2006). The following themes emerged from the interviews:

- the code of the streets;
- effects of incarceration;
- being street cool;
- re-entry;
- Bu's story.

The code of the streets

The 'code of the streets' is a street-level 'survival of the fittest' philosophy (Anderson, 1999). It revolves around the ability to navigate the perils of violence, gang culture, drugs, and extreme social deprivation. Individuals who understand and manage the 'code of the streets', use extreme menace and intimidation to control sections of the communities in which they reside.

As Byron highlights, there are no hard and fast rules about the 'code of the streets', other than you have to survive at all costs: 'You gotta do what you gotta do. Shit's real. Ain't no sense worryin' bout a future you don't have.' Byron's sense of not thinking about the future would suggest that the 'code of the street' is less about planning a future or looking back, but more of living in the moment, as you never know what is around the corner. Ishmael sees his desire to get off the streets as being connected to the problems associated with being black in America. He sees the streets as a place to have some control over his life:

> Yeah, I want out, but what am I supposed to do? This is America. It ain't no place for black people. We don't have anything. At least on the streets I can have some level of control over my life.

Ishmael sees the streets, in spite of being a dangerous space to occupy, gives some purpose to his life. Paradoxically he also intimates that he would like to get off the streets. The problem with the 'code of the streets' is that it demands loyalty and creates very few exit strategies. Rahim illustrates this point: 'It's hard, this street hustle. Real fuckin' hard, but it's got to be done. No-one here's gonna give you shit.' Although Rahim acknowledges the difficulty of street life, he also accepts that there's no way out, as well as accepting that no-one cares about his plight. A form of street level 'Double Consioussness'.

Another feature of the code of the streets is the way many black men in Baltimore struggle in school. As Tyrone points out, poor schooling drove him onto the streets:

> I felt the white teachers looked down on me as they had low expectations. Something that followed me throughout my education. I suppose then I discovered the seduction of the streets. Street life became more exciting and gave me a sense of belonging.
>
> (Tyrone)

Tyrone's seduction by the streets was less of a conscious choice, but one that came about as a consequence of being rejected by white teachers. Katz (1988) also argues that some individuals are seduced by street life and criminal activity. He further argues that researchers who have never engaged with those individuals at times fail to look critically at that seduction, and spend more time trying to disprove any notion that some criminals actually like being involved with crime. An example here is Byron who sees himself as a soldier, defending his territory:

> You gotta defend your territory. Like soldiers, we go out on the streets. It's dog eat dog out there. And I ain't gonna get eaten for no-one. You feel me? You can't be actin' all soft an' shit.
>
> (Byron)

By equating his role to that of a soldier, it could be argued that Byron sees himself as an alternative police force, designed to keep order in his community, with a strong sense of duty and loyalty. This sense of purpose, albeit flawed, highlights the importance to Byron of establishing a role in the community, where society has not enabled him to acquire one. Byron's hyper-masculine posture also reveals a darker element to the 'code of the streets', namely, notions of strengths and weaknesses. Being physically and psychologically tough is the currency of survival on the streets of Baltimore. Ishmael too explains why being tough is an important part of the 'code of the streets':

> I see young brothers all around me dyin' for a beef, slingin' rocks. Ain't no way out. No-one cares, so why should we? You can't be showin' fear. You have to lock it off. Can't think too much. This is too fucked up. You wanna survive out here, you can't be weak.
>
> (Ishmael)

Ishmael's nihilistic view is borne out a sense of helplessness and despair, where death is ever present. Death seems to be casually accepted as a by-product of occupying the streets.

Thus, the ability to be around death without it affecting you is important here. Here, Rahim recounts his experiences of loss: 'I've lost a lot of my friends out here. Too many. It hurts, but you gotta maintain. Yeah, it's stressful, but they're family. They've always got my back. So I gotta have their's. You feel me?' Rahim sees losing his friends as a price that has to be paid. On the flipside, Barry reveals a darker truth, a 'kill or be killed' mindset:

> Whoever steps to you does so at their own risk. I have no problem puttin' a cap in someone's ass. The streets ain't a nice place. It's survival of the fittest. It's how we roll. It's just the way it is.
>
> (Barry)

Barry's casual acceptance of death as the 'norm' is as painful as it is disturbing. This would suggest life on the streets equates to playing a game of chess that requires the development of a clear and achievable strategy of reducing the possibility of dying by the code of the streets. Rahim reveals the implication of violating the code:

> You cross me and it's on. I'll do whatever I have to do. If you can't take pain, don't get in the game. That's all I say. On the streets, it's ain't about actin' bad. You gotta be able to do it.
>
> (Rahim)

Rahim's view also highlights the importance of gaining and maintaining a 'street reputation'. Tyrone also adds weight to Rahim's argument:

> When I got involved in crime, I felt I was someone. People looked up to me and quickly I built a strong crew. I was living large. I had guns, money, women, and most of all status. Growing up, I felt I was a nobody. Then I became a somebody.
>
> (Tyrone)

Tyrone highlights the deeper need to become someone at all costs. Using menace to gain status would not usually be seen as a legitimate way to gain respect, but the 'code of the streets' places the same value on achieving respect, but according to the rules of street survival. He continues:

> The problem with it all is when you want to come out of the game, and you have left so much destruction out there. You've hurt people really bad. How can that be good? How do they get into the side of the community that's doing good? Now things are different, but you can't bring back the past. If you look around the city, it's getting worse because

young guys looked up to people like me and developed their way of being bad. So we don't really have a sense of community. With so much crime, poverty, drugs and violence, communities are being destroyed. I suppose I saw myself as an outsider to the community and have to establish myself and surround myself by my own community.

Most interviewees' lives in this section are tinged with loss, sadness, and a search for a sense of identity. The streets provides a refuge for 'bad' men; those who exert extreme control over the lives of others, as well as giving rise to a culture of street respect, that requires individuals to risk their lives in order to do so. In spite of the desire to terminate their criminal behaviour, the overwhelming view was the barriers towards desistance were too great to consider, while the seduction of crime was seen as a simpler option.

However, for those who do not end up dead, or have the protection of gangs, prison becomes a site where many black men end up. This next section explores the experiences of black men who have served time in the US prison system.

Effects of incarceration

Al spent many years in San Quentin and the experience of incarceration has had a significant impact on his life:

> It makes no difference if you committed the crime or not, you are still denied every human right. Chained and shackled, I was taken away from my family, away from my freedom, shipped, stripped, stacked and packed into small cells of a jail where my true test of mental survival would be tested and my endurance for sadistic torture would be put under experimentation. I was told when to shit, shower, and shave, fed slop not worthy of feeding pigs, psychologically abused and misused, in some cases beat upon and then even killed.
>
> (Al)

Al reveals a system that is unfair where the loss of liberty ultimately diminishes his psychological state and mental well-being, creating a very isolated individual. Neville also questions whether the system works and suggests that incarceration has a more sinister motive, to damage the psyche of prisoners: 'Few prisoners get better in these overcrowded compounds. Often they vegetate in whatever level of psychosis they are beaten into, and they never change, never worse, never better, for year after year.' Neville highlights yet again how prisons generate and maintain a sense of 'psychic deprivation' that in itself can push prisoners to vegetate. Alexander (2010) argues a different point, accusing prisons for black men as creating 'a new slavery'. Her analogy rests on an understanding that destroying the minds of slaves made them compliant, controlled, and incapable of contemplating any challenge to their captors. Neville reaffirms Alexander's view with the recounting of his own experiences of incarceration. Brian expresses the view that prison is worse than the streets, and in prison he finds the same type of behaviour as he did when he was free:

> Prison was fucked up. Worse than the streets. Can't get no peace. You can't escape the shit of street life in there. People up in ya business and shit. Fuckin' hustle in prison like the streets. That's all you can do to stay alive when ya locked up.
>
> (Brian)

However, perhaps the difference in Brian's prison behaviour was that it was motivated by the need to preserve his mind from being overtaken by the oppression of the prison system and, ultimately, becoming sedated by his deteriorating psychic condition. Al highlights the importance educating the mind while incarcerated: 'It is a time of educating oneself on surviving on little or nothing and developing shameful habits. I found killing time is no art. Keeping yourself sane while doing time is.'

Al shows how sanity on the streets and in prison have parallels. They are both ruled by fear, codes of violence, and respect. Neville also reminds us that prison is supposed to be about providing rehabilitative opportunities, but paints a cold reality of what it is really like being locked up as a black man in a US prison:

> If you provide them with nothing but walls and bars, then you create a very frustrated and troubled human being. However, if you give them an education, job skills, forgiveness and caring, in general, rehabilitate them, what is created is someone you will not fear but respect because they have learned how to respect themselves and others.
>
> (Neville)

Neville's view sees rehabilitative processes that can enable a prisoner to learn about respect as a possible factor required in the trajectory towards desistance. However, Byron brings out another aspect of the impact of incarceration, when a prisoner is separated from friends and family:

> There are numerous adverse psychological effects which result from incarceration, but none quite as devastating as those which result from the separation of family and friends. It is not just a problem for friends and family, but society as a whole.
>
> (Byron)

Byron sees this separation as a form of control as part of an on-going conspiracy regarding black men's incarceration in the USA, and is eager to point out the human aspect of being locked away that at times is missed. Likewise, Al views this state of affairs as a form of regression:

Prisons and jails, like no other institutions, have a way of reducing a person to a form of adolescence, which takes years to recuperate, and regain consciousness of self as a functioning adult. They create a sense of dependency, through certain forms of brainwashing, reconditioning of the mind, and sadistic treatment.

(Al)

Al highlights how continuous exposure to the prison environment can lead to a shift in mood that at times would be seen as depressive. It could be argued that producing this state of being acts as a form of social control or sedative, designed to disable prisoners' minds from contemplating freedom, escape, or challenge. Neville, likewise, sees incarceration as a slow death: 'The slow, meticulous march towards death a prisoner experiences daily is far more uncivilised and criminal than the acts for which we are charged and eventually executed for.' The experience of incarceration has forced Neville to question the criminal justice process. By equating his crimes on the same level as those of flawed criminal justice agencies, he is questioning who the real criminals are.

No one desires to exist in this imprisoned state, though with some, it may be the only state of existence in which they can function properly. But if we are to ever reach a state of rehabilitation and reconciliation, then the circumstances surrounding our existence within the prison environment must drastically change to promote a positive atmosphere for re-entry into society.

(Al)

Al cites the factors that will position him in relation to re-entry back to the community and, clearly identifies what is right for him. He continues:

With the present influx of incarceration, the conditions of jails and prisons continue to decline. The overcrowded, stuffed cells, the inability to provide decent hygienic care, the brutal treatment and the sadistic and violent behavior of the guards rob an inmate of his/her dignity, pure and simple, it makes me ask a question, how are we supposed to do better, if better is not done to us?

Al is obviously angry about his incarceration and demonstrates an eloquent and insightful view of life as ex-offender. His statement raises another deeper question about the role of the ex-offender in looking effectively at pathways towards desistance. Al, like other interviewees, seems to know the experience of incarceration intimately, which would suggest they have something important to contribute to what would enable them to understand how the racialisation of the US prison system impacts on the desistance process. However, Byron reminds us of the wider structural concerns that invalidate the possibility for ex-offenders to point the way towards their own desistance:

Imprisonment rates for black people stem from the nature of black imprisonment in the US. It is a major social problem. While the entire social fabric is disintegrating, schools and hospitals are closing, housing is increasingly unavailable, jobs are disappearing, life expectancy for young black men is low, and more prisons are being built.

(Byron)

Byron raises an important question: how many criminologists have ever sat down with men like him, as a way of understanding the impact of incarceration and the difficulties of re-entering the community? He continues:

In California, an inmate appears before a board, who then evaluates his behaviour. If he fails to perform, he will be sent to an institution which is hundreds of miles from his home. This practice serves as a control mechanism in terms of inmate behaviour.

(Byron)

Byron highlights the unfairness of the system and sees it as a furthering of control exercised by the system. Neville pushes the argument further when he slams the attempts to rehabilitate prisoners as empty gestures:

Whilst I was inside I thought about things long and hard. Now I'm released, I still don't feel free. They made a mockery of any meaningful attempts at rehabilitation, which is, after all, the so-called purpose of incarceration. If anyone is callous enough to say, 'Who cares?', please be warned that these degraded souls will return to society in time, and we will then reap what we have sown.

(Neville)

Neville sees the prison experience as creating space for him not only to reflect. He also grounds himself in the reality of where he's at. He also warns of what will happen to returning offenders who have had no rehabilitation. Al also reminds us of the humanity of those who have offended and argues that incarceration is not always as a result of a conscious act of criminality, but as the result of poor choices:

Inmates have aspirations just like everyone else. The desire to take care of family doesn't escape their consciousness. We are people, we have loved ones, we have people who love us, this makes us people, not unlike yourself. Some prison inmates are not really bad, they just made a bad choice and ended up in prison.

(Al)

The men interviewed in this section remind us that being incarcerated for a long time inside a hostile prison environment can and does take its toll on prisoners. Like most encounters with released prisoners who have served long sentences, there is a reluctance to revisit their pasts. As Alexander (2010) points out, prison is a control mechanism which has as its purpose the goal of subordinating people of colour and other disaffected sections of the community. This suggests the need to consider the importance of social and community bonds in relation to creating a stronger pathway towards desistance than incarceration. With looking at the 'code of the streets' and the 'negative effects of incarceration', how do black men rise above these experiences to chart a pathway towards desistance? Although it's clear that though many of those interviewed are coping, managing, and surviving, there is also something deeper clearly operating below the surface, and would best be described as 'street cool'. This section hears from individuals who are operating with 'street cool'.

Street cool

Neville offers an interesting scenario. The move from the South to the North forced him to make the kind of readjustment that pushed him slowly towards a life of crime:

> I grew up in the South where there were very strong community connections. Life was slower and easier. When my parents moved into Baltimore, it was a rougher place. People weren't as friendly. Life was tough. Baltimore was place where black and white didn't get on, drugs flowed freely and everyone was on the hustle.
>
> (Neville)

Neville reveals that where once there was a sense of belonging in his life, moving to a big city changed that dynamic. It is evident that the weakening of his social bonds increased the likelihood of an individual like him being pushed into a life of crime and constructing notions of 'street cool' to cope with the pressure. Al likewise focuses on the importance of having a sense of community:

> Inner city living wasn't and still isn't good. In the world I lived, you had to have strong connections for personal safety. It was a 'dog eat dog' way of living. Community connections were about fear, control things, and being cool in the way you managed it. The more fear you generated, the more street respect you generated, and the cooler it made you.
>
> (Al)

Al reflects on how his community used to be, revealing the notion that the 'code of the streets' almost becomes the norm. He highlights being bad isn't enough, but there's a style that accompanies it that in turn gains the respect.

Tyrone discards any notion of being positive:

> Growing up I couldn't see the point of being positive. I suppose what I was doing is rebelling against what was right. Doing right was for fools, back then. No-one on the streets respects if you ain't carrying yourself correct.
>
> (Tyrone)

This benchmark of 'street cool' masks another important issue, like in the UK, that of 'father absence' as Rahim reflects:

> I wasn't born this way. I was made this way. No pops, like most around here. Mom did several jobs, sisters ain't around. What chance did I have? Fuckin' racist place like this forces you out onto the streets. It's like you ain't gotta a choice. I'm a survivor.
>
> (Rahim)

The desire to be a man without being given adequate guidance can lead to the kind of destructive behaviour outlined by both Tyrone and Rahim. However, normalising negative type of behaviour in the name of 'father absence' and being cool can only serve to create more tension on the streets, the community, and society as a whole. Ishmael questions the role of parents in his life:

> In Baltimore, there ain't shit for us. Everyone talks about gangs as negative. At least they take care of business. They're like my family. Sure, it's harsh, but they keep shit tight. What can parents do? We ain't got no sense of community out here.
>
> (Ishmael)

Ishmael highlights a deeper problem, namely having no sense of community creates a legion of isolated individuals, connected by loss and no sense of belonging. Hence the propensity to join a gang. If the gang then becomes the replacement family and part of the normal socialisation of young men like Ishmael, then this situation will fracture the possibility of developing the meaningful and positive social bonds required to create a successful pathway towards desistance. Here Barry, Rahim, and Jason talk about the need for the love and security of a family:

> Never had no family or security in my life. That's when I became the devil's child. The daily struggles of life on the corner prepared me for this life. Yeah, I'd like a better life, but who's gonna give me one? More importantly, whose gonna show me?
>
> (Barry)

I've lost a lot of my friends out here. It hurts, but you gotta maintain. Yeah it's stressful, but they're my family. They've always got my back. So I gotta have their's. You feel me? We all need a family, but when you don't have yours at hand, you have to create one.

(Rahim)

Future, what future? I take things a day at a time. Out here, every day could be ya last. Never had a good start in life. It's like an epidemic. I don't know anyone with a secure background. They say you don't miss what you don't have. That's shit! I miss my moms and pops.

(Jason)

The issues facing Barry, Rahim, and Jason are complex, as they feel powerless, alienated, and disaffected from society.

Constructing a street persona that they define as cool can be seen as a coping strategy in light of their circumstances, but the absence of guidance from family and community only drives them further into seeing crime as a way out. As Rahim argues: 'Yeah, I'd like an older man to talk to, but round here they're either on drugs, drinkin', fuckin', and that ain't good. We're all fucked up. I blame the older guys.' Sustainable intergenerational development could be a way to assist the hunger Rahim has for older teachers who support, mentor, and guide. He continues:

For lots of guys, they have no reason to live. They also come to a point in their lives where they can't face doing one more prison term. So they wanna get off the streets and the corners, but they don't know how to. I didn't know what I was going to do, but then I remembered my parents and my brothers. I had a family that I had rejected. Shock, fear of death, and other stuff helps you make that decision.

Rahim highlights an important point here that the aspiration to go straight can be thwarted by not having the appropriate tools to do so. Prison provides little in the way of rehabilitative processes, as already outlined, and this is all combined with an absence of meaningful family and community guidance and support. It then becomes hard to see how an individual can develop coherent strategic pathways towards desistance. So a closer examination of the constraints or opportunities that can be created by re-entry back to the community is important here

Re-entry

This section focuses on the journey back to the community. Jason reflects on how he felt on release and the importance of gaining his freedom:

On my first day of freedom, I was engulfed in the silence of my thoughts, treasuring the collected memories of the morning's experiences, and abhorring the thought of the reality which awaited me around the next few turns in the road. As I returned back into the reality of leaving prison behind, the sights and wonders of the day slowly settled into that dimension of time and place known as memories, where only such dreams will allow me to visualise, retrace, and enjoy the world beyond those walls that were home for such a long period of my life.

(Jason)

Although Jason revels in the experience of being released, Neville highlights the problems that lead to his recidivism:

As life seem to always have its up and downs, my downfall was just around the corner. I had been out no more than a couple of months, then I was back in trouble again, this time myself along with some other guys who would pull off a robbery. We would then go around spending money, having fun and not realising that we are slowly becoming what was soon to be hoodlums.

(Neville)

Neville's lack of preparation or ability to adjust to a new situation would suggest that rehabilitative processes, if they were present whilet incarcerated, were not in place on release. Al sees the inability to manage the prison experience as another possible threat to maintaining a successful re-entry back to the community:

Then these so-called authorities release people like us into a demanding society and then expect them to function and act as independent individuals.
    Left in an incarcerated society such as this, it is far wiser to fall and remain, than to rise and be knocked down repeatedly. I've seen many break, both mentally and physically, and go straight back to prison.

(Al)

Al sees a culture of neglect and a failure to provide a duty of care to returning prisoners as fuelling the failure of the US penal system. Rahim also highlights this position:

When I got out, I became more restless, and started to get deeper in criminal life. There was no support, no guidance, nothing for me to do. I never had the chance to do stuff in prison, so hell called me back.

(Rahim)

Rahim further suggests the level of anxiety that can arise when there is a lack of available support post release. Not having anyone to meet you on release is also another factor that can be debilitating for men returning back to the community. As Barry reflects:

My first day of release from prison was hard. I had no family, no-one to meet me at the gate, and an uncertain future. In the past I have expressed my sadness at not being able to see any forms of plant life and growth, as well as other such things and experiences which every free person sees and experiences within the travels of everyday life on the outside.

(Barry)

Barry's state of affairs is also compounded when the returning prisoner, excited by the prospect of a new life, realises that he is in effect returning to an environment that has remained unchanged since being locked away. Al testifies to how demoralising it can be knowing that things have got worse and not better:

Returning to the community I noticed my old neighbourhood was over-fed with narcotics, supplied and controlled by the very same so-called law enforcement officers. Our schools no longer held the vitality of academic education, but rather a formal introduction into the criminal element.

(Al)

Al reflects on an unchanged community and feels even more isolated. Rahim's scathing attack on the community is even more damning, when he cites his own community as inflicting more damage on his already broken life:

On my release I tried to re-connect to the so-called community. Those fuckers who come around here and want to put us into programs, and shit, they're just like the police. Those black motherfuckers who come around here tryin' to tell us to behave. Fuck off, that what I say. That's why the hustle and the streets become the place where you have to make it. Many don't come back. Here one day, then you're gone.

(Rahim)

Rahim's view is painful as it is highlights a more disturbing feature and a challenge to black men's desistance. Namely, if the community remains unaltered, which had originally led to the justification for involvement in criminal activity for men like Rahim, how do they then motivate themselves to consider a life free from crime? Tyrone comes to the conclusion that sometimes re-entry is a dead road, with no comeback:

I'd been gangster, done lots of bad things, and actually never got caught. I was living large. I had everything. When it came down to it, no-one was there. And still aren't. Most of my friends are dead.

(Tyrone)

These testimonies highlight how the agents of criminal justice agencies are determined to show offenders that they're firmly in control and will get tough on anyone who breaches their boundaries. This brings us to one of the most significant interviews that took place in very difficult circumstances. Without exception, the notorious and feared gangs in Baltimore, the 'Crips' and the 'Bloods', pose one of the biggest threats to the trajectory towards desistance. This final section recounts a meeting with a significant Baltimore gang member, 'Bu', and takes the form of a reflexive account of the encounter. Even though I had to declare my intentions upfront and reveal to Bu what I was doing, why I was doing it, and other related ethical concerns, it was mutually agreed for me to listen to him, and then reflect on the experience. Bu told me that so many people have attempted to interview him and made pre-determined assumptions that at times clouded the interview.

Based on Bu's senior gang member status, I also felt gaining important insights might emerge with a less structured, but no less ethnically grounded approach. Access to Bu was mediated through a gang mediator. Based on his profile and possible risk in terms of my own safety, it was important to demonstrate to Bu that my motives were honourable and not part of a deeper plot of entrapment. The interview attempts to engage a serving senior gang member in a serious dialogue about the racialised context of why gang members in Baltimore exist, and become a serious threat to activities designed to enable others to journey towards their desistance. The importance of Bu's story is one of accessing a story, seldom accessed by outsiders such as myself. Gangs have an important perspective to add to our study of desistance.

Bu's story

Night has descended; 'T' and I are in a car park, face to face with a man sporting a red bandana. My first encounter with a member of the 'Bloods' gang is surreal, challenging, and insightful. Being granted an audience with him, followed by a meeting I will never forget was one of the most powerful experiences of my life. He was charismatic, intelligent, and truly a leader. The conversation did not focus on gangs, but more on fatherhood and society in general. The mixture of fear and exhilaration ran through my veins. All the way through the conversation I wondered about his childhood, dreams, aspirations, and what led him into such a lifestyle. Bu felt less of an avenging angel and more as someone who decided that a history of oppression and limited life chance for a suffering community gave him a mandate to operate in opposition to the forces of law and order. In some respects it felt like an act of defiance with menace and consequences. Eventually, I plucked up the courage to ask him how I could prevent my own son from joining a gang. He quickly told me that if I stayed at home with him, ensured he was loved, combined with supporting his education, he would escape the lure of gang life. I concluded by asking Bu if it was all worth it. To my shock, he lifted up his shirt, to reveal a mass of bullet holes, and then calmly said, 'What do you think?' The meeting ended, Bu went on his way, and I was back sitting next to 'T', where we began to debrief. I was truly impressed not only by 'T's unswerving commitment to trying to make Baltimore a better place, but the gang member's openness to reasoning and dialogue.

Be under no illusion, any male US gang member is no saint. However, they are men and fathers, who have made a choice that many find offensive, scary, and wrong. Be that as it may, they exist alongside us, occupying the same space, going to the same shops, taking their kids to school, and trying to survive in their own way. We can all have an opinion, view or judgement as to what is right and wrong. What I would say is, until you have stood face to face with someone like the guy I have just met, we will continue to believe the hype and moral panic that surrounds gang culture. Yes they are menacing individuals who have done all sorts of stuff. The truth is that the solution for changing them will not be found in more incarceration, biased media coverage, or ignoring their existence. Gangs are a complex social phenomenon that requires more than just rhetorical posturing to sort it out. I don't have the solution, but what I did learn today, is that it starts with dialogue. But first you have to gain access. That access was created by 'T'. The sad fact remains there are many guys like 'T', who don't get paid, supported, and validated for what they do. Yet he saves as many lives as any paramedic or surgeon.

After 12 hours on the road 'T' says he will drop me home. Suddenly an incident involving five White police officers arresting a young black woman forces 'T' to stop, pull over, take out a video camera and record what they're doing. 'T' archives stuff that happens on the streets as he wants to make a documentary on the abuses that take place on a regular basis. Lo and behold, it is taking place opposite Little Melvin's shop front. We stop off and talk with Little Melvin for about an hour before making our way home. I am thoroughly exhausted and take several hours to decompress reground myself.

Conclusion

Analysing these interviews indicates that while the process of desistance maybe a gradual one, the overwhelming feeling of helplessness burst through all these interviews. Desiring to break away from crime for many of those interviewed may be motivated at first by a strong aversion to viewing themselves as negative and not liking who and what they have become. But before some of them were willing to give up their identity as a lawbreaker, they had to perceive this identity as unsatisfying, thus weakening their commitment to it.

The problem tended to focus on the unfairness of the system and how racialisation was used to continually re-criminalise black men at every layer of the criminal justice system.

Those who were seeking to break from crime slowly began to consider a new identity and move towards a more pro-social life. They developed new, non-criminal preferences and realigned their social networks to suit their aspirations to become crime-free. I would argue that those wishing to quit crime are more likely to be successful at desistance if they are embedded in social networks that not only support their new identities and tastes, but also isolate them from those who would oppose them quitting crime or induce them to continue in their criminal ways. This position would suggest that success in desisting from crime is more likely when black men who have made the decision to leave crime become more pro-social.

However, racism, the code of the streets, and the general disappointment of living in unchanged, resource-stripped communities ensured that, for some of the participants, crime became a renewed choice based on a 'counter-response' to the way they perceived they were being unfairly treated. My own observation of the African-American situation was one of degree. Although both black Britons and African Americans share similar and contrasting histories, their experiences of contact with criminal justice systems differed on a whole series of levels. This position led me to explore some of the common features of the experience of racialised criminal justice processes and their impacts on the desistance process to create a unity of understanding, in this case, masculinities. Chapter 8 presents a theoretical model in relation to black men's desistance that emerged through examining the data with specific reference to the role played by the dynamics of masculinities presented by black men in the research, shaped by the racialisation of the criminal justice systems. It suggests that assessing the impact on black men's masculinities is an important consideration when looking at their trajectories towards their desistance.

8 A theoretical model of masculinities in relation to black men's desistance

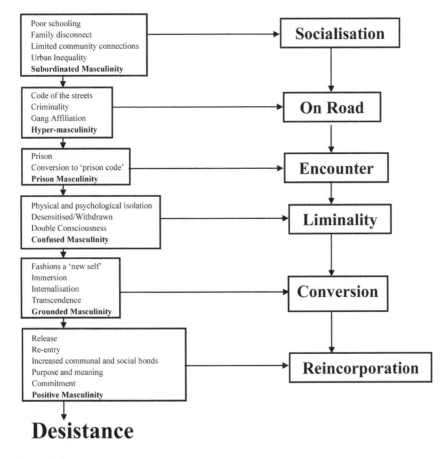

Figure 8.1

West and Zimmerman (1987) argue that masculinity is not something that just 'happens to men' or is 'done to men', but masculinity is seen more as something that 'men do'. Coleman (1990: 191) sees the acquisition of masculinity as a learned process of 'masculine socialisation' and suggests that masculinity is 'performed' or 'acted out' and occurs during social interactions between other men, and this display of masculinity should then be based on shared understanding between men. Messerschmidt feels that masculinity is an on-going process where he states: 'Masculinity is never a static or finished product. They are influenced by the gender ideals that we have come to accept as proper' (1993: 67). Connell further argues that 'when conditions for the defence of patriarchy change, the basis for the dominance of a particular masculinity are eroded. New groups may challenge old solutions and construct a new hegemony' (1995: 77). Connell's perspective is echoed by Hill-Collins (2005) and hooks (2003b) who view hegemonic masculinity as the basis for the 'subordination' and 'marginalisation' of black men and their masculinities. Figure 8.1 presents a model of the different types of masculinity involved in the trajectory to desistance that emerged out of my research.

Messerschmidt (1993) not only states that there are power relations that exist between and among different types of men, but he sees this state of affairs as a product of masculine responses to crime when other resources are unavailable to accomplish socially acceptable masculine norms. Messerschmidt further says that when looking at the relationship between masculinity and crime, and why men commit crimes, it needs to be acknowledged that 'subordinated' masculinities in relation to crime will emerge. Hill-Collins (2005) likewise sees Messerschmidt's position as providing the conduit by which a power dynamic between white and black men involved in criminal activity is the result of a racialised interplay in relation to how crime among different groups of men is generated.

Connell (1987), like Hill-Collins (2000), clearly understands that not all masculinities are seen equally. Both Hill-Collins (2005) and Alexander (2010) see black men as situated near the bottom of the masculine hierarchy, while white men predominately have the power. This creates both 'subordinated and marginalised masculinities' driven by notions of racialised masculine identities (hooks, 2003b). Brown (2002) similarly argues that criminology seldom if ever deals with notions of racialised identities among black men involved in criminal activity. This paucity of research information and data when theorising black masculinities not only weakens the discourse on masculinities as a whole, it also relegates black men to a category defined as 'excluded masculinities' (Glynn, 2005). Connell criticises those social scientists who fail to recognise race within masculinity and does concede that racialised identities within masculinity are under-theorised (Connell and Messerschmidt, 2005).

Baraka (1963) suggests that white theorists have little interest in representing black masculinities, based on a racist construct designed to maintain and sustain 'white privilege'. Baraka states, 'When black people got to this country, they were Africans, a foreign people. Their customs, desires, were shaped by a different place and a radically different life' (ibid.: 1). Baraka's assertion places the production of 'rebellious masculinity' as a counter-masculine position to that of white masculine identity, placed within a socio-historic context. Sale (1997), like Baraka, explains that the creation of 'marginalised' and 'subordinated' masculinities for black men emerged from nineteenth-century slave ship revolts by slaves resisting attempts to be enslaved. Alexander (2010) also sees the socio-historical context to understanding black masculinity as operating a colour-blind approach (Delgado and Stefancic, 2000). Alexander (2010) sees this colour blindness as a way of understanding the marginalisation of black masculinity in relation to mass incarceration of black men as a whole.

Alexander further states, 'In the era of colorblindness, it is no longer socially permissible to use race, explicitly, as a justification for discrimination, exclusion, and social contempt' (ibid.: 2). Alexander continues, 'As a criminal, you have scarcely more rights, and arguably less respect, than a black man living in Alabama at the height of Jim Crow. We have not ended racial caste in America; we have merely redesigned it' (ibid.: 2). Du Bois (1938) further argues that Africans in America struggled with the inability to shake off a 'dual masculine identity' within the confines of the so-called 'American Dream', which excluded black men under the US Constitution. Du Bois referred to this state of being as 'double consciousness'.

Du Bois states it is a peculiar sensation, this 'double consciousness', this sense of always looking at oneself through the eyes of others (ibid.: 8). Du Bois continues: 'One ever feels his two-ness, an American, a negro, two souls, two thoughts, two un-reconciled strivings, two warring ideals in one body' (ibid.: 8). To counter the impact of 'double consciousness', Du Bois emphasised the need to train black men as a way of creating a more grounded masculine identity. Fanon (1952) extends Du Bois's position when explaining the plight of black men under colonialism. Fanon states, 'The black man has two dimensions. One with his fellows, the other with the white man. Negro behaves differently with a white man and with another Negro' (ibid.: 8). Fanon further argues that Du Bois's 'double donsciousness' leads to what he referred to as 'dual narcissism'. 'Dual narcissism', as Fanon sees i, is the entrenchment of 'White men in their Whiteness' as having a knock-on effect by creating 'black men locked into their blackness' (ibid.: 7). The interplay between the two racialised masculine identities is designed to keep black and white men apart, and ultimately play a role in establishing 'subordinate masculinities' (Hill-Collins, 2005).

Frazier (1957) argues that the way to counter the impact of a subordinate masculine position for black men is through gaining and sustaining employment. However, Frazier claims poverty through chronic unemployment in the black community as the major causal factor that led to a rise in both rebellious black masculinity and black male criminality. Frazier also sees the so-called 'American Dream' as being beyond the reach of many black men, based on the devastating impact of slavery, combined with the failed attempts of America to include those black citizens it had historically and systematically excluded. Frazier further argues that crime becomes an oppositional masculine response to white oppression. Liebow (1967) also sees the lack of employment opportunities not only as a factor that has destroyed black men's self-esteem, leading to an erosion in the desire to find work, but also as responsible for black men engaging in criminality as a way of restoring their lost masculine pride.

Clark criticises the professional training of social scientists involved in researching black masculinities as inadequate, and argues that white researchers struggle to 'understand, cope with or to change the normal status in ghetto communities' (1965: xv). Pietila (2010) points out that it is researchers, who are 'backroom wheelers and dealers', who keep US cities segregated, through poor housing, lack of employment opportunities, and claims it is policy-makers who have pushed many black men to abandon conformity and law-abiding attitudes, in favour of 'corner' behaviour in defiance of oppressive white society. Pietila provides the backdrop against which we can see how Clark (1965) argues for an academic clarity about how black men are looked at, investigated, and understood, in a society that refuses to see who they really are (see Alexander, 2010). Like Pietila (2010), Majors feels that 'rebellious masculinity' is the result of black men rejecting society's rules, due to the cumulative impact of racism, denied access, and marginalisation (Majors and Billson, 1992).

Majors further states that cumulative oppressions placed on black men create confusion about how unfair rules apply to black men, which in turn opens the door that leads to systematic deviance, much the same as what Agnew (2006) refers to as 'general strain'. Majors sees black men adopting an alternative masculine coping strategy in the face of general strain which he refers to as 'cool pose'. hooks (2003a) also feels black men develop a 'cool masculinity' as a way of not caving in under the pressure of being marginalised in a racist society. hooks also questions if black men develop these notions of a 'cool masculinity' as a way of reducing the propensity to be seen as deviant in society's eyes, and falsely coming across as socially compliant.

Grier and Cobb feel that black men struggle to acquire manhood 'as [they] must penetrate barriers and overcome opposition in order to maintain a masculine posture' (1968: 50) and suggest that reconstructing a stronger sense of manhood is dependent on developing stronger social bonds. If those social bonds are weak as a consequence of racist oppression, then Grier and Cobb argue that the result is that some sections of the community turn into hyper-masculine identities. Benyon (2002) highlights that social rejection as experienced by black men can lead to serious violent offending (Sampson and Wilson, 1995). Benyon further argues that the structural concerns of white society are internalised by many black men who may feel they are not equal stakeholders in society, and hence the emergence of positive masculinity is arrested. West (1993) argues that hyper-masculinity has become a significant feature in black subculture, located within popular culture such as hip-hop. Marriot (2000) also sees black hyper-masculine tendencies as being framed within a racist construct, not rooted in a position defined by black men themselves and therefore questions whether black men acquire hyper-masculinity, but sees it as being imposed upon them.

Marriot sees the representation and portrayal of black hyper-masculinity as the way that black men defend their right not to be defined in terms of the host culture that wants to continue to operate from a position of pacifying black men's resistance to society, and restricting their self-determination. hooks challenges Marriot's assumptions and contextualises how black men historically have defined their own sense of masculinity as a consequence of 'confronting the hardships of life without allowing their spirits to be ravaged' (2003a: 147). hooks suggests that when racist constructs short circuit the development of positive masculinity for black men, then it may be time for black men to construct a new and improved masculinity that can better respond to the increasing social pressures placed upon them, as opposed to playing out the 'hyper-masculine roles, that lead to mass incarceration' (Alexander, 2010).

West (2004) cites the lack of understanding and changing notions of black hyper-masculinity as flaws within society itself, not as problems associated with black men *per se*. West further argues that society's compulsive need to disable black men by placing the burden of changing attitudes towards race on the oppressed and not the oppressor will continue to distort any notions of an authentic black masculine identity. West expresses the view that the hyper-masculine worldview eventually becomes nihilistic and places black men in a state of eternal liminality (see Turner, 1969: 95). West (2004) attacks the failure of white people to create the space and conditions for black men to reach their full potential, claiming it is a core component in the construction of hyper-masculinity for black men. Mauer (1999) concurs with West (2004) when he highlights how the criminal justice system has both labelled and incarcerated black hyper-masculinity (see Alexander, 2010) as an extension of US criminal justice policy following the legacy of slavery and sustainable white privilege (Brown *et al.*, 2003).

Hill-Collins (2005) identifies the need for alternative black masculinities as a priority to move beyond the confines of subordinated masculinities (see Connell, 1987). Hutchinson (1994) feels the image of black masculinity has been pushed deeply into the American psyche and lays the blame at the door of the media that distorts images of black masculinities for personal gain. Mutua (2006) questions whether the discourse on masculinities is undermined by racism and highlights a possible a new position, namely, 'what qualities does it require to be a black man in the 21st century? and what are the contemporary ways of responding to that position?' (ibid.: 25). In light of the dilemma faced by many black men in framing and acquiring masculinity, the question of explaining how those same black men can desist from criminal activity must also be addressed.

Socialisation

The socialisation of the black men in this study is related to how the intersection of class, race, and gender relations is constituted in relation to the social structure that governs and at times constrains their lives. This state of affairs can and does have a negative impact on some aspects of the 'structured action' undertaken by black men. Messerschmidt (2005) argues that when the divisions of labour and power among black men is constrained by white privilege, then the outcome will invariably be criminal activity. He further argues that social structures organise the way individuals think about their circumstances and generate methods of dealing with them. Therefore, black men articulate notions of their masculinity according to the social situation they find them-selves in. When black men cannot find opportunities to demonstrate a positive masculine identity, then crime becomes an option when other masculine resources are not available. The pressure of expectations placed on black men by their families and communities is made worse if the racialisation of those 'social structures' blocks meaningful and productive opportunities.

The result is that some black men construct ways of articulating their masculinity in opposition to those social structures that relegate them to a position of 'subordinated masculine' identities. Shaw and McKay (1942) argue that 'residential mobility', or lack of it, is a structural factor that accounts for the variation in crime rates. They further reject individual explanations of crime and focus on social disorganisation and weak social controls. Sampson and Wilson (1995) also suggest that research conducted on the individual rarely questions whether community-level processes are at fault. They further argue that residential inequality gives rises to social isolation, which in turn leads to structural barriers that undermine social organisation and place limitation on the ability to desist.

Sharkey (2008) argues that persistent inequality should be seen as the failure to conceptualise the role that race plays in the production and maintenance of inequality across multiple dimensions. He further argues that families become connected to places and these places offer a unique set of advantages within the social structure. If those unique opportunities are blocked, then the 'life course' can be dramatically altered. The growing social and spatial con-centration of limited opportunities has created a significant set of obstacles for the black men in this study. This structural entrapment plays a significant role in the barrier to desistance for black men. Blau and Blau (1982) argue that negative structural relations within inner-city communities lead to an increase in interpersonal violence. It is my view that the present concentration on the treatment of individual offenders may serve to obscure much of the truth about the nature of crime and so absolve us of blame for those social conditions and practices which are equally culpable. Black men can so easily become the social scapegoat and reinforce hegemonic assumptions but fail to solve the problems of social disorganisation within inner-city communities, where all of the men in this study reside.

With severely limited education and skills, black men have little chance to participate in the regular economy. Young blacks in particular are caught in an employment bind. To many young men, the underground economy of drugs and vice is an attractive proposition. The interpersonal trust and moral cohesion that once prevailed have been undermined, and an atmosphere of distrust, alienation, and crime pervades the area, further disrupting its social organisation. A new role model emerges and competes for 'turf', 'territory', 'endz' or 'on road'. He is young, often a product of the street gang, and at best indifferent to the law and traditional values.

On road

When those same subordinated masculine identities connect to the streets, some black men use the structured action of criminality to challenge the existing social structures that exclude them. In doing so, some black men join forces and create an alternative form of 'social structure', namely, 'street gangs'. These street gangs may operate within a framework that is both hyper-masculine and nihilistic. To be part of a gang means being prepared to lose your life in exchange for the gains from criminal activity. Being 'on road' is governed by the code of the streets, where respect, toughness, fearlessness, and loyalty are the benchmarks for measuring the masculine resources individuals have to possess in order to be part of the gang. Black men who subscribe to this way of being justify their decision by arguing that the available routes to becoming men are blocked, and therefore the gang becomes a way of accomplishing their manhood, in spite of the risks involved. Winlow (2008) argues that some criminals get pleasure from some of their crimes. He further argues that the adrenaline rush of criminality relates to aspects of masculinity, which in turn reflects the nature of contemporary social life. In essence, 'doing wrong' can be thrilling and intrinsically enjoyable and it can also be linked to forms of status attainment and identity.

The lack of practical opportunities identified by the black men in this study highlights how many of these men have been left outside of the institutions of social control and with little hope of entering the new disciplines of the market and consumption. Similarly, Katz (1988) argues that there are 'moral and sensual attractions in doing evil'. Katz sees crime less as a background factor and believes the answers lie in delving deeper into the criminal act itself. He argues that the various mechanisms which move actors between 'background factors and subsequent acts' have been a kind of 'black box', assumed to have some motivational force but left essentially unexamined.

Rather than view Katz's work simply as resurrecting one side of this binary framework, I wish to argue a differing viewpoint. It is my contention that Katz's analysis is not so much about agency versus structure, but rather about prioritising emotionality. This position would also suggest that some black men see the 'code of the streets' and 'on road' as part of a dangerous game, where they do draw some psychic pleasure from outwitting the forces of law and order, combined with exercising control over those who try to stop them. Unfortunately, the engagement with the streets is short-lived, as many are caught, charged, and sentenced. Prison becomes the next stop on their journey. On the local street corners, black men attempt to impress people through displays of material success such as expensive clothes and fancy cars. For some who follow this model, great though often fleeting financial success may be in store. More often a trail of unfulfilled dreams, broken lives, and jail awaits.

Liminality

While in prison black men express the desire not to return to a life of crime. The dislike of the prison environment, not wanting to repeat old patterns of behaviour, having acquired the tools required (via prison education) to go back into the community, and fear of the unknown (can I still cut it on the out?) push the prisoner's inner desire to 'go straight'. This is combined with the prison regime's vision of enabling the prisoner to undergo a new journey of reintegration and resettlement, via a productive time spent in prison. As the primary purposes of the prison environment are confinement, containment and security, the racialised social order in prison can push black men into adapting a 'prison code' of behaviour, based on menace and the fear of strength, where violence and the fear of violence promote exploitation and govern much of their behaviour.

The conversion into another layer on hyper-masculinity also reproduces a form of prison social action, where the 'prison code' is also responsible for assisting in the creation of an informal social structure governed by the prisoners themselves. The prisoner's vision of his intended new journey enables him to see the road ahead as tricky, but, if conquered, will make him a hero in the eyes of friends, family, and in turn the community he has hurt. However, when faced with the challenges and difficulties of prison life, the incentive to 'go straight' can be thwarted and is initially met with opposition if the prisoner feels ill equipped to meet the new challenges that lay ahead. This conflict creates notions of 'double consciousness'. On the one hand, the prisoner wants to do well and keeps his head down, but, on the other hand, the allegiance to his gang and other vested interests places severe restrictions on his ability to make the right choice.

The resulting outcome can push some black men to become desensitised as a survival mechanism, while others can become withdrawn and fearful. In the latter case, individuals can opt to put themselves into a segregated wing, away from the turmoil of wing politics. However, this position has implications for the prisoner when they return to the former wing.

Racialised/spiritual conversion

The development of a positive identity while in prison is part of an on-going socialisation process shaped by experiences with one's family, community, school, group and social affiliations. The prisoner undergoes trials and tests to serve to make him feel his identity is focused and stable by making life predictable. While change in the environment is tolerated and sometimes welcomed, a change in our identity can be disturbing and difficult. For many black men in prison, the desire to change for the better, and not go back to prison, can be undermined if a new identity cannot be forged. Cross (1991) argues that having a racial identity is essential in enabling black men to transcend the negative impact of racism and white privilege. The following are brief summaries of Cross's 'nigrescence' model (ibid.).

Stage 1: Pre-encounter

Black men in the pre-encounter stage exhibit a racial attitude that ranges from race neutral to anti-Black. These individuals are socialised to favour a Eurocentric cultural perspective. For black men in prison, their socialisation has pushed them away from seeing blackness as important, as their reality demonstrates that being black is a barrier in a white society in terms of gaining the benefits. So an internal decision emerges. To develop a cognitive shift away from the dominance of white norms and values. This stage is referred to as 'the encounter'.

Stage 2: Encounter

This stage is usually identified by a series of incidents, episodes, or circum-stances that erode or transform the individual's present outlook or worldview. The individual must personalise the encountered information in a way that changes the way the person sees the world and themselves. For many black men in prison, this process can be actualised during black history month, where they are exposed to a history that has been denied to them in their formative years at school. This experience also reunites black men with the importance of education and reading resources in the library. This encounter nudges the individual outside his or her comfort zone and may cause them to be perplexed, apprehensive, or even depressed. The person may seek addi-tional information and validation for their newly developing identity. This state may be accompanied by emotion, guilt, and anger that are generalised toward Whites. There is a commitment to replace the old worldview with a new one, but the new self is not clearly defined.

Stage 3: Immersion-emersion

Symbols and attitudes that represent the development of the new self now come into play. Symbols such as styles of dress, hairstyles, increased involve-ment in productive activities in the prison, such as writing and reading groups typify individuals in this stage. The vernacular that at times which may have been coarse and vulgar is now replaced with a stronger awareness of language and its content. As the individual *immerses* themselves in the developing world and exploration of their social, cultural, and historical past, they *emerge* with the essence of a new sense of being. The journey then moves from one of external shift into something that becomes more introspective and is internalised.

Stage 4: Internalisation

Internalisation represents a sense of contentment with the self that calms the internal struggle of the previous stages. The militant and radical attitudes are transformed into thoughtful examination of oppression and racism. The individual connections are fully made to, and accept, the new-found blackness. Internalisation accompanies a healing of past internal psychological distress. This then leads to the shift of the individual's basic personality, notions of blackness merge with other role identities, such as embracing the spiritual, being more thoughtful, philosophical, or purposeful. The journey of transformation culminates in a substantial degree of time and effort forging the individual's new worldview in relation to emerging blackness.

Stage 5: Commitment

Having now acquired a new consciousness shaped by the acquisition of a new value system, the individual then occupies a new cultural space, where there is a 'commitment' to sustain their black consciousness as an instrument to contest and challenge racist norms within society.

The activation of the 'nigrescence' journey, like desistance, is led by an individual trajectory. It is not the same for all black men. The vast majority of the participants in my research felt that racial socialisation was important and necessary to prepare themselves for the reality of confronting and transcending racism in prison and the community. In essence, it gives an impetus to fashion a new identity that is less 'anti-white' but more 'pro-black'. A word of caution here, though, some black men's views of society are so narrow and devoid of life experiences, that their internalisation attitudes may be premature and idealised rather than based on experience and thoughtful analysis.

Reincorporation

Leaving the prison gates, a taxi ride home, driving through the old community that hasn't changed, can and does create internal responses that can bring a euphoric moment of release to the realms of self-doubt on achieving freedom. Internally, the ex-prisoner asks themselves a range of question: can I do this? Will I stay out of trouble? What if temptation comes back to me? Do I have the discipline to get me back on track? Will I get a job? Can I take care of my family? At this moment in the journey, the enormity of the task begins to set in. The ex-prisoner finds a range of personal and professional support designed to boost confidence, develop new skills, as well as urging him to be compliant with society's rules. Individually or collectively, the support structures attempt to prepare the ex-prisoner for the journey ahead (agency and structure). However, a mentor in the form of a close friend, partner, family member, or concerned professional uses wisdom to reassure the ex-prisoner that the real challenge to begin a new life, and ultimately the destination of desistance, should be seen as an adventure.

This mentor equips the ex-prisoner with the inner tools to take up the challenge and urges him to be fearless in pursuit of acquiring a new status beyond the label ex-prisoner. If the mentor's work has been done correctly, the ex-prisoner pledges to himself and others to journey towards desistance with the understanding that the road ahead will be full of challenges ahead. The ex-prisoner feels empowered and inspired to continue, but self-doubt still lurks in the psychic experience of the prison experience. The ex-offender is free of the world he left behind (prison) and has now returned to the community, a place of wonder and marvel. Things have changed.

The sweet smell and taste of freedom enable the ex-prisoner to envision a new reality, where he can live in this special world, not only free, but knowing that the journey towards a new status will bring new rewards, via employment, increased social bonds, and the restoration of positive masculine status. The ex-prisoner meets new individuals who issue him with the challenges that lie ahead, pushing him towards forward movement of the journey. This person is his probation officer, who gives the ex-offender a list of criteria that society expects, and warns him about going back to his old ways. Old friends taunt the ex-prisoner by questioning whether he will stay out of trouble. The ex-prisoner comes to the realisation that there is a range of vested interests in determining what journey he should make. The needs of the state begin to outweigh the needs of the individual himself, who is reminded of his time in prison.

The ex-prisoner begins the journey towards a new life and faces numerous tests. He struggles with gaining employment, furthering his studies, managing family life, adjusting to life outside of prison, meeting old adversaries, and experiences the cumulative impact of everything around him. During this time he encounters numerous obstacles and barriers. These characters and circumstances can emerge from the ex-prisoner's personal, social, and professional circles. They become symbolic of the challenges ahead that must be overcome in order to pursue the 'golden fleece', which is desistance. His ability to negotiate the challenges successfully or unsuccessfully will determine whether he continues the journey towards desistance or recycles old patterns of behaviour that invariably will land him back inside. It is a time of turmoil, distress, and tests the potential of the ex-offender in terms of his potential as a hero.

To continue to be in contact with negative associates, the pressure of having to be accountable to society and the system, dealing with increased labelling, lack of social acceptance, limited access to resources, start to make life difficult. The inability to manage and control one's life becomes apparent. Internally, this is a difficult time for the ex-prisoner as the temptation arises to go back to a life of crime and take a risk. A desire for short-term gratification kicks in. The mentor arrives on the scene, recognises the potential arising crisis, and gives the ex-offender some much needed wisdom. The mentor warns the ex-offender that if he walks back into the dark forest, he may not be able to assist him any more.

A fight between good and evil, light and dark, right and wrong takes place. This moment places the ex-offender on the cusp of self-destruction and provides the ultimate test of strength, self-determination, and mastery over his situation. The system begins to let the ex-offender down. The restrictions prove too much and provide extreme pressure in the form of convincing the ex-offender he has nothing to lose, based on being let down by the 'so-called' right social forces. The intrusion of these negative forces pushes the ex-offender's masculine defences to breaking point. Several questions emerge 'Am I a man if I back down?', 'If I can't make ends meet, does that make me less than a man?', 'If I do go straight, will the system really make me better off?' The tools for doing the negative force's bidding are made available: money, drugs, weapons, etc. The ex-offender spends a period in hibernation contemplating his options. The competing forces, good versus bad, are replayed constantly. Internally, the ex-offender is in conflict with himself, which starts to create delusional and painful thoughts. The mentor is informed and reinforces his previous message. The ex-prisoner is completely alone with his thoughts. Internally, there is a massive amount of confusion where clarity is sought, but the responsibility for making the necessary changes lies with the ex-offender.

It is at this moment that the cognitive skills developed in prison education via enhanced thinking skills provision become a potential source of assistance. The ex-prisoner begins to weigh up the pros and cons, and begins to assess his options, balanced against what tools he has to sustain and maintain his journey towards desistance. The ex-prisoner reflects on his family, his real friends, his children, and in turn what freedom means to him. He also reflects on his skills, abilities, hopes, dreams, and aspirations, and connects that to a purpose that is culturally and spiritually driven. He decides that it is better to be 'poor and free', than 'live life a slave'. However, the fear of having to deal with the negative vested interests generates another layer of fear and self-doubt.

The reward, though achievable, seems a long way off. The ex-offender decides to confront his old past and cut it off. In doing so, he encounters hostility, aggression, rejection, and conflict. The ex-offender engages with a range of new people, who can give him access to a new life: faith leaders, sports and cultural practitioners, educators, employers, voluntary agencies. His encounter with them is painful at times, but he is determined to shed his old life. The ex-prisoner knows he must make adjustments that centre around the rebuilding of trust, combined with focussing on a renewed sense of purpose and achievable aspirations. In essence, notions of heroism kick in, as he realises that to achieve this, he will have to make sacrifices. The ex-offender starts to place the needs of others above his own selfish individualism. This position has a new reward, namely, community acceptance and a reincorporated status that validates his sense of masculine courage. Over a period of time, the ex-prisoner begins to fashion a new identity formed by the past, but shaped by journeying towards a new future.

The label ex-prisoner has now been both rejected and replaced with the reclamation of his name and new masculine status. He feels reborn and celebrates making those choices that have made it possible. The ex-prisoner now looks back on the journey and vows never to return to the dark forest. This acknowledgement that he has travelled from descent to ascent becomes a new internal narrative that in turn becomes wisdom for someone he may encounter who is also journeying towards desistance. The ex-prisoner now becomes someone's mentor in turn. The ex-prisoner turned mentor is now a valuable resource in the community and is seen by a range of vested interests as having value. The journey has taken the individual from a liability and made them into an asset. For men like these, the support systems in the home and in the community at large were not sufficiently strong to prevent their treading a path that led to prison.

Desistance

My theoretical framework suggests that the structural context of crime and the level of social disorganisation within the community may be at the core of the problems associated with black men and desistance. Namely, it may be that the community itself needs to change in order to facilitate the changes made by black men who have served their time well while being in prison. The challenge of returning ex-prisoners is much more than their physical relocation into their home community. Instead, the real challenge is reintegrating former prisoners into the community from which they come. Understanding the impact of racism on the desistance process requires regime delivery to play a greater role in equipping black men with the tools required to navigate this hurdle. Healy (2010) argues that when examining desistance, it is important to consider the influence of local cultures and how membership of powerful street cultures fractures the possibility of desistance in inner-city communities.

Healy further argues that during emerging adulthood, young people explore a variety of possible identities, experiment with risky behaviours and rarely form ties to social institutions. Paternoster and Bushbay (2009) likewise argue that before individuals are willing to give up their working identity as a lawbreaker, an individual must begin to perceive this identity as unsatisfying, thus weakening their commitment to it. They further argue that those wishing to quit crime are more likely to be successful at desistance if they are embedded in social networks that not only support their new identities but also protect them from those who would oppose them quitting crime or induce them to continue in their criminal ways. By providing encouragement, opportunities and structures through which they can function as full members of the community, ex-prisoners can become positive contributors to community life.

These reintegration aspirations are built on two premises: first, that the ex-prisoner has skills, abilities and talents that can and should be used for the benefit of the community to which they return; and consequently, second, that rather than seeing them as 'community liabilities', communities should view them, and enlist and deploy them, as 'community assets'. Successful re-entry is about providing what has been missing in the lives of most of ex-prisoners; a strong sense of connection to, and respect for, their communities as places to flourish, prosper and grow. To promote a successful, positive return of ex-prisoners to their home communities, we must first change their value systems in ways while in prison that will increase their appreciation of the challenges facing the communities they have affected, and then connect them to real and meaningful opportunities to make a difference and effect positive change. Making black men desist could pose a threat to the maintenance and enforcement of white privilege in terms of control and power.

Portraying black men as deviant and threatening to the social order protects the interests of white people. The intersection of race, gender, and class must be considered if we are to understand the wider social context in which black men operate. Hegemonic masculinity, while offering the understanding of power over others, can also negate the internal oppression working in different types of black men. Jefferson (1994) argues for the need to theorise masculine subjectivity in order to understand how masculinities are experienced within cultures. Jefferson offers the prospect of looking at black masculinity not just as a subordinated construction in relation to white men, but claims that by seeing black men as an 'in group', we can begin to explore a deeper layer of black masculinities. The following is a case example of my theoretical model of masculinities in relation to black men's desistance.

Case study: Ibrahim

If prison works, then desistance should be a natural outcome of positive rehabilitation and re-entry. However, for black men who are exposed to a criminal justice system that is racially oppressive, there may be a need to reframe the context in which they desist. The data confirm that black men in my research understand that the criminal justice system treats them less fairly. The inability to have their masculine aspirations realised, being an involved father, loving partner, dedicated son, and numerous other roles, may require support agencies, such as probation, to reframe some of their thinking in relation to what black men need in order to stay crime-free. Webster and Mertova (2007) argue that people make sense of their lives according to the narratives available to them. They also contend that we all have a basic need for story, to organise our experiences into tales of important happenings. In narratives, they argue, our voices echo those of others in the world, and evidence membership of society, both through our ways of crafting stories and the content of our stories.

A 'critical event', as told in a story, reveals a change of understanding or worldview by the storyteller and becomes almost always a 'change experience'. This 'change experience' can come about as a storyteller encounters some difficulty in integrating their idealised worldview with the reality of their real lived experience. This conflict of belief and experience promotes the development of a critical event as the storyteller struggles to accommodate a change to their worldview. Ibrahim's story could be seen as a critical event, as he contrasts life as a free man and compares it to life as a prisoner.

Ibrahim is a 32-year-old ex-gang member from Birmingham in the West Midlands. He has served six and a half years in prison for gang-related offences. While serving time, he underwent a faith-based conversion and embraced Islam. On his release he came back to his old community and faced a range of challenges in terms of re-entry and resettlement issues. Over a period of time, Ibrahim managed to get his life back together, settled down, had a family, and is in a new place.

Socialisation

When Ibrahim couldn't find opportunities to demonstrate his positive masculine identity, then crime become became an option when other resources were not available. He felt the pressure of his family's and the community's expectations and this was made worse as the racialisation of his access to the social structures prevented meaningful and productive opportunities. With severely limited education and skills, Ibrahim had little opportunity to participate in the life of the community and thus he turns into a product the streets and indifferent to the laws of society.

Ibrahim says:

> I was crap at school. Always fighting and angry all the time at the teachers. It's only when I left school I found out I was dyslexic. Everyone thought I was stupid. Dad wasn't around. Nuff and sisters. Plus mum did more than one job. So I never got any attention. No guidance. All my friends at the time were going through the same thing. So it was just a matter of time before I started to stray. I used to sneak out of the house. Back then my brothers and sisters used to tell my mum, which made it worse. Basically I was out of control. That's when the streets called me out.

On road

When Ibrahim connected his masculine identity to the streets, he used the structured action of criminality to challenge the existing social structures that had excluded him. In doing so, he created an alternative form of 'social structure', namely, joining a 'gang'. His gang was both hyper-masculine and nihilistic. To be part of his gang meant Ibrahim had to be prepared to do everything for the gang in exchange for the gains from criminal activity. Being 'on road' is governed by the code of the streets. Black men who follow this way of being justify their decision by arguing that the available routes to becoming men are blocked, and therefore the gang becomes a way of accomplishing their manhood, in spite of the risks involved.

Ibrahim says:

> I was about 13 when I started doing robberies and burglary. Never got caught. It wasn't anything major, but after a while certain bigger manz in the community heard about what was doing. I suppose I got a bit of a

rep. I wasn't interested in gangs at that point in my life, just making money, coz mum never had any. At school, things got bad and I got expelled for fighting. That's when I decided to join a gang. Never went back to school and got deep into the gang runnings. Had to do some dark stuff to get in, but once I did, they became my new family. Mum went mad, so I left and went to live with my Nan. I never brought no badness to her house, as I respected her. Although she didn't like what I was doing, she did try to talk to me. Things on road got hectic. I saw things that were horrible, but I became like a mad man. I didn't care about anything. To tell the truth I didn't feel anything either. On road you can't show weakness, so you have to block stuff out, or you can't be a soldier. I was cool for a while. Rollin' with the older guys, doin' all sort of crazy shit. I was makin' money, had nuff women, and I had the lifestyle. I thought I had it locked. Got away with it. Then some proper madness went down, and then it really hit. When I heard the judge give me 9-year sentence, I was gutted. I saw my family in court, crying. I felt ashamed. Trust me. When they took me down, I knew my nightmare had just begun. But at the time I still thought I was bad man.

Liminality

When in prison Ibrahim decided not to return to a life of crime. The dislike of the prison environment, not wanting to repeat old patterns of behaviour, having acquired the tools required through an education acquired in prison, and his wish to return to the community, pushed his inner desire to 'go straight'.
   Ibrahim says:

I hated prison. Reminded me of school. Only this time it was white screws instead of teachers. Plus you had to deal with manz from other endz, as well as beefin' with racist prisoners. It was a mad one. Couldn't take the loneliness or isolation. Hardly got any visits and when I did, it was pure arguments with my mum. None of my old crew ever came to see me. Neither did my Nan as she was too upset to see me. There were times when I thought I was goin' crazy.

Conversion

Ibrahim spent a lot of time reflecting and delving into his troubled past; as he knew failure to confront his inner demons would result in perpetuating the same type of behaviour that had landed him in prison. It was at this point Ibrahim underwent a crisis that acted as a turning point for his soon-to-be new journey.

Then I started to read. It was even harder trying to read when I got older, but I had nuff time on my hands. So I went down the prison library and took it slow at first. I was pissed at first, as they had no black books. In fact, the only thing that was black whilst I was in jail, were the prisoners. After a couple of years I started doing some courses and started to get my education sorted. By this time I began to go to the chapel on Sunday, but I wasn't feelin' it. Then one day I met a Muslim and we got talkin'. All I remember is I started to move with him and his bredrins on the wing. What I liked about them is the Muslims weren't beefin' like we were. So I converted.

After that, my life changed. I became a listener, wing rep, and I began to feel useful. I started writing to my mum, and she started to visit more. I felt different. Still used to get beef from my old bredrins but after a while they left me alone, now I was a Muslim. I suppose in a strange way prison made me think about my life. In some respects it was a good thing, coz I felt I was better than I used to be.

Reincorporation

Ibrahim noticed that the society hadn't changed when he got out of prison. However, he actively sought out personal and professional support designed to boost his confidence, help him develop new skills, as well as urging him to be compliant with society's rules. His former friends try to tempt him back into street runnings and question whether he will stay out of trouble. It is at this moment that the cognitive skills that he developed in prison education become a potential source of assistance. He states:

> I'll be honest, when I knew I was getting released, I felt nervous as hell. It had been a long time. I know I had changed, but whilst I was inside was all the crap on road. I didn't know what I would be like. Although I'd got qualifications, had a good group of people around me, and I also had good links at the mosque. But I still felt weird. I never felt that nervous when I was on road. I knew I couldn't go back to what I was. I kind of felt with my faith I had nothing to worry about. I knew all I wanted to do is come back into the community and do the right thing. I didn't want no drama in my life. I felt ready.

Desistance trajectory

Ibrahim begins to weigh up the pros and cons, and begins to consider his options. He reflects on what his freedom means to him. He also reflects on his skills, abilities, hopes, dreams, and aspirations. He wants to have a better life but fear of facing his old past makes him nervous. He knows he will be tempted to return to his old ways, in order to reinforce his masculinity. He says:

> So I came out. My mum picked me up. I remember I just hugged her. My little sister was there too. I felt good. Trust me. That feeling didn't last

long. Things still looked the same. I saw some my old bredrins standin' on the same corner I stood on all those years back. I felt bad. I couldn't believe it. When I got to my mum's house, there were a few people waiting for me, especially my Nan. I cried. I didn't feel no way. I was so relieved. I'll never forget my first night of freedom. I couldn't sleep. I kept thinkin' about my bredrins in prison and what my future was gonna be. It took me ages to get work and settle back into things. But my faith kept me goin'. Probation didn't help, plus my old bredrins were trying to rope me back in to the old ways, but I resisted the temptation, when it got rough. Some of the brothers had a barber shop, and I started doin' some trimmin' and made a little change to keep me goin'. Eventually me and some of the other brothers who'd become Muslims opened a little shop, where we cut hair, sold books, and tried to do something in the community. That's how I met my wife. Three years later, I've got daughter, my own place, and I'm goin' back to college to study business. I know there's a possibility that I can always get into trouble, but with the right support, it's possible.

Conclusion

I have suggested that the structural context of crime and the level of social disorganisation within the communities may be at the heart of the problems associated with black men's desistance. Therefore, it may be that the community itself needs to change in order to facilitate the changes made by black ex-prisoners. The challenge for the community returning ex-prisoners is much more than their physical relocation into their home community, instead, the real challenge is reintegrating former prisoners like Ibrahim back into the community. Understanding the impact of racism in the trajectory towards desistance also requires the prison regime delivery to play a greater role in equipping black men with the tools required to navigate this hurdle.

Successful re-entry is about providing what has been missing in the lives of most of ex-prisoners: a strong sense of, connection to, and respect for their communities as places to flourish. So how can we view black men's desistance with a lens which can both contest and challenge the racialisation of criminal justice systems, alongside creating a counter-narrative for black men to speak for themselves on issues where historically they have been rendered invisible? Chapter 9 therefore attempts to respond to that question by looking at Critical Race Theory (CRT) and its relevance to black men's desistance.

9   A Critical Race Theory of desistance

It is my contention that any future research into desistance must acknowledge the central and intersecting roles of racism, sexism, class and other related fields that maintain inequalities in the study and understandings of desistance as a whole. It must also challenge dominant social and cultural assumptions regarding black men's ability to name their own reality in relation to their insights and understanding of their desistance aspiratons. A paradigm shaped by notions of 'intersectionality' could also provide a complementary theoretical lens and pedagogical possibility that would help us better comprehend the issues associated with black men's desistance. Until such time the 'counter-narrative' may be the only avenue open to researchers to give a platform to those voices rendered invisible by the continuing imposition of white privilege within criminology itself.

The counter-narrative

Sampson and Wilson (1995) see the systemic and ecological failure in relation to black men as partly responsible for stripping them of the possibility of securing a renewed sense of purpose in their community, post release. With no sense of belonging, legions of black men wander around aimlessly with little meaning to their lives. In capturing the experiences and privileging of the voices of black men, it was evident that their stories were both reflexive and informative. Critics could argue that representing your story or 'personal narrative' maybe subject to edits, omissions, and distortion. However, their testimonies form the basis of further investigation.

For many of the participants of my research, these systemic failures were seen as the enemy to their success and their criminal behaviour became a 'metaphor' for defiance, much the same way as slaves did while being held captive on plantations. As argued throughout this book, many black men have traditionally been denied a voice, so the need to create a 'counter-narrative' as an act of political transformation and definance is important here. Therefore, privileging the voices of black men in relation to desistance may be something for criminology to consider. This position would not abandon existing theories on race and crime, but instead would provide a complementary framework designed to increase insights and knowledge in an under-theorised area of criminology. The justification is borne out of the acknowledged negation of white criminologists to engage in a significant dialogue on issues of race and crime.

Only through a critical examination of black men's own understandings can their desistance be appropriately identified and understood. It was identified that a persistent weakness of previous research is its failure to examine how processes of racialisation in desistance do not privilege the voices of black men. A researcher who is sensitive to the needs of black men, who wants them to be the 'authors of their own lives', is also an important consideration in enabling black men to talk, free of judgement or recrimination. The inability of black men to acquire a positive self-concept is a causal factor in the way black men engage in criminal activity and gives white society the justification for extreme punishment. Researching with black men should be both political and transformative as a way of challenging the dominant narrative that places black men disproportionately in the confines of the criminal justice system. The inability of black men to challenge, address, and transcend their differential treatment could be partly to blame for the creation and sustainability of stereo-types of black masculine identities as aggressive and threatening.

This distortion and absence of a racialised narrative for black men to flourish highlight a flaw and a significant gap within the current knowledge base and, ultimately, the understanding of black men in its widest context. Privileging the voices of black men would create new, and reframed 'life events' that have meaning and significance rooted within a symbolic, metaphoric, and allegorical context. The occupation of a different personal space to 'be' creates a newly constructed 'self' that could be articulated using performance as the conduit. Performance not only provides the opportunity for 'self-reflection', but scope for transforming into a new 'constructed self'.

Glynn (2005) described how enabling black male inmates to explore and narrate their own social realities in dramatic form in prison assisted in con-fronting hostility, racism and opposition by white prison officers. Belton (1995) expresses the view that the duty of black men is to alter the relation-ship of power that makes them subordinate to white men. The black men in the research explored who they are: gang affiliations, attitudes towards vio-lence, and how contact with the criminal justice system is having an impact on their masculinity. They highlighted that there are many characteristics and experiences that define black masculinity but their personal struggles to attain and define their manhood in relation to desistance is both misunderstood and under-researched. The complexity of black men's lives, combined with the lived experiences of black masculinities, therefore demands to be placed in a context not governed by white privileged theorising. Therefore, the need to locate black men's experiences, understandings, and insights of their desis-tance within a culturally competent analytical framework is important here. This counter-narrative construction is designed to both privilege the voices of black men, while at the same time contesting some of the assumptions made by criminologists who seldom take into consideration the 'collective narrative' of the 'experts' and 'knowers'.

It is also a way of enabling black men to transcend their silences in a way only they understand. CRT may provide some much needed clarity.

Black men's desistance and Critical Race Theory

Delgado and Stefancic (2005) cite several tenets that locate CRT as an analytical framework for creating counter-narratives of black men's desistance. Valdes *et al.* (2002: 244) also acknowledge that CRT 'resists the subordinating messages of the dominant culture by challenging stereotypes and presenting and representing people of colour as complex and heterogeneous'. Valdes further suggests that CRT may not only enable the subordinated persons (black men) to narrate, to interpret events in opposition to the dominant narratives (white men), but also recognises the complexity of the issues being addressed. The narrative potential of CRT therefore lies in 'its ability to re-story the past and to then re-imagine the future much the same as black feminism has done' (ibid.: 246). Critical Race Theory not only offers new insights with which to explore and explain the understanding processes of the racialisation of crime/criminal justice systems and its impacts on the desistance process, but it uses storytelling as the basis of its analytical framing. This provides a unique creative opportunity for looking at black men's desistance that has previously not been explored.

CRT operates with two distinct storytelling paradigms. 'Majoritarian stories', as told by privileged white people, and 'counter-stories', as told by subordinated black people (Solorzano and Yosso, 2002). Hill-Collins (2000) also sees the internalised oppression for black women as a journey that leads towards a need for self-definition. She further suggests that black women can gain a richer self-definition if they strive to tell their own stories, free from the oppressive gaze of white women.

It could be similarly argued that the understanding processes of the racialisation of crime/criminal justice systems and its impacts on the desistance process are more effectively revealed if efforts are made to free this telling from white oppression. McAdams (1988) provides a further context that demonstrates that beginning the process of desistance requires black ex-offenders to make sense of their lives in the form of a 'life story' or 'self-narrative'. In essence, McAdams advocates that ex-offenders must gradually interrogate their 'own story' and create a space to rework it by providing their own 'counter-story'. hooks (1991) highlights that black men's 'counter-stories' of the racialisation of crime/criminal justice systems and its impacts on the desistance process, could contest white men's accounts of maintaining their privileged position, and in doing so be seen as posing a threat to challenging their subordinate status. hooks suggests: 'Often when the "radical voice" speaks about domination, we are speaking to those who dominate' (ibid.: 80). hooks' assertion suggests it may be a better proposition for black men themselves to 'name their own reality' and to further consider how they can encourage and institutionalise 'outsider within' ways of seeing, to overcome the struggle to transcend their 'subordinate status' (Hill-Collins, 2000: 29).

My CRT of black men's desistance identifies that the perceptions and experiences of black men within the criminal justice system shape their worldview and ultimately their motivation towards desistance as an agency choice. It also understands that those experiences and perceptions must be located and situated within individual stories and a collective narrative that has been impacted on by racism, colour-blindness, white privilege, and invisibility. The cumulative impact of the previously mentioned symptoms have formed the backdrop through which black men have been stigmatised, over-represented, leading to overt disproportion representation in the criminal justice system.

For black men it is the belief that criminal justice processes are inherently racist, that places a significant barrier on the desire to desist from criminal behaviour. A 'counter-narrative' becomes an important way of validating and naming their own reality, as well as contesting and challenging white privilege. This in effect means that the counter-narrative acts as a catalyst for 'politicising' the struggle not just for black men's desire to desist, but also, more importantly, as part of a wider campaign for social justice. Using culturally sensitive research methods where participants hear their own stories and the stories of others assists this process of transcending black subordination, much the same way as music and dance operated during slavery. By doing this black men can develop coping strategies, and respond more effectively to exploring pathways towards desistance.

The findings of the research would suggest that rarely are the social, political, and historical experiences of black men taken into consideration. All of this is compounded by the absence of available academic information/data, which is also a continuing, unaddressed problem. Put simply, black men's desistance is undermined by a criminal justice system that treats black men unfairly based on race and processes associated with racialisation. It may also be apparent that the promotion of stereotypes of black men can create the kind of psychic response that manifests in anger and defiance, that when these are expressed becomes criminalised. The negative portrayal and labelling of black men via the media may also reduce the interaction black men have with white institutions. Unable to find a place to be respected and validated, crime becomes a way of 'getting back' at a society that rejects them. It could be argued that black men offer more resistance in relation to their gendered, enhanced racial subordination, based on early racial socialisation and the constraints of being negatively gender-stereotyped.

Central to any rehabilitative process is that individuals make sense of their world and organise it, in a way that will enable them to cease their offending and make different choices. It is assumed that some black men may start the journey towards desistance (termination of offending) while being incarcerated and experience a transformation into a 'replacement self'. In prisons, like the community, stories hold the key to memory and purpose. Everyone must participate and submerge themselves in stories to process the world around them, and make sense of it. Stories open up our world, boost imagination and give us self-knowledge. Without stories we cannot function adequately in understanding who we are and why we're here. Stories bind people together and allow each individual to better comprehend what their place is in the world, and how their place holds everything else together.

Hearing and making their stories told in their own words reaffirm a sense of humanity that enables them to consider different ways of constructing new ways of seeing the world. Likewise, the occupation of a different personal space to 'be' creates a newly constructed 'self' that acts as a 'rite of passage'. From the findings in this study it is clear that the current positioning of black men within prisons provides very little outlet for them to articulate the trauma of historical misrepresentation, denied access, social exclusion, and disaffection. Hence black men have little or no opportunity to reframe notions of their self-concept. This CRT of black men's desistance underpins a template of understanding that is familiar to the men who are the subjects of this inquiry. Much of the research structure was based on shared societal and cultural values, and reflected my personal values too. The labels 'black prisoner', 'black offender', 'black gang member', and so on were at times unhelpful and did not assist black men 'naming their own reality'.

My CRT of black men's desistance must challenge and contest negative assumptions about black men by arguing that a sense of racial pride and improvement of self-concept are necessary for black men to be motivated towards desistance. It also argues that prison is an under-researched site when looking at black men's desistance. The development of a counter-story, and a critical narrative such as CRT may offer insights into how black men construct their own understanding of desistance in relation to a racialised and gendered context. My CRT of desistance is also built on the idea that racism and power oppress black men, and in doing so create the conditions where the outcomes to that oppression at times result in criminal activity. This position in essence means my CRT of black men's desistance must do the following:

1 Foreground racialisation in relation to crime/criminal justice systems, black men, and its impact on the desistance process.
2 Challenge the traditional research approach in theory when explaining the experiences of black men in relation to their desistance from crime.
3 Offer a transformative solution that will contest, challenge, and remove the racial subordination of black men by white men in relation to the racialisation of criminal justice systems.
4 Focus on racialised, gendered, and class-based experiences of black men in relation to their desistance from crime.
5 Create a counter-narrative to highlight and contextualise black men's experiences of the racialisation of criminal justice systems and its impact on the desistance process.

My CRT of black men's desistance also necessitates that the stories of black men's desistance operate as a way of transcending their silences, inasmuch as these stories are not often told or heard. These counter-stories must expose stories of racial privilege. They must further challenge the dominant discourse on race within criminology and demand for significant change in terms of the struggle for racial reform in the criminal justice system. To create these counter-stories data has to be found. Strauss and Corbin (1998) use a concept called 'theoretical sensitivity' and refer to it as a personal quality of the researcher. It indicates an awareness of the subtleties of meaning of data. One can come to the research situation with varying degrees of sensitivity depending upon previous reading and experience with or relevant to the data. It can also be developed further during the research process.

Theoretical sensitivity refers to the attribute of having insight, the ability to give meaning to data, the capacity to understand, and ability to separate the pertinent from that which is not relevant. Counter-stories not only reiterate dominant meanings or power relations, but through retelling also contribute to the process of social change. It is also important within the development of counter-stories to examine, explore, and expose notions of colour-blindness. All of this is intended to move beyond the narrow confines of criminological research that struggles to validate, acknowledge, and indeed understand that the racialisation of crime is something that cannot be ignored. By examining the colour-blind perspective more closely, this analysis teases out the differences within the colour-blind position. Colour-blindness ignores racism and bolsters white privilege. Colour-blindness hides in the unspoken landscape of human and social relations, distorting racial discourse and preventing awareness of knowledge that already exists in the real lived experiences of black men.

My CRT of black men's desistance should also provide a wealth of material to analyse how racism operates in the culture and to understand how individual experiences link to and reproduce broader social patterns. If we are ever to alter the social institutions that compel racism, then we must get to grips with the mindsets of the systemic contexts that perpetuate it. How then can black men begin to imagine a new narrative that moves beyond the divisions that shape their lives? My CRT of black men's desistance needs to validate the kind of story that celebrates the diversity of black men, combined with embracing their humanity. It asserts that factors associated with race, racialisation, and racism operate within the UK and the USA and understands that these factors help explain racial inequality in the wider criminal justice system. Before black men are willing to cease their offending behaviour they must begin to perceive that what they are doing is unsatisfying, thus weakening their commitment to the sustainability of criminal activity. In essence, black men seeking to break free from crime must fashion a new identity and develop a more 'pro-social' life. Black men who desire to quit crime are more likely to be successful at desistance if they are embedded in networks and activities that not only support their new identities but keep them away from those who are opposed to them quitting crime or have a vested interest in enabling them to continue in their criminal ways.

How do black men acquire and tell their own authentic narrative when it has been shaped by a history of oppression? It is therefore right to assume that meaningful reintegration of incarcerated black men back into communities requires a deeper commitment to culturally competent rehabilitative processes, that could lead towards a culture of desistance. My CRT of black men's desistance found that the black men in this inquiry found themselves constantly having to defend their 'racialised identities' throughout their engagement with, and journey through the criminal justice system.

The need to challenge white privilege by validating the black contribution to criminology is also on-going, while occupying space with those who fear black assertion continues to throw up challenges. As an insider researcher I felt the irony coming from the field of criminology that, on one hand, profits from identity politics by acknowledging there is disproportionality and over-representation of black men in the criminal justice system, but, as the men in this inquiry attested, on the other hand, there is little understanding or desire to see things change. My CRT of black men's desistance sees a more multi-dimensional approach to understanding black men's experiences of criminal justice systems. A starting point could be the need to validate criminological data within the 'lived experiences' and embrace notions of black men's subjectivity using interpretative methodologies. This should be combined by using processes of knowledge production by and for black men.

What influence, if any, do racism, poverty, ethno-cultural group membership, etc., have on both the broader distribution of opportunities across society, and the ability to recognise them as such as opportunities for black men to desist? It is also important that as part of a process of rehabilitation, incarcerated black men should engage with institutional processes and practices that are 'pro-social' that will lead to a challenge in their criminal values and behaviour, designed to increase their capacity to consider desistance. A journey towards desistance 'by which individuals come to know themselves and their purpose' may help personal transformation and ultimately desistance. By doing so black men could be reintegrated back into the society, without prejudice or labelling.

So what lessons have been learned in the course of this book? And more importantly where do we go from here? What direction should criminologists take to look critically at black men's desistance? Chapter 10, the final chapter, may have something to offer in relation to these questions.

10 New directions for black men's desistance

The previous chapters have painted a vivid portrait of key issues associated with important insights and understandings of the racialisation of crime/criminal justice systems and its impacts on the desistance process for black men. While these insights and understandings have been varied and detailed, the need to discuss critical emerging themes is important here. This chapter contains some additional perspectives that have already been addressed but are presented here in a context that calls for more investigation. It is also important that in summarising the need for new directions that the participants in the research continue to (re) present their views by way of locating their voices at the centre of this book. I have previously argued that social science research must include rich and personal accounts by black men, and further suggest that interpretative studies using racialised methods of analysis such as CRT are particularly appropriate for addressing specific knowledge of participants' detailed subjective experiences such as black men's desistance. A key concern that requires more research is that of fatherhood arrested.

Fatherhood arrested

The term 'fatherhood arrested' encompasses issues of black men who have not been fathered, combined with their inability to provide connected 'fathering' to their children as a consequence of their criminal lifestyles and incarceration.

Interestingly, the vernacular used to describe this situation differed according to each research site. For example, African Americans would frequently say that 'poppa was a rollin' stone', whereas in HMP Grendon, black men were a little more forgiving as the therapeutic experience had equipped them with the capacity to talk about their pain openly, resulting in the use of the word 'father' being used. However, in stark contrast, the participants from Birmingham used the term 'waste man' to describe a feckless father, who is labelled a 'waste of space'. The diverse use of the vernacular highlighted different ways black men expressed notions of their own lack of fathering and how it impacted on their own attempts at fathering.

As illustrated by Leroy: 'Why can't you be a fucking man? What makes you not want to be involved in your own son's life? My dad's a "waste man".'

I have no respect for him.' While Leroy has lost respect for his father, Chris blames his father for him going to prison: 'He's a waste man and it's all his fault I went to prison. From day one he hasn't said anything to me. What am I supposed to do but just get on with my life?'

Although Leroy and Chris lay some of the blame for their plight at their fathers' doorsteps, this assertion suggests that they see the importance of having a father masked by their anger reflecting a deep sense of hurt and loss. It appears that without strong 'father figures' to guide their behaviour, young black men like Leroy and Chris will create new models of what it means to be a father when they themselves have children. In their case, there is the connection to a darker extended family, namely, the gang.

Here Jason expresses his sense of loss at not having his father around to teach him basic values:

> I haven't really had a father–son relationship that any normal child would have with their dad. I don't like him and I hold it against him. He could have taken time out to see me but my man still don't business about me.
>
> (Jason)

Jason is resentful at not having a connected relationship with his father as he feels robbed of not having someone to guide him. This would suggest that the feelings of upset are underpinned by the rejection experienced by a father that plays a limited role in the lives of their children. David also highlights how not having a father played a role in him going to prison:

> If my father was around, I could be in a better position than I am now. I could have avoided situations being 'on road' and getting locked up. He could have helped me, talked to and shown me things from his past, like how he was, and what he was involved in.
>
> (David)

hooks (2003) suggests that if a father is absent, then the image young children will have of who they are will be flawed as illustrated by David. Here, Yusef focuses on the issue of what a present father should be:

> Not having a father is negative. He should have told me stuff. If he had, I wouldn't be in the position I'm in now. A father can help by just being there. You should still look after your son. See your son grow and being there would have make a big difference, trust me.
>
> (Yusef)

Yusef reveals the importance of a father just being there and spending time with his son. Kieran, on the other hand, reflects on his father's absence in a touching way regardless of his absence: 'I wanted him to pick me up from school, go to the park, these thing are strange to me, I've never had it.' Kieran highlights that in spite of being a grown man, he has missed out on something that he should have had as a child. hooks (2003) also points out that unless there is a collective response to the crisis of black fathers in society, a feeling of despair and hopelessness will continue to embed itself in the consciousness of subsequent generations. Her view underpins the need to address this issue to reduce the possibility of father absence becoming the norm in black communities. Robert points out the psychological pain of not having a father and demonstrates his coping strategy for this state of affairs is, in effect, to cut his father out of his life.

> I missed out not having a dad in my life. If I see him, I see him. It hurts, coz obviously when I'm on road and I see him, it's not like he's even my dad, he's just another person on the road.
>
> (Robert)

Although Robert refuses to use the term 'father', he does acknowledge the pain of his absence, which suggests that he really misses him.

On the other hand, Jay reveals a darker side to the way some black men respond to their father's absence, namely, the construction of a hyper-masculine identity. 'Without a dad, you have to be bad, I have to be masculine and ready for anything, I've had to grow up quick time. I ain't had no fathering so I gotta fill that void and I fill it myself.'

Jay demonstrates how the lack of a positive experience of fathering can push an individual into a nihilistic frame of mind. The context here is the paradox between the need and hunger for a 'present and engaged' father, and the implications when the absence creates a void. Jay continues:

> Maybe being 'on road' is not the best thing but this is all we know, we ain't had no guidance, we ain't had the father or the positive role models who society would say was positive, there's no other form of good role models, so we just look after each other.

Jay identifies that without adequate role models in his life, he is faced with turning to life on the streets with others like him. Ishmael once again illustrates the difficulty of not having a father as a role model present to guide, shape, and mentor his son: 'Absent fathers is a big issue with black people. Look at it like this, all of us have absent fathers, we haven't really had anyone, we had to teach ourselves.' Ishmael is placed in an impossible situation. Without his father's presence, he has no alternative but to act alone. Belton (1995) argues that black men are not monoliths and experience the impact of their father's absence in many different ways. This in turn, he further suggests, will leave many black boys feeling emotionally neglected or abandoned, as illustrated by Noel and Rahim:

> My dad not being around has caused me lots of problems. I know if my dad was there for me, I would not have done the things I've done.

If my dad was about, he would have been that authority figure in my life, so I had to provide for myself. All my friends are like me, we come from broken homes. We come from rough life, no money, no dad, no education, surrounded by crime.

(Noel)

My father ain't no male role model. I just need to survive. It's either you're with the gang, if not, how are you gonna survive? If he was there, then maybe I would have made a different choice. We all need family.

(Rahim)

To build meaning into their involvement with children, men reflect on how other important family relationships have changed over time. In this process of meaning-making, men's relations with their own fathers take on new significance. Reflection on these father–son relationships suggests that, during the course of personal development and family transitions, the older you get, the more you need your father (Wideman, 1994). This is consistent across all three sites. Sampson and Laub (1993) also argue for a deeper understanding of the role of absent fathers in providing a turning point in men's narrative identities and subsequent criminal behaviour.

So what happens when there is no good future to look forward to? Where does that leave black men in relation to a crime-free future? Robert does not see his father as a stable influence in his life and has no ready-made image to construct a story of involvement: 'Not having a father is bad. I don't love him and he don't love me. I don't want nothing from him. All he's done is bring pain to my family. I've taught myself not to care, it's survival.' Men like Robert who have never known the love of a father, only have a model of complete absence resulting in rejection and anger. In doing so Robert has also decided that his father doesn't deserve any love from him. It is clear that absent fathers have a significant impact on the lives of their sons who feel at times lost, and bereft of any sense of belonging. It could also be that the level of anger due to abandonment pushes some black men into creating their own rules in relation to their manhood. Although not conclusive, this section highlights that experiencing positive fathering may result in some black men making choices away from engaging with crime. But for some of those interviewed, there is a 'disconnect' between these 'lost sons' and their fathers, where there is a lack of a secure family network. It could be argued that for black men to desist from crime, they must overcome not just external barriers, but also the internal battles that lurk in the subconscious as a consequence of seeing the world in a negative way. The continuing separation from their fathers and their children then become a battleground, played out on the streets, culminating in levels of extreme social disorganisation, where spaces occupied by some black men become toxic and dangerous places to be.

One marked difference in the wider experience of the pain of 'father absence' was rooted in notions of distance. For example, in the USA, the sheer distance between prisons, combined with the cost of travel, made it impossible for some families to stay connected. On the other hand, men who were in HMP Grendon felt stigmatised and shamed by being in a therapeutic community, and tended to distance themselves from their family and loved ones. Interestingly, many of those interviewed in the community, in spite of not having restrictions of space, chose to disconnect fully from their fathers and their children, for a variety of reasons, ranging from fear of rejection, reprisals, and the length of separation.

Invisibility and self-concept

It may be that the improvement of how black men see themselves in relation to their fathers' absence is one way of transcending black men's negative self-expectations brought about by their absent parent. How then does the issue of father absence impact on the wider issue of black men's self-concept? Furthermore, how does the notion of a poor self-concept for black men increase or decrease their propensity to commit themselves to the trajectory of their desistance? Akbar (1991) argues that black men must structure their world in such a way that they are constantly reminded who they are and what they want to be. Hill (1992) also argues that black men must create, develop, and sustain and transform their lives that will address those needs that have suffered at the instigation and maintenance of 'black invisibility'. He further argues that any model designed to address these issues must penetrate the racialised norms which permeate society, and in turn, subordinate black men. Allen (2001) argues that individuals possess many self-concepts that operate in particular situations producing multiple self-conceptions. He further argues that black men should develop a more resilient self-concept that enables the transcendence of external importations of a history of 'white oppression' and 'black subordination'.

However, for many of those interviewed, the feeling of 'invisibility' in prison, in the lives of their families, and well as the communities they came from, was acute. As noted previously, the concept of invisibility was put forward by the African-American novelist, Ralph Ellison. Ellison (1947: 7) states:

> I am an invisible man. No, I am not a spook like those who 'haunted' Edgar Allan Poe; nor am l one of your Hollywood movie ectoplasms. I am a man of substance, of flesh and bone, fibre and liquids – and I might even be said to possess a mind. I am invisible; understand, simply because people refuse to see me.

Ellison's notion of invisibility becomes a metaphor for how black men perceive their self-concept in the eyes of some white people, as explained by Donovan: 'They're not letting me be black. They're not letting me have my culture. They're trying to take that away from me.' Donovan feels the control over the projection of his black identity is not within his grasp and is being eroded.

Porter and Washington (1979) argue that black men tend to define aspects of their identity with regard to economic and social status issues, but use the black community as a frame of reference for their self-esteem and worth. Donovan is separated from the black community, so it is understandable that he is fearful of having his sense of identity eroded in a predominantly white environment such as a prison. According to Demo and Hughes (1990), being a black man in a white society means occupying a subordinated racialised status within society. Leroy agrees:

> I'm a black man. Not a white man. My family is black. The community I lived in was black. That's all I know. So why do I feel I'm not treated equal? You tell me. My parents came here from abroad to do better, but I don't feel I've done better. I don't feel like a proper man. Being a black man never feels like being a proper man. You're always fitting into someone else's agenda. Why should I always have to do that? White people don't fit into our way of doing stuff.
>
> (Leroy)

Leroy sees acquiring a positive black self-concept may enable him to transcend negative social expectations. Stefan also highlights how the pressure to assimilate can remove traces of a positive black identity: 'When I came to prison, I was the only black person on the induction wing. I could tell straight away that the ethos of this place was that they want you to fit in with white people.' Stefan's experience highlights how being a minority person in a prison can be very isolating, as one has to contend not only with being a prisoner, but also being a minority person in the institution itself. Problems arising from stereotypical judgements based on cultural differences, and a general lack of understanding of black male social reality, are also revealed by David:

> I know that I'm supposed to be here to look at what I've done, but I didn't know that I would lose my identity. Being a black man is important to me. I don't want to give that up for no-one. Being black keeps me grounded and gives me a sense of pride that white people can't take away from me.
>
> (David)

Donovan reveals, like others, that at times the negation of their cultural heritage compounds an already deep sense of isolation and loneliness within the ethos of the prison regime. Like many of those interviewed, black men occupy several differing linguistic communities – street, cultural and prison. They all struggled in negotiating the language of authority and power within both prison and the community. Leroy illustrates the importance of having language as a sense of personal power:

> As black men we speak differently. My parents were from the Caribbean. They spoke different and it affected the way I spoke. I also grew up on

the streets and we speak different there too. In here you can only speak that way in front of others that understand it. My language is part of who I am. If you take that away from me, I feel I would be lost.

(Leroy)

The use of 'street slang' and the black vernacular enabled black men to both speak and express themselves freely. In essence, the participants expressed the importance of not having to defend their racial or cultural identity when immersed in their own linguistic communities. Neville states:

As an African American from the South, my accent differs from other African Americans, but to white people we all sound the same.

In fact, we are stereotyped because of how we speak. The police think we're all rap artists. Bullshit!

Neville highlights that even if there is recognition of having a different linguistic patterning, white people do not make the distinction.

Wilson (1994) argues that a black man like Neville with a poor self-concept will be motivated by self-alienation, will exhibit an ignorance of his blackness, and engage in hedonism that will manifest in an erosion of positive masculine feelings. So too, Al sees being in an exclusively white environment while serving time in prison as a factor that forced him to conceal a sense of his black identity and push it underground:

Whilst inside, I was aware of being in a majority white male prison where there was a minority of black or ethnic inmates. Because they didn't understand me, I've had to change the way I spoke and the way I socialised.

(Al)

The negation of Al's cultural heritage made him feel invisible. Those experiences have had a profound effect on how he attained a positive self-concept on release from prison. In essence, he had to operate in one way in prison and another in the community. The lack of consistency in terms of self-concept would suggest that men like Al at times struggle to know which identity would be deemed positive in relation to re-entering the community. Here Robert talks about how his Rastafarian beliefs are compromised and sees himself as becoming 'deculturalised', when he was in a predominately white prison regime:

Psychologically, I've been deculturalised because I have limited access to my culture. Rastafarian is a subculture when you're in prison that you're being denied. The first thing I heard when I came here was that you couldn't speak my language because they say it's aggressive. I've seen white inmates get more privileged jobs and get out of the system easier.

(Robert)

Robert sees the system as unfair and has a clear understanding that when his difference is visible, it is seen as subversive, which is similar in orientation to many black men in HMP Grendon. Here we see that the inability to share thoughts, be listened to, or to feel understood, generates the kind of internal oppression that all too often leads to isolation and withdrawal. This can and does develop internal negative perceptions of 'self'. This 'absence of being' is made worse by being held captive inside a racialised system that treats black men differently to white men. Goggins (1997) argues that the process of discovery and appraisal of one's talents, character, relationship to the cosmos, and purpose as the basis for one's sense of self is best rooted within a framework that recognises a historical past free from white oppression. Here Robert reflects on life as a black prisoner.

> As black people we can be lawyers, doctors, and teachers, it may take a long time but you can succeed. But I do know it's going to be hard, as white people don't really want us to succeed. However, I'm not going to let that stop me from pursuing my dreams. I've come too far to turn back now.
>
> (Robert)

Robert clearly sees that achievement is possible and begins to envision a new future where black men will be treated equally within a society that has traditionally created disadvantage and blocked opportunities for them. By reframing and altering a worldview that is restrictive and closed, there may be more of an openness to consider new choices in relation to the journey towards desistance. Spence (2010) also argues that black men need to have space in which they do not have to defend their racial existence or humanity.

Spence further advocates that this space is essential to building a reconstructed black identity, defined in terms of a black man's own vision on how he should be. Most of the participants in both the UK and USA expressed the view that the impact of being held within a racist environment in prison drove the need to be part of a culturally diverse community in the prison itself, and exclude themselves from mainstream activities that at time were pathologised by the prison itself. Winston, Yusef, Pablo and Tyrone, have a view on this:

> It's hard when you're not around your own people. It's not that I don't like the white guys here, but it's not the same as being with your own.
>
> (Winston)

> I had racism at school, when I left school, and I get it in here. It wears you down, and makes you forget who you are. Although there's a few of us in here, you can't deal with the crap you have to face. They just don't get us.
>
> (Yusef)

Too much racism in here. It's subtle though. I get on with the white people here, which ain't that bad. But we don't get our food, books, or learn anything about our history and culture.

(Pablo)

In the US, we have a history of segregation. In the schools, in the community, in church, in society. We grow up not mixing. I didn't make the rules. It's just the way it is. All I've known is white people treating me differently. I feel that's why I began to act differently. They saw me as evil and bad, so that's what I did, act wild.

(Tyrone)

These black men's combined narrative illustrates the subtle aspect of racist practices that can go undetected by a regime that does not see its expression, or impact on black men. It is also evident that a majority white prison population or a regime predominately run by white people was seen as an inhibiting factor for some interviewees who struggled to integrate into the wider prison ethos. Very often the issues presented by black men in prison appear to be no different from those of other prisoners and are therefore often misinterpreted, not addressed or dismissed. More importantly the experience for black men in this area is uniform, but differs only according to the harshness of the regime, not by geographical location. In essence, racism does not discriminate because of distance. However, coping strategies do differ according to where the individual is located within their respective community.

Stefan states: 'I need to be around my own people. It makes me feel better. White guys don't have to worry about that as there's more of them than us.' Stefan also highlights that having a sense of community is also about numbers. Even if there are a few black men among a small group of white men, it can erode a sense of belonging, as the minority group feels they are now part of a 'subordinate' community. Also as important was that some black prisoners in HMP Grendon at times suppressed both cultural features of their identity on account of being stereotypically labelled as 'yardie', 'gangster', 'thug', and so forth. This suppression forced many of them to 'opt out' of programmes and other related services important to their rehabilitation, as the negation of their racial and cultural identity is a risk they were not prepared to make. What this situation revealed is that the prison environment places additional strain on how to cope with this type of labelling.

Being located in community networks can enable black men to retreat into the comfort of their darkness. Du Bois (1938) argues that black men who are constantly defined in the gaze of others will end up in a state of confusion. For men who occupy an oppressive space, stripped of identity and status, the search for a space just to be can become a priority. Hence many black men interviewed in HMP Grendon, Birmingham, and Baltimore retreated into their blackness, with others who shared the same worldview. This retreat provided a comforting experience away from the constant defense of their racial and cultural identities. The importance here that for those black men who successfully desist, being validated for who you are is an important feature that helps when returning to friends, family and, in turn, the community, where there are no judgements, combined with not having to defend who you are, what you eat, what you listen to, or how you express your cultural and racial identities. Tyrone falls back on his faith as a way of bolstering his self-concept:

> My faith as a Christian is what brings me peace and it helps me to become a calmer person. I got tired of walking around with hatred in my soul and needed a different outlet. Having a faith goes way beyond my colour. However, the way black people worship God is different, so we still get viewed with suspicion. No-one really questions white people's beliefs.
>
> (Tyrone)

Tyrone highlights the importance of having a faith as strengthening his self-concept, while at the same time revealing a paradox. Namely, he feels that white men are seldom if ever challenged about their right to conform or integrate into groups of black men. Not seeing oneself reflected in a prison regime or community that is racialised can have a detrimental effect on the way that some black men perceive themselves in relation to others.

The recurring issue here is one of 'invisibility'. Invisibility is defined by Franklin (1997: 23) as 'feeling that one's genuine persona is not seen, respected, or considered of value'. Many of those interviewed talked about the impact of black or racialised 'invisibility' throughout their lives and how this experience had left them feeling powerless. This in turn had stifled many of their desires to be compliant in a society that they see as creating the conditions to keep them in a subordinated position, as explained by Winston: 'I'm tired of the way there was nothing for us. No food like ours, no books, nothin'. Makes me sick. I'm a black man, so why can't they treat me like a human being? Tired of bein' stereotyped.'

Winston talks about being continuously bombarded with negative images of himself that fed into already created negative stereotypes. Therefore, if the cultural and racial identity of black men is driven underground, then their subordination by white men will be inevitable. Robert, however, takes the view that being invisible or hiding his true self is a better option than having his blackness judged: 'I can't show who I really am. They might see me as too black. You know what happens then? It's like they don't see us as black men, until we do something wrong.' Robert reveals something even more disturbing. If black men suppress their identity for fear of being judged, the resulting outcome will by default, maintain and sustain a 'colour-blind' approach to both their prison life and the social, and cultural reality that makes the oppressive nature of racism both hard to detect and see.

This may then push their level of 'invisibility' into a psychic space, making some black men angry and reactive. Gaining acceptance and a feeling that one is a person of worth plays a significant role in countering notions of invisibility, especially within the TC and the community, both in the UK and Baltimore. However, Yusef reminds us of the importance of understanding, not just acceptance of one's racial and cultural identity, which is central to maintaining a positive self-concept.

> It's harder for us. I have to put my culture aside and adopt the British culture in order to survive. Because a lot of people in here do not understand my background or my culture, they think Jamaica is only about drugs and smoking weed, that's all. So there is a limited view or expectation from somebody with my background.
>
> (Yusef)

Hearing and validating black men's stories told through their own words reaffirm a sense of humanity that will enable them to consider different ways of constructing a new and improved way of being that could act as an enhancing factor in their desistance. However, for some black men the desire to stop playing the fool for the sake of gaining acceptance from white men, who want them to be non-questioning, can and does push many further into a liminal state (Turner, 1969). 'Invisibility' and 'colour-blindness' work hand in hand to create a level of internal distress for black men who can spend a significant amount of time trying to get white people to see them. Ishmael has a more confrontational view on the issue:

> Fuck white men. They think I'm bad, then that's what I'll be. I ain't gonna surrender who I am coz of them. Yeah, I like my gangster rap, reggae an' shit, but that's part of my culture. They ain't gonna take it away from me, no way.
>
> (Ishmael)

Ishmael projects a self-fulfilling prophecy, where the stereotypical assumptions about black men will prevail. The need to become 'visible' at all costs would suggest that for men like Ishmael 'Invisibility' is neither fictional nor made up, but is more of an option not to be considered, even if it leads towards an increase in criminal activity.

> Pure stereotypes. That's all we're seen as. Yeah, I know I did wrong, but white men do wrong things too. Here in the US, its white people who take the big decisions, not us. But we're still as the bad ones.
>
> (Neville)

Many participants saw black stereotypes as leading to white people feeling a direct 'threat' from assumptions that were not only distorted, but designed to block opportunities in crucial areas of their lives, both in prison and the community post release. Steele and Aronson (1995) defines this as a 'stereotype threat'. They define a 'stereotype threat' as 'being at risk of confirming, as self-characteristic, a negative stereotype about one's group' (ibid.: 797). They further suggest that stereotypes can disrupt personal performance, produce doubt about one's abilities, and cause an individual to dis-identify with their ethnic group. A term used to identify the actual features of the stereotype threat is 'self-handicapping', which is a defensive strategy black men use to erect barriers to their performance to provide attributions for failure.

As Steele and Aronson reason, this identity distancing reflects a desire not to be seen through the lens of a racial stereotype. As this 'stereotype threat' arises from negative expectations that black men at worst can underperform if the situation puts their threatened identity in the spotlight. Winston discusses this position:

> Sometimes I have to play fool to catch wise. When I'm with the other black guys and I can be myself, but if they see us all talking together they think we're plotting something. They don't do that with the white guys.
>
> (Winston)

In other words, black men like Winston feel their identities are threatened when stereotypes are invoked, either blatantly or subtly, in a range of settings such as prison or in the community. Situations where black men believe that they will be evaluated in a stereotypical way create a strong sense of group identity and 'stereotype threat'. 'Stereotype threat' may also lead to distraction and loss of motivation which, in turn, can negatively affect black men's performance. If black men expect to do poorly at something, they might not be able to perform as well as when confidence is high. These experiences highlight that activating gender stereotypes can undermine positive masculine identity development for black men. The battle to counter stereotypes for black men is on-going and has been managed badly. As articulated by Ishmael, Rahim, and Stefan:

> They think I'm a bad man, so I act like one. It don't serve no purpose to act cool, if you ain't treated like that.
>
> (Ishmael)

> Damned if you do, damned if you don't. Don't make no difference if you act proper, you're still gonna get treated like a piece of shit.
>
> (Rahim)

> I got treated like shit in school, on road, and now prison. How is a man supposed to be positive if the only treatment you get is negative? I ain't gonna let them push me around. I'm not a dog.
>
> (Stefan)

Ishamel, Rahim, and Stefan reveal how at times they played up to the stereotype as an act of defiance, when they felt tired of being judged by others.

A significant problem associated with black stereotypes is how the media use, promote, and maintain them. Some of the participants argued that the press prejudiced the public's perception of them by distorted or exaggerated reporting of their cases. It could be argued that black men with poor self-concept, who feel powerless and disconnected from themselves and each other at times can feel a lack of motivation towards personal change, a central tenet of the trajectory towards desistance. How can this state of affairs be challenged by black men? Some see the need for the initiation of black males and goes on to argue that the lack of 'a confirming community' leaves the individual stranded in a liminal state.

Once again it is evident that the experiences of living in a racialised context are uniform, consistent, and ubiquitous for black men. A new ontological position may be required if black men are to move beyond the confines of the racist construct that blights their lives. Asante (1987) cites a move away from Euro-centric hegemonic knowledge to a grounded form of Afro-centricism that may start to bring some significant change within the current 'misplaced consciousness' of men of African descent. Hare (1973) suggests that there is a need to develop African-centred 'rites of passage' programmes and ceremonies as a counter to the socially reactive way that many black youths live their lives. Paul, Tyrone, and Ishmael reflect on the important of culture and history in their lives:

> I didn't learn about my culture and history at school. If I did, I probably wouldn't have ended up involved in badness.
>
> (Paul)

> What little I knew about black people came from my parents who were involved with the Civil Rights movement.
>
> (Tyrone)

> I didn't really go to school. I learned about my history from people on the streets, but it didn't mean shit, as it never helped me get a job or anything constructive, so I didn't see it as important.
>
> (Ishmael)

However, the exposure to different worldviews and historical legacies, if not handled correctly, can create confusion among black men, as highlighted by Paul, Ishmael and Tyrone. On one hand, they're are told that black history will be a tool for liberation and challenge in relation to hegemonic assumptions, but the reality of the imposition of white privilege undermines any positive momentum towards desistance. Once again there is a uniformity of experience which suggests black oppression is constant wherever black men reside. As Noel and Jason recount:

> Sometimes I get confused about who I am. I'm a black man in a white society, but I don't know anything about my past. All the black men I

know are involved in street runnings. I've read a bit, but I need to know more.

(Noel)

It don't make any difference what you know. You're black and that's it. We were born slaves and we're still slaves. The difference is we're slaves to drugs, money, badness, and all that shit. White people still control us, but now they control our minds, which is worse than our bodies.

(Jason)

Both Noel and Jason highlight that in order for black men to begin to create a new template for living, they will have to disrupt that part of their journey which is still controlled by the racist constructs that continue to subordinate them. Challenging negative values and codes of behaviour must therefore become a priority for black men. Developing a stronger sense of being black and male involves learning how to organise their world, make appropriate decisions, and create meaning and purpose from things that affect their lives.

Under the oppressive conditions of society, the code of the streets and prison, many black men find themselves in situations where they have internalised masculine scripts and definitions of self, and coping styles that are obstructing the trajectory towards desistance (Anderson, 1999). Black men need to develop a sense of identity that is grounded in their own soul and not simply a reaction to racism or to stereotypical roles that they are expected to act out. Spence (2010) and Hill-Collins (1986) advocate that space where one doesn't have to defend who one is should be enshrined within the overall ethos of any institution that prides itself on good race relations. Paul comments: 'Why can't we have more things for black people in this jail? It's the same in all the other jails I've been. It's like they don't care about what we need.'

Linton also expresses the desire to be part of a culturally diverse community in prison and also recognises that some white people may be interested too. Could giving white prisoners access to black culture provide a tipping point for more regime sensitivity towards black needs? Linton says: 'We should be able to listen to our music, learn about our history and culture. There's also some white guys in here who wanna know about our culture as well.'

Linton offers an interesting proposition that white prisoners appropriating black culture could assist in validating his own desires to have his culture recognised. Ishmael and Tyrone, however, state how white appropriation of black culture can at times make it difficult for black men to develop a strong culturally appropriate identity and positive sense of self. Not being able to see oneself in a positive light may be responsible for driving many black men back onto the street corners, where in spite of engaging in dangerous and risky activities, there is a sense of the familiar, which creates an idea of safety and belonging.

On release, you're hungry to learn about your culture, but there is nothing in the community to help you, as most of the projects are run down and don't offer stuff to ex-offenders. Also a lot of black projects are at times run by black people, but controlled by white funders.

(Tyrone)

Black history to me is like what the Chinese do. They never serve you real Chinese food. Most of the stuff we get told is what white people want us to know. If you can't read, how do you know what's in books about us? Most of the history books are written by white people. So they can see how we are from their version of events.

(Ishmael)

This emphasises the understanding that the ownership, production, and distribution of one's own image and cultural context are important to black men, both in the UK and the US context, in community and prison alike. Many of those interviewed expressed the wish to see African-centred processes in operation while in prison. Again, in the UK and the US, the desire to be free of the oppression of white men created a unified cultural position of wanting to shed the attachment to their country of origin. However, whereas in the US the term African American is enshrined in the vernacular of communities and the consciousness of America, the UK constituents felt that black had limited use in terms of positive perception. Therefore, there was less emphasis on a term that defined notions of blackness, but more of a cultural identification with either African or Caribbean roots, expressed through cultural activities such as music, dance, and literature. The need to develop an 'African-centred worldview' as a way of countering racism was universally accepted as both a counter-cultural response, combined with positioning it as an act of defiance for not being or acting 'white'.

An African-centred worldview

Oliver (1989) sees African-centred socialisation as an interactive process that promotes values of love of self, via awareness of one's African cultural heritage. Developing a stronger black self-concept must involve the re-organisation of damaging beliefs and values. Since the late 1960s, African-American psychologists have been examining the development of ethnic awareness as a culturally based empowerment process that reaffirms self-worth and enhances personal efficacy in black men.

Karenga (1980) created a set of values that has become enshrined in the movement towards African-centred rites of passage. The following principles underpin his theory, which are used across the world in communities that feel that African values have more to teach and offer than engaging with a system that continues to marginalise black aspirations:

1   *Umoja* (Unity) – Striving and maintaining unity within the family, community, nation, and race.

2 *Kujichagulia* (Self-determination) – Defining one's own needs, goals, aspirations, etc.
3 *Ujima* (Collective work/Responsibility) – Collective work designed to solve problems in maintaining the community.
4 *Ujamaa* (Cooperative economics) – Community-centred enterprise. Recycling community monies.
5 *Nia* (Purpose) – Build, develop, and cultivate a position in the community.
6 *Kuumba* (Creativity) – Improving the community intrinsically and aesthetically.
7 *Imani* (Faith) – Steadfast determination and belief in ourselves.

Karenga (1980) suggests a shift in the values acquired by black men that have been shaped by a history of racist oppression may offer the solution. However, the impact of white oppression that leads to black subordination may push African-centred approaches that will assist black men's desistance to the margins. This was particularly noticeable in HMP Grendon where prisoners felt that asserting an African-centred approach to their prison reality would label them even further. In essence, this is 'double consciousness' personified (Du Bois, 1938). As Byron argues: 'I'm a Muslim. I know my African heritage, but it doesn't help you survive the white man's onslaught of oppression in relation to your soul. If they have your soul, they have your mind.'

Tyrone also highlights that however well intentioned African values are, they are not strong enough when dealing with racist oppression. He states:

> My parents taught me about Africa and I grew up with feeling proud of my past, but my experiences with white people who didn't understand or respect my history made me realise that it makes no difference what you believe in. Once a nigger, always a nigger.
>
> (Tyrone)

Both Byron and Tyrone see knowledge of Africa as positive, but acknowledge it is not able to arrest the onslaught of racism. Jason too sees the futility of acquiring a new value system, by confronting the reality that the power of the system outweighs anything that a cultural value system might offer.

> Out on the streets Africa don't count for anything. This is America. The only colour that matters is green. I know my ancestors were great, but slavery got in the way. So how I see it, knowing about my ancestors ain't goin to help a brother deal with the Ku Klux Klan, the police, courts, the prisons, or another gang.
>
> (Jason)

Jason reminds us that a history of racial subordination clearly makes black men more vigilant and defiant in the face of continuing and sustainable pressure coming from forces designed to keep black men down. Having to seek permission, gain access, go through intermediaries, and negotiate with gatekeepers clearly has a negative impact. Human beings who are denied a voice will speak without fear of recrimination, others will break unjust laws, while freedom will be the pursuit of individuals who refuse to obey the dictates of those in power whose motivation is to control and oppress. Central to this proposition is the way the black men have produced and produce change. Without a clear, precise, and focused approach to challenging power within society, it may be that some black men will merely replicate a reactionary approach to our oppression, and not a transformative one. Leroy brings home a stark reality echoed by many black men in this study: 'I can't be arsed to try and change things. Where am I supposed to go to change who I am?

For black men like Leroy to seek transformation as a way of transcending their subordination, they must seek transformative spaces where the interrogation of the obstacles and barriers to freedom are given voice, complete with the development of an action plan designed to translate a counternarrative into a strategy for change. This strategy must not replicate a structure that has kept black men down, but instead create a more equitable and empowering way to function and live in a society that still privileges different groups over each other. Prison does not seem to offer that space. Likewise, the tough inner city communities of Birmingham and Baltimore seem to offer no respite from the constant struggle for validation inside a racialised social structure. According to Pablo: 'It's hard out there. Being a black man inside a white system means that when you rebel you end up inside like me.' Black men like Pablo may require a greater level of self-investigation into the different ways they experience the everyday world from their position in society and how that impacts on their relationships with white men. Therefore, the complexities of black men in prison and community must also be more fully comprehended. Nowhere is this more important than in expanding the understanding and perspectives around desistance studies that have routinely focused on issues such as family links, employment prospects and moving away from criminal friends, but have said less about the structural issues that might facilitate or impede the transition of black men to the status of more mainstream members of civil society. Yet, in light of the interaction between 'agency' and 'structure' in producing processes of desistance, a consideration of racialised social structures and the implications of changes in structures is clearly of some importance here. Gadd and Farrall (2004) argue that the 'risk-based' criminal careers literature is so preoccupied with statistical prerogatives that it often makes generalisations that are either vague or not typical of any particular case existing in reality. Similarly, Maruna (2010) argues that reintegrating prisoners back into the community acts as a form of justice ritual that is meant to reaffirm and strengthen the wider moral order. Neville has a word of caution: 'The community should be a place to change, but, hell, we're all in the same struggle. So what can they do? They're trapped just like me.'

One way to ensure that men like Neville thrive may be for community members to play a key role in the reintegration rituals, hence strengthening the possibility of building social capital for black men. To do so, 'culturally competent' services will be required to do most of the actual reintegration work. However, if the strict controls in prisons, where the maintenance of white privilege is the dominant feature in many black men's experience of incarceration, it is questionable whether the community will be able to mount a credible challenge to racialised blocked opportunities. A deeper questioning of the role that the building of social capital plays in assisting black men to desist is relevant here.

Building social capital

Rose and Clear (1998) argue that it is commonly accepted that in the absence of effective controls, crime and disorder flourish. They further argue that controls operate at the individual, family, neighbourhood, and state levels; and the safest neighbourhoods are thought to be those in which controls work at each of these levels. As stated previously in this research, the racialisation of criminal justice processes can and do impact on all of the categories mentioned above. How do the racialised state social controls that are typically directed at individual behaviour have important secondary effects on family, neighbourhood structures and the desistance trajectory for black men reentering the community after release from prison? Henry, Nathan, and Al have their own insights:

> In and out of prison the system gets you. If ya black, turn back.
>
> (Henry)

> You can't get a job, place to live, you can't do shit. Although I'm in prison, there ain't nothin' here for me either. It's crap.
>
> (Nathan)

> When I came out, it was worse than it was before I went in. So what did I come back to? Nothin, absolutely nothing!
>
> (Al)

Thus, at the ecological level, the side effects of policies intended to fight crime by controlling black men may exacerbate the problems that lead to crime in the first place. How does this state of affairs affect the trajectories towards desistance for black men if the journey is disrupted as previously outlined? 'Social capital' therefore refers to the social skills and resources needed to effect positive change in neighbourhood life. It is group structure that increases the capacity for action oriented toward the achievement of group goals. Goals are accomplished by transforming resources gathered in one forum for one purpose, into resources for another forum and for another purpose.

High levels of social capital augment the ability and efficacy of the community to sanction transgressors. Sampson and Laub (1993) concluded that social capital in institutional relationships dictates the salience of informal social control at the individual level. More important, they found that trajectories of crime and deviance can be modified by these bonds. It follows that communities rich in social capital also will experience relatively low levels of disorganisation and low levels of crime. Social capital relies upon (and in turn promotes) human capital. Human capital refers to the human skills and resources individuals need to function effectively, such as reading, writing, and reasoning ability. It is the capital that individuals acquire through education and training for productive purposes. In a sense, social capital contextualises human capital (and vice versa) because neighbourhoods rich in social capital exert more control over individual residents, thus helping to produce more highly educated, employable, and productive members of the community.

But what happens if there are no social networks, support structures, tools for change, etc.? Marvin, Donovan and Jason reveal more compelling testimony that challenges the possibility of black men being able to build successful social capital on account of the wider erosion of the communities' racialised social structure.

> Shops are shut down. Churches don't want us, and our families don't want nothing to do with us.
>
> (Marvin)

> I can't do nothin' from here. I've got so long to go. So I can't do anything to help me get back in the community. That's in the hands of others.
>
> (Donovan)

> I got in trouble coz the way I had no sense of community. It ain't changed. All that's happened is I've got older.
>
> (Jason)

As their truths testify, neighbourhoods deficient in social capital are areas conducive to crime because they are characterised by many individuals who are undereducated, unemployed, and more likely to be criminal. Events that disrupt the relational networks and systems so fundamental to the development and maintenance of social capital reduce the neighbourhood's ability to self-regulate and in turn will invariably affect the capacity of black men to develop a coherent strategy regarding their desistance trajectories. Many disorganised communities have networks disrupted through incarceration and the impact felt may be more devastating than in flourishing communities beacuse they have a lower threshold due to depleted supplies of social capital.

It could be argued that the rebuilding of social capital requires a conceptual framework on which to build the kind of human resources required to aid and complement the trajectories towards black men's desistance. Societal constraints and individual choices in the process of desisting from criminal activity may depend on opportunities and resources to support black men.

Considerations within the desistance process might see the acquisition of 'social capital' as a critical element in the process of transition from offender to desister. As argued previously, social capital can provide opportunities and links to those aspects of society which can support a decision to desist, yet they may not be available to some black prisoners on release. The acquisition of sufficient 'social capital' for it to be useful in a movement away from crime raises a number of issues about the availability of social capital and other support for desistance to members of marginalised groups, such as black men.

Can black men therefore acquire sufficient social capital in prison to assist in overcoming the structural constraints which may operate as barriers to successful desistance on release? Are the opportunities to desist, and access to resources available to all those serving time in prison? What aspects of black men's life history, personal circumstances and social conditions make available recognisable opportunities to desist? What influence, if any, does racism have on both the broader distribution of opportunities across society, and the ability to recognise them as opportunities for desistance? By eroding employment and other related opportunities based on racism, incarceration may also provide the motivation and subsequent pathway back into crime. In this context, the experience of imprisonment by black men emerges as a key social division marking a new pattern in their lives.

If black men have not been able to realise their potential as men or have not been guided to a place where they feel a strong social or community connection, then it is hard to see how they can vision a new future, if their current situation does not reflect optimism and light. The lack of social involvement, the persistence of family breakdowns through father absence, and increasing nihilistic tendencies articulated by some black men in this study would suggest that the understandings of desistance whilst in prison is patchy and requires more investigation. Akbar (1991) sees prison as a way of arresting black men's development and in doing so, destroys the type of consciousness required to live a crime free life.

Desistance as a rite of passage

This section propeses that black men's desire to desist is part of an on-going 'rite of passage', that becomes a search for a reclamation of a 'new self', combined with finding a newly defined role in the community. Van Gennep (1960) argued the significance of a 'rite of passage' as a transitional stage of a man's life, as it acts as a process of pro-social transformation. Pinnock (1997) further argues that a 'rite of passage' is part of a wider process of community restoration and provides liberation for the returning offender, as well as providing much needed healing for the community who have been affected by destructive behaviour. Maruna (2010: 1) also sees that ex-prisoner reintegration should focus on the development of notions of a 'rite of passage' as a symbolic element of 'moral inclusion'. It could be that key 'life events' and 'socialisation experiences' in adulthood can counteract, at least to some extent, the influence of early negative life experiences, and that desistance from criminal behaviour in adulthood can be improved by strengthening strong social bonds in adulthood.

However, the racialising experience of incarceration suggests there is a need to challenge white criminologists' assumptions in relation to the racialisation of crime and criminal justice systems and its impact on the desistance process, before making any claims about black men's desistance as a whole. As part of a process of rehabilitation, incarcerated black men should engage with institutional processes and practices that are 'pro-social 'that will not only challenge their criminal values, but also prepare them for life on the outside. The result is that some black men may leave prison transformed by the experience, never to return again. In essence, if prison can be effective, then desistance could be a natural outcome of positive rehabilitation and re-entry. Nonetheless, for other black men who are exposed to a criminal justice system that is racially oppressive, there may be a need to reframe the context in which they desist.

Glynn (2005) argues that when black men have reflective time and space (when in prison), not only can they change the way they think and act, but that space can form the basis of developing a new life strategy. Therefore, as stated previously, prison becomes an important consideration for examining if the trajectory towards desistance for black men starts while in prison. The participants in this study who had desisted drew heavily on their experience of prison, as a significant factor that either hindered or enhanced their understanding and experience of the 'journey' associated with black men's desistance. How can black men begin to construct a new identity that will carry them forward towards a journey that will enable them to be crime-free? And does the journey towards black men's desistance start when they are locked up? Is black men's desistance starting while in prison a realistic proposition when the barriers imposed seem out of their control?

McNeill (2012) argues for a more interdisciplinary understanding of desistance and sees rehabilitation as a social project as well as a personal one. He further argues that desistance requires 'psychological rehabilitation' (which is principally concerned with promoting positive individual-level change in the offender). In essence, for McNeill, this is part of the cognitive rite of passage, where the transitions to be made are part of a personal strategy to transcend the impact that invisibility, colour-blindness, and white privilege have on the 'psychological rehabilitation' of black men. This paradigm should be complete with a pre-determined set of rules, principles, or expectations that will enable black men to negotiate the barriers to their desistance based on the racialisation of the criminal justice systems. Through the introduction of processes designed to improve the qualities or characteristics to improve their 'self-concept', it may be possible for some black men to redefine notions of purpose and meaning that will transcend negative social expectations, as well as reincorporating them back into the 'village' they were removed from. This is referred to as the P.O.S.E strategy:

- *PURPOSE – Black men should be encouraged to establish a clear sense of meaning and purpose that will enable them to ground who they are, where they're at, and where they want to be.* To do this would require intense work on working on improving the damage that has been inflicted while they were incarcerated. Engaging in activities such as learning about black history, combined with serving the community via volunteering, is also encouraged.
- *OWNERSHIP – Black men need to be encouraged to take responsibility for shaping their journey in life, and to own its formulation, development, and implementation, beyond negative social expectations.* This would involve black men studying and acquiring the skills and abilities required to become self-determined. In essence, it is about enabling black men to undergo an intensive period of self-work, designed to remove the shackles of institutionalisation.
- *SUSTAINABILITY – Black men need to be able to sustain the development of their journey in a transformative and holistic way, via the acquisition of a faith/cultural value system rooted in a reality that enables black men to manage negative social expectations.*
- *EVALUATION – Black men to regularly update, reframe, and rework aspects of their personal journey, using creative forms of expression that will enable the processing of new needs, thoughts, and visions required to transcend negative social expectations.*

This new journey aims to push them beyond the boundaries of that scared child hiding in the corner, to a child who wants to explore new things without living in fear of taking risks.

Like an adrenalin rush, new desires, thoughts, and feelings need to push their curiosity to new heights, where mediocrity has no place in their lives. Like marathon runners they are poised to begin a long arduous journey where the route is mapped out, but their training while being locked up has not prepared them well. Black men need to become more philosophical, gain new wisdom, and acquire a mind not held captive by oppressive and dark forces. The need for validation and self-acceptance is more important than the emptiness of seeking the approval of others who oppress. Evident in those black men who had successfully desisted was the improvement of their self-concept where they had spent time working out their 'status frustration' (Cohen, 1965). Hill (1992) feels an African-centred 'rite of passage' would connect black men to Africa and its traditions in a concrete way that would lead to the development of positive black masculinity as well as offering a way out of the racist oppression that currently exists for many black men.

Both Hill and Akbar understand that black men operate within a white supremacist context, and by acquiring a direct experience of an African value system may be better equipped to transcend their oppression and create a new template for living. However, the disproportionality of black men in prison both here in the UK and the US would suggest that African-centred approaches may be far too idealistic a proposition. A challenge comes from Pinnock (1997) who sees traditional 'rites of passage' have been adapted as a method of 'gang initiation' that replaces the traditional family unit. He states, 'Gangs provide more emotional support than the youths' often-dysfunctional families. Adolescent boys face ordeals and trials that test their manhood and courage. Where ritual is absent, it is created' (ibid.: 20). It could be that by reintroducing and reframing the context in which a 'rite of passage' is actualised for black men, transcendence of subordination may be the outcome.

While most of the prisoners taking part in this research accepted their position and role within both prison and community, many have encountered problems, arising from stereotypical judgements based on a general lack of understanding of black male social reality. At times, some felt that the negation of their cultural heritage compounded a deeper sense of isolation and loneliness where they were in a minority, not just in terms of numbers, but within the ethos of the regime itself. These men also occupied several differing linguistic communities – street, cultural and prison. They struggled in negotiating the language of authority and power. In essence, the participants expressed the importance of not having to defend their racial or cultural identity. Spence (2010) and Hill-Collins (1986) advocate that space where one doesn't have to defend who one is should be enshrined within the overall ethos of any institution that prides itself on good race relations.

Black prisoners interviewed expressed the desire to be part of a culturally diverse community in the prison itself, while at the same time many black men suppress cultural features of their identity on account of being stereotypically labelled. Socio-historical marginalisation and psychological invisibility also present difficulties for some black men, while mono-cultural and eurocentric notions of therapeutic intervention can at times make it difficult for black men to develop a strong culturally appropriate identity and sense of self. Rather than developing a colour-blind approac, there is a need for the prison regime and reentry services to fully recognise and respond to racialised differences so that these are visible rather than invisible. Developing a stronger black self-concept must involve the re-organisation of damaging beliefs and values.

Since the late 1960s, African-American psychologists have been examining the development of ethnic awareness as a culturally based empowerment process that reaffirms self-worth and enhances personal efficacy in black men. Listening to black men's life stories, there is a need to address the impact of 'double consciousness', an 'outsider within' perspective and 'black invisibility' to enable black men to be confident in, and able to satisfactorily express, their black identity and culture in order that a positive self-concept/construct may be achieved. This would then assist the trajectory on their release towards desisting from criminal activity by establishing a pattern of life that takes account of their past lifestyle and provides a culturally acceptable alternative. For black men who have been labelled and stereotyped, there is a need for them to create a new template for living. Prison regimes and community support services that do not see, acknowledge, or understand the impact of race and processes of racialisation on black men will only serve to perpetuate the difficulties that some black men experience.

Denzin suggests that 'at the beginning of a new century it is necessary to re-engage the promise of qualitative research as a form of radical democratic process. We know the world only through our representations of it' (2010: 6). Therefore, it seems that black men's desistance should be viewed through a more radical lens. The need to create a space that will enable a 'subordinated individual or community' to both narrate and interpret 'real-life events' in the form of a 'counter-narrative' in opposition to oppressive 'dominant narratives' may 'bring coherence and validation' to their lives. In doing so, it is hoped that representations and presentations of black men's understandings and insights into their desistance will be brought to a heightened prominence.

The future for research of black men's experiences of re-entry and desistance should therefore involve listening and hearing the 'narrative' of black men themselves. This 'narrative' must address itself to the process of both social and political change for men in relation to criminal justice policies that affect them. How do black men acquire and tell their own authentic narrative when their voices are conspicuously absent at a strategic level? As stated previously, it may be that black men have to re-frame what is right for black men.

Bibliography

Abbott, J. (1997) 'On the concept of turning point', *Comparative Social Research*, 16: 85–105.

Afshar, H. and Maynard, M. (2000) 'Gender and ethnicity at the millennium: from margin to centre', *Ethnic and Racial Studies*, 23: 805–19.

Agnew, R. (2006) 'Storylines as a neglected cause of crime', *Journal of Research into Crime and Delinquency*, 43: 119.

——(2011) *Toward a Unified Criminology*, New York: New York University Press.

Akbar, N. (1991) *Visions for Black Men*, Florida: Mind Productions.

Akom, A. (2008) 'Black metropolis and mental life: beyond the burden of "acting white": toward a third wave of Critical Racial Studies', *Anthropology and Education Quarterly*, 39(3): 247–65.

Alexander, M. (2010) *The New Jim Crow: Mass Incarceration in the Age of Colour-blindness*, New York: The New Press.

Allen, R. (2001) *The Concept of Self: A Study of Black Identity and Self-Esteem*, Michigan: Wayne State University Press.

Alvesson, M. and Skoldberg, K. (2009) *Reflexive Methodology: New Vistas for Qualitative Research*, London: Sage.

Andersen, M. and Collins, P. (2004) *Race, Class, and Gender*, 5th edn, Belmont, CA: Wadsworth.

Anderson, E. (1999) *Code of the Street*, New York: W. W. Norton.

——(2011) *The Cosmopolitan Canopy: Race and Civility in Everyday Life*, New York: W. W. Norton.

Angrosino, M. (2007) *Doing Ethnographica and Observational Research*, London: Sage.

Arroyo, C. and Zigler, E. (1995) 'Racial identity, academic achievement, and the psychological well-being of economically disadvantaged adolescents', *Journal of Personality and Social Psychology*, 69: 903–14.

Asante, M. K. (1987) *The Africentric Idea*, Philadelphia, PA: Temple University Press.

Atkinson, R. (1998) *The Life Story Interview*, Thousand Oaks, CA: Sage Publications.

Babbie, E. (2002) *The Basics of Social Research*, Belmont, CA: Wadsworth Publishing.

Back, L. and Solomos, J. (2009) *Theories of Race and Racism: A Reader*, London: Routledge.

Baldwin, J. A. and Bell, Y. R. (1985) 'The African self-consciousness scale: an Africentric personality questionnaire', *The Western Journal of Black Studies*, 9: 61–8.

Balsa, A. and McGuire, T. (2002) 'Prejudice, clinical uncertainty and stereotyping as sources of health disparities', *Journal of Health Economics*, 22: 89–116.

Banton, M. (1987) *Racial Theories*, Cambridge: Cambridge University Press.

Barak, G., Flavin, J. and Leighton, P. S. (2001) *Class, Race, Gender, and Crime: Social Realities of Justice in America*, Los Angeles, CA: Roxbury.

Baraka, A. (1963) *Blues People: Negro Music in White America*, New York: William Morrow & Company.

Baszile, D. (2008) 'Beyond all reason indeed: the pedagogical promise of critical race testimony', *Race, Ethnicity and Education*, 11(3): 251–65.

Becker, H. (1963) *Outsiders: Studies in Sociology and Deviance*, New York: Free Press.

——(1967) 'Whose side are we on?' *Social Problems*, 14: 239–47.

Bell, D. (1992) *Faces at the Bottom of the Well: The Permanence of Racism*, New York: Basic Books.

——(1995) *Critical Race Theory: The Key Writings that Formed the Movement*, New York: The New Press.

——(1996) *Gospel Choirs*, New York: Basic Books.

Bell, L. (2003) 'Telling tales: what stories can teach us about racism', *Race, Ethnicity and Education*, 6(1): 3–28.

Belton, D. (1995) *Speak My Name: Black Men on Masculinity and the American Dream*, Boston, MA: Beacon Press.

Bennett, P. (2007) 'Why do relatively few BME residents choose to come to Grendon? Introduction to the third Grendon winter seminar', *Prison Service Journal*, 173: 5–8.

Benyon, J. (2002) *Masculinities and Culture*, Buckingham: Open University Press.

Berger, P. and Luckmann, T. (1966) *The Social Construction of Reality: A Treatise in the Sociology of Knowledge*, London: Penguin.

Bernasco, W. (2010) *Offenders on Offending*, Cullompton: Willan Publishing.

Bhui, H. (2009) *Race and Criminal Justice*, London: Sage.

Billson, J. (1996) *Pathways to Manhood: Young Black Males' Struggle for Identity*, New Jersey: University Press for New England.

Birt, R. (2002) *The Quest for Community and Identity*, Lanham, MD: Rowman and Littlefield.

Blau, R. and Blau, P. (1982) 'The cost of inequality: metropolitan structure and urban crime', *American Sociological Review*, 47: 114–29.

Bonner, A. and Tolhurst, G. (2002) 'Insider/outsider perspectives of participant observation', *Nurse Researcher*, 9(4): 7–19.

Bosworth, M. and Hoyle, C. (2011) *What Is Criminology?*, Oxford: Oxford University Press.

Bottoms, A., Shapland, J., Costello, A., Holmes, D. and Muir, G. (2004) 'Towards desistance: theoretical underpinnings for an empirical study', *The Howard Journal*, 43(4): 368–89.

Bowling, B. and Phillips, C. (2002) *Racism, Crime, and Justice*, London: Longman.

Bracken, D., Deane, L. and Morrissette, L. (2009) 'Desistance and social marginalization: the case of Canadian Aboriginal offenders', *Theoretical Criminology*, 13 (1): 61–78.

Brah, A. (1996) *Cartographies of Diaspora: Contesting Identities*, London: Routledge.

Brewer, R. and Heitzeg, N. (2008) 'The racialisation of crime and punishment: criminal justice, color blind racism, and the political economy of the prison industrial complex', *American Behavioral Scientist*, 51(5): 625–44.

Brill, N. Q. (1999) *Being Black in America: A Multi-Perspective Review of the Problem*, Springfield, IL: Charles C. Thomas.

Bromley Briefings (2011) *Prison Fact File*, London: Prison Reform Trust.

——(2012) *Prison Fact File*, London: Prison Reform Trust.

Brookes, M. (2010) 'Putting principles into practice: the Therapeutic Community regime at HMP Grendon and its relationship with the "Good Lives" model', in R. Shuker and E. Sullivan (eds), *Grendon and the Emergence of Forensic Therapeutic Communities: Developments in Research and Practice*, London: Wiley-Blackwell.

Brookes, M., Glynn, M. and Wilson, D. (2012) 'Black men, therapeutic communities and HMP Grendon', *The International Journal of Therapeutic Communities*, 33(1): 16–26.

Brown, K. (2002) *The Colour of Crime*, New York: New York University Press.

Brown, M., Carnoy, M., Currie, E., Duster, T., Oppenheimer, D. and Shultz, M. (2003) *Whitewashing Race: The Myth of a Colour Blind Society*, Berkeley, CA: University of California Press.

Bryman, A. (1988) *Quantity and Quality in Social Research*, London: Unwin-Hyman.

Bushway, S. D., Piquero, A. R., Broidy, L. M., Cauffman, E. and Mazrolle, P. (2001) 'An empirical framework for studying desistance as a process', *Criminology*, 39: 491–515.

Bushway, S. D., Thornberry, T. P. and Krohn, M. D. (2003) 'Desistance as a developmental process: a comparison of static and dynamic approaches', *Journal of Quantitative Criminology*, 19: 129–53.

Butler, J. (2006) *Gender Trouble*, London: Routledge.

Byran, M. (1997) *The Prodigal Father: Reuniting Fathers and Their Children*, New York: Potter.

Calhoun, L. and Tedeschi, R. (2006) *Handbook of Posttraumatic Growth: Research and Practice*, New Jersey: Psychology Press.

Calverley, A. (2013) *Cultures of Desistance: Rehabilitation, Reintegration, and Ethnic Minorities*, London: Routledge.

Cardinal, D., Hayward, J. and Jones, G. (2004) *Epistemology: The Theory of Knowledge*, London: Hodder Education.

Carlsson, C. (2012) 'Using turning points to understand processes of change in offending', *British Journal of Criminology*, 52(1): 1–16.

Chapman, R. and Rutherford, J. (1988) *Male Order: Unwrapping Masculinity*, London: Lawrence and Wishart.

Charmaz, K. (2006) *Constructing Grounded Theory*, London: Sage.

Chevannes, B. (1999) *What We Sow, What We Reap: Problems in the Cultivation of Male Identity in Jamaica*, Kingston: Grace Kennedy Foundation.

Chilisa, B. (2012) *Indigenous Research Methodologies*, London: Sage.

Christian, B. (1989) 'But who do you really belong to, Black studies or women's studies?', *Women's Studies*, 17: 17–23.

Christian, M. (2002) *Black Identity in the 20th Century*, London: Hansib Publications.

Christians, C. (2000) 'Ethics and politics in qualitative research', in N. K. Denzin and Y. S. Lincoln (eds), *Handbook of Qualitative Research*, 3rd edn, Thousand Oaks, CA: Sage, pp. 139–64.

Clark, K. (1965) *Dark Ghetto: Dilemmas in Social Power*, New York: Harper and Row.

Clark, R. (1973) *The Brothers of Attica*, New York: Links Books.

Clarke, A. (2005) *Situational Analysis: Grounded Theory after the Postmodern Turn*, Thousand Oaks, CA: Sage.

Cohen, K. (1965) 'The sociology of the deviant act: anomie theory and beyond', *American Sociological Review*, 30: 5–15.

Cohen, L., Manion, L. and Morrison, K. (2000) *Research Methods in Education*, 5th edn, London: Routledge.

Cohen, S. (1973) *Folk Devils and Moral Panic*, London: Routledge.

——(1985) *Visions of Social Control*, Cambridge: Polity Press.

Cole, M. (2009) *Critical Race Theory and Education: A Marxist Response*, New York: Palgrave Macmillan.

Cole, M., Gay, J., Glick, J. and Sharp, D. (1971) *The Cultural Context of Learning and Thinking*, New York: Basic Books.

Coleman, W. (1990) 'Doing masculinity/doing theory', in J. Hearn and D. H. Morgan (eds) *Men, Masculinities and Social Theory*, London: Unwin Hyman Ltd.

Connell, R. W. (1987) *Gender and Power*, Stanford, CA: Stanford University Press.

——(1995) *Masculinities*, Cambridge: Polity Press.

Connell, R. W. and Messerschmidt, J. (2005) 'Hegemonic masculinity: rethinking the concept', *Gender and Society*, 19(6): 829–59.

Connor, M. (1994) *What Is Cool? Understanding Black Manhood in the US*, New York: Agate.

Conroy, S. A. (2003) 'A pathway for interpretive phenomenology', *International Journal of Qualitative Methods*, 2(3): 1–43.

Crenshaw, K. (1999) 'Mapping the margins: intersectionality, identity politics and violence against women of color', *Stanford Law Review*, 43: 1241–99.

Creswell, J. W. (1994) *Research Design: Qualitative and Quantitative Approaches*, Thousand Oaks, CA: Sage.

Crewe, B. and Maruna, S. (2006) 'Self-narratives and ethnographic fieldwork', in D. Hobbs and R. Wright (eds), *The Handbook of Fieldwork*, London: Sage.

Cross, W. E. (1991) *Shades of Black: Diversity in African-American Identity*, Philadelphia, PA: Temple University Press.

Cruse, H. (1967) *The Crisis of the Negro Intellectual*, New York: Quill.

Cusson, M. and Pinsonneault, P. (1986) 'The decision to give up crime', in D. B. Cornish and R. V. Clarke (eds), *The Reasoning Criminal*, New York: Springer Verlag, pp. 72–82.

Daly, K. (1995) 'Reshaping fatherhood: finding the models', in W. Marsiglio (ed.), *Fatherhood: Contemporary Theory, Research, and Social Policy*, Thousand Oaks, CA: Sage, pp. 21–40.

Darder, A. and Torres, R. (2004) *After Race: Racism After Multiculturalism*, New York: New York University Press.

Davis, A. (1998) *Masked Racism: Reflections on the Prison Industrial Complex*, New York: Color Lines.

——(2001) 'Race, gender and prison history: from the convict lease system to the supermax prison', in D. Sabo, T. A. Kupers and W. London (eds), *Prison Masculinities*, Philadelphia, PA: Temple University Press.

Day, A., Casey, S., Ward, T., Howells, K. and Vess, J. (2010) *Transitions to Better Lives: Offender Readiness and Rehabilitation*, Cullompton: Willan Publishing.

Day, K. (2005) 'Being feared: masculinity and race in public spaces', *Environment and Planning*, 38: 560–86.

Deane, L., Bracken, D. and Morrisette, L. (2007) 'Desistance within an urban Aboriginal gang', *Probation Journal*, 54: 125.

Delgado, R. and Stefancic, J. (2000) *Critical Race Theory: The Cutting Edge*, Philadephia, PA: Temple University Press.

——(2005) *The Role of Critical Race Theory in Understanding Race, Crime, and Justice Issues*, New York: John Jay College.

DeLyser, D. (2001) '"Do you really live here?" Thoughts on insider research', *The Geographical Review*, 91(1, 2): 441–53.

Demo, D. and Hughes, M. (1990) 'Socialisation and racial identity among black Americans', *Social Psychology Review*, 53(4): 364–74.

Denzin, N. (2003) 'Performing (auto) ethnography politically', *The Review of Education, Pedagogy and Cultural Studies*, 25: 257–78.

——(2010) *The Qualitative Manifesto: A Call to Arms*, Walnut Creek, CA: Left Coast Press.

Denzin, N. K. and Lincoln, Y. S. (eds) (2000) *Handbook of Qualitative Research*, 2nd edn, Thousand Oaks, CA: Sage.

Devlin, A. and Turney, B. (2001) *Going Straight*, Winchester: Waterside Press.

Dickerson, D. (2004) *The End of Blackness*, Toronto: Penguin Books.

Dilworth Anderson, P., Burton, L., and Boulin Johnson, L. (1993) 'Reframing theories for understanding race, ethnicity and families', in P. Boss, W. Doherty, R. LaRossa, W. Schumm, and S. Steinmetz (eds), *Sourcebook of Family Theories and Methods: A Contextual Approach*, New York: Plenum Press, pp. 627–46.

Dixson, A. (2006) *Critical Race Theory in Education*, New York: Routledge.

Du Bois, W. E. B. (1938) *The Souls of Black Folk*, New York: W.W. Norton.

——(1978) *On Sociology and the Black Community*, Chicago, IL: University of Chicago Press.

Dunbar, P. (1892) *Lyrics of a Lowly Life*, New York: Citadel Press.

Duncan, G. (2002) 'Critical Race Theory and method: rendering race in urban ethnographic', *Research Qualitative Inquiry*, 8(1): 85–104.

Duneier, M. (1992) *Slim's Table: Race, Responsibility, and Masculinity*, Chicago, IL: University of Chicago Press.

——(2006) 'Voices from the sidewalk: ethnography and writing race', *Ethnic and Racial Studies*, 29(3): 543–65.

——(2007) 'On the legacy of Elliot Liebow and Carol Stack: context-driven fieldwork and the need for continuous ethnography', *Focus*, 25(1): 33–8.

Dwyer, O. and Jones, J. (2000) 'White socio-spatial epistemology', *Social and Cultural Geography*, 1(2): 209–22.

Dyer, R. (1997) *White*, London: Routledge.

Edin, K., Nelson, T. and Paranal, R. (2001) 'Fatherhood and incarceration as potential turning points in the criminal careers of unskilled men', paper presented at the Institute for Policy Research, Northwestern University.

Elder, G. H. (1985) 'Perspectives on the life course', in G. H. Elder (ed.), *Life Course Dynamics*, Ithaca, NY: Cornell University Press, pp. 23–49.

——(1994) 'Time, human agency, and social change: perspectives on the life course', *Social Psychology Quarterly*, 57(1): 4–15.

Elder, G. H. and Pellerin, L. (1998) 'Linking history and human lives', in J. Giele and G. H. Elder (eds), *Methods of Life Course Research: Qualitative and Quantitative Approaches*, Thousand Oaks, CA: Sage, pp. 264–94.

Ellison, R. (1947) *Invisible Man*, London: Penguin.

Evans, K. and Jamieson, J. (2008) *Gender and Crime: A Reader*, Maidenhead: McGraw-Hill.

Ewick, P. and Silbey, S. (1995) 'Subversive stories and hegemonic tales: towards a sociology of narrative', *Law and Society Review*, 29(2): 197–226.

Fanon, F. (1952) *Black Skin, White Masks*, London: Pluto.

——(1961) *The Wretched of the Earth*, London: Penguin.

Farrall, S., Bottoms, A. and Shapland, J. (2010) 'Social structures and desistance from crime', *European Journal of Criminology*, 7: 546–69.

Farrall, S. and Bowling, B. (1999) 'Structuration, human development, and desistance from crime', *British Journal of Criminology*, 39(2): 252–67.

Farrall, S. and Calverley, A. (2006) *Understanding Desistance from Crime*, Maidenhead: Open University Press.

Farrington, D. P. (1986) 'Age and crime', in M. Tonry and N. Morris (eds), *Crime and Justice: An Annual Review of Research*, 7: 189–250.

Fekede, T. (2010) 'The basis of distinction between qualitative and quantitative research in social science', *Ethiopian Journal of Education and Science*, 6(1): 97–108.

Fenton, K., Johnson, A. M. and Nicoll, A. (1997) 'Race, ethnicity and sexual health', *BMJ*, 314: 1703–6.

Ferrell, J., Hayward, J. and Young, J. (2008) *Cultural Criminology*, London: Sage.

Fine, M. and Weis, L. (1998) 'Crime stories: a critical look through, race, ethnicity and gender', *Qualitative Studies in Education*, 11(3): 435–59.

Flynn, N. (2010) *Criminal Behaviour in Context: Space, Place, and Desistance from Crime*, Cullompton: Willan Publishing.

Ford, C. (1999) *The Hero with an African Face*, New York: Bantam Books.

Fordham, S. and Ogbu, J. (1985) 'Black students' school success: coping with the burden of "acting white"', *Urban Review*, 18: 176–206.

Foucault, M. (1972) *The Archeology of Knowledge*, London: Tavistock Publications.

——(1998) *The History of Sexuality, Vol. 1: The Will to Knowledge*. London: Penguin.

Franklin, A. (1997) 'Friendship Issues between African American men in a therapeutic support group', *Journal of African American Men*, 3(1): 29–41.

——(2004) *From Brotherhood to Manhood*, Hoboken, NJ: Wiley.

Franklin, A. and Franklin, N. (2000) 'Invisibility syndrome: a clinical model of the effects of racism on African American males', *American Journal of Orthopsychiatry*, 70(1): 33–41.

Frazier, E. (1957) *Black Bourgeoisie*, New York: Free Press.

Freire, P. (1970) *Pedagogy of the Oppressed*, London: Penguin.

——1998) *Pedagogy of Freedom: Ethics, Democracy, and Civic Courage*, Lanham, MD: Rowman & Littlefield.

Fryer, P. (1984) *Staying Power: The History of Black Britain*, London: Pluto Press.

Gabbidon, S. (2007) *Criminological Perspectives on Race and Crime*, New York: Routledge.

Gabbidon, S. and Taylor-Greene, H. (2009) *Race and Crime*, London: Sage.

Gabbidon, S., Greene, H. and Wilder, K. (2004) 'Still excluded? An update on the status of African American Scholars in the discipline of criminology and criminal justice', *Journal of Research in Crime and Delinquency*, 41(4): 384–405.

Gadd, D. and Farrall, S. (2004) 'Criminal careers, desistance and subjectivity: interpreting men's narratives of change', *Theoretical Criminology*, 8(2): 123–56.

Garner, S. (2009) *Racisms: An Introduction*, London: Sage.

Gates, H. L. (2002) *Unchained Memories: Readings from the Slave Narrative*, New York: Bullfinch.

Gause, C. (2010) 'Black masculinities', *Journal of Black Masculinity*, 1(1): 1–112.

Genders, E. and Player, E. (2010) 'Therapy in prison: revisiting Grendon 20 years on', *The Howard Journal*, 49(5): 431–50.

George, N. (1998) *Hip Hop America*, New York: Viking Press.

Gerrish, K. (1997) 'Being a "marginal native": dilemmas of the participant observer', *Nurse Researcher*, 5(1): 25–34.

Gibson, J. J. (1979) *The Ecological Approach to Visual Perception*, Boston, MA: Houghton Mifflin.

Giddens, A. (1984) *The Constitution of Society*, Cambridge: Polity Press.

Gilroy, P. (1987a) 'The myth of black criminality', in P. Scraton (ed.), *Law, Order and the Authoritarian State: Readings in Critical Criminology*, Milton Keynes: Open University Press.

——(1987b) *There Ain't No Black in the Union Jack*, London: Routledge

Giordano, P., Cernkovich, A. and Rudolph, J. (2002) 'Gender, crime, and desistance: toward a theory of cognitive transformation', *AJS*, 107(4): 990–1064.

Giordano, P., Longmore, M., Schroeder, R., and Seffrin, P. (2007) *A Life Course Perspective on Spirituality and Desistance from Crime*, Bowling Green, OH: The Center for Family and Demographic Research: Bowling Green State University.

Glaser, B. and Strauss, A. (1967) *The Discovery of Grounded Theory: Strategies for Qualitative Research*, Chicago, IL: Aldine Publishing Company.

Glynn, M. (2005) 'Passages: black men, masculinity, and the search for a contemporary rite of passage', MA thesis, U.C.E.

——(2007) 'Breaking the fourth wall: black men, rites of passage and desistance', unpublished paper.

——(2010) *Breaking the Fourth Wall: The Impact of Fatherlessness*, London: Winston Churchill Trust.

——(2011) *Dad and Me: Father Deficit, Young People and Substance Misuse*, London: Addaction.

——(2013) 'Black men's desistance: the racialisation of crime/criminal justice systems and its impacts on the desistance process', unpublished doctoral thesis, Centre for Applied criminology, Birmingham City University, Birmingham.

Goffman, E. (1959) *The Presentation of Self in Everyday Life*, London: Penguin.

——(1961) *Asylums: Essays on the Social Situation of Mental Patients and Other Inmates*, New York: Penguin.

Goggins, L. (1997) *African Centered Rites of Passage and Education*, New York: African American Images.

Goldberg, D. (2009) *The Threat of Race: Reflections on Racial Neo-liberalism*, Malden, MA: Blackwell.

Goode, J. (2002) 'How urban ethnography counters myths about the poor', in G. Gmelch and W. Zenner (eds), *Urban Life: Readings in Anthropology in the City*, Illinois: Waveland Press, pp. 279–95.

Gottfredson, M. and Hirschi, T. (1990) *A General Theory of Crime*, Stanford, CA: Stanford University Press.

Green, J. and Thorogood, N. (2004) *Qualitative Methods for Health Research*, London: Sage.

Green, L. (2010) 'The sound of "silence": a framework for researching sensitive issues or marginalised perspectives in health', *Journal of Research in Nursing*, 16(4): 347–60.

Grimes, R. (2000) *Deeply into the Bone*, Berkeley, CA: University of California Press.

Grier, W. and Cobbs, P. (1968) *Black Rage*, New York: Basic Books.

Grover, C. (2008) *Crime and Inequality*, Cullompton: Willan Publishing.

Gunaratham, Y. (2003) *Researching Race and Ethnicity: Methods, Knowledge, and Power*, London: Sage.

Haley, A. (1965) *The Autobiography of Malcolm 'X'*, London: Penguin.

Hall, S. (2002) 'Daubing the drudges of fury: men, violence and the piety of the hegemonic masculinity thesis', *Theoretical Criminology*, 6(1): 35–61.

Hallett, M. (2006) *Private Prisons in America: A Critical Race Perspective*, Chicago: University of Illinois Press.

Halsey, M. (2008) 'Risking desistance: respect and responsibility in custodial and post release contexts', in P. Carlen (ed.), *Imaginary Penalities*, Cullompton: Willan Publishing, pp. 218–51.

Hammersley, M. (1995) *The Politics of Social Research*, London: Sage Publications.

Hammersley, M. and Gomm, R. (1997) 'Bias in social research', *Soc Res Online 2*, available at: www.socresonline.org.uk/socresonline2/1/2.html.

Hare, N. (1973) 'The challenge of a black scholar', in J. Ladner (ed.), *The Death of White Sociology*, Baltimore, MD: Black Classic Press, pp. 67–78.

Harper, C. and MacLanahan, S. (2004) 'Father absence and youth incarceration', *Journal of Research of Adolescence*, 1(3): 369–97.

Healy, D. (2010) *The Dynamics of Desistance: Charting Pathways Through Change*, Cullompton: Willan Publishing.

Heddon, D. (2008) *Autobiography and Performance*, Basingstoke: Palgrave.

Helms, J. (1990) *Black and White Racial Identity: Theory, Research, and Practice*, New York: Greenwood Press.

Hill, P. (1992) *Coming of Age: African American Male Rites of Passage*, Chicago, IL: African American Images.

Hill-Collins, P. (1986) 'Hearing from the outsider within: the sociological significance of Black feminist thought', *Social Problems*, 33(6): 14–32.

——(2000) *Black Feminist Thought*, New York: Routledge.

——(2005) *Black Sexual Politics: African Americans, Gender and the New Racism*, New York: Routledge.

HMSO (1985) *The Swann Report: Education for All*, London: HMSO.

Hollis, J. (1994) *Under Saturn's Shadow: The Wounding and Healing of Men*, Toronto: Inner City Books.

Hollis, M. (1994) *The Philosophy of Social Science*, Cambridge: Cambridge University Press.

Home Office (2004) *HM Prison Grendon: Report on a Full Announced Inspection*, London: HMSO.

——(2006a) *HM Prison Grendon: Report on an Unannounced Short Inspection*, London: HMSO.

——(2006b) *Young Black People and the Criminal Justice System*, London: Blackwell Systems.

Hooks, B. (1991) *Yearning: Race, Gender, and Cultural Politics*, Boston, MA: South End Press.

——(1992) *Black Looks: Race and Representations*, London: Turnaround.

——(2003) *Inner Wounds: Abuse and Abandonment*, New York: Washington Square Press.

——(2004) *We Real Cool: Black Men and Masculinity*, New York: Routledge.

Hopkinson, N. and Moore, N. (2006) *Deconstructing Tyrone: A New Look at Black Masculinity in the Hip-Hop Generation*, San Francisco, CA: Cleis.

Howells, K. and Day, A. (2006) 'Affective determinants of treatment engagement in violent offenders', *Journal of Offender Therapy and Comparative Criminology*, 50(2): 174–86.

Hughes, M. (1998) 'Turning points in the lives of young inner city men forgoing destructive criminal behaviours', *Social Work Research*, 22(2): 143–51.

Hutchinson, E. (1994) *The Association of Black Male Image*, New York: Simon & Schuster.

——(2007) *Dimensions of Human Behavior: The Changing Life Course*, London: Sage.

Hylton, K. (2005) '"Race", sport and leisure: lessons from Critical Race Theory', *Leisure Studies*, 24(1): 81–98.

Ifekwunigwe, J. O. (1997) 'Diaspora's daughters, Africa's orphans? On lineage, authenticity and "mixed race" identity', in H. S. Mirza (ed.), *Black British Feminism: A Reader*, London: Routledge.

——(2004) *Mixed Race Studies: A Reader*, London: Routledge.

Jacobson, J., Phillips, C. and Kimmett, E. (2010) *Double Trouble: Black and Asian and Minority Ethnic Offenders' Experience of Resettlement*, York: Clinks.

Jahn, J. (1961) *Muntu: An Outline of the New African Culture*, New York: Grove Press.

Jefferson, T. (1994) 'Theorising Masculine Subjectivity', in T. Newborn and E. A. Stanko, *Just Boys Doing Business?: Men, Masculinities, and Crime*, London: Routledge.

Jensen, R. (2005) *The Heart of Whiteness*, San Francisco, CA: City Lights.

Johnson, E. (1998) *Brothers on the Mend*, New York: Simon & Schuster.

Jones, J.M. (1972) *Prejudice and Racism*, Reading, MA: Addison Wesley.

——(1988) 'Cultural differences in temporal perspectives: instrumental and expressive behaviors in time', in J. McGrath (ed.), *The Social Psychology of Time: New Perspectives*, Thousand Oaks, CA: Sage Publications, pp. 21–38.

——(1997) *Prejudice and Racism*, 2nd edn, New York: McGraw-Hill.

——(1999) 'Cultural racism: the intersection of race and culture in intergroup conflict', in D. Prentice and D. Miller (eds), *Cultural Divides: The Social Psychology of Cultural Identity*, New York: Russell Sage Foundation.

Kanazawa, S. and Still, M. (2000) 'Why men commit crimes (and why they desist)', *Sociological Theory*, 18(3): 434–47.

Kardiner, A. and Ovesy, L. (1951) *The Mark of Oppression*, New York: W. W. Norton.

Karenga, M. (1980) *Kawaida Theory*, Inglewood, CA: Kawaida Publications.

Katz, J. (1988) *Seductions of Crime: Moral and Sensual Attraction of Doing Evil*, New York: Perseus Books.

Kazeman, L. (2007) 'Desistance from crime: theoretical, empirical, methodological, and policy considerations', *Journal of Contemporary Criminal Justice*, 23(1): 5–27.

Kelley, R. (2002) *Freedom Dreams*, Boston, MA: Beacon Press.

Kimmel, M. S. and Messner, M. A. (eds) (2001) *Men's Lives*, Boston, MA: Allyn and Bacon.

Kitwana, B. (2002) *The Hip-Hop Generation: Young Blacks and the Crisis in African American Culture*, New York: Perseus Books.

Kroeber, A.L. and Kluckhohn, C. (1952) *Culture: A Critical Review of Concepts and Definitions*, New York: Random House.

Lacey, C. J., Merrick, D. W., Bensley, D. C. and Fairley, I. (1997) 'Analysis of the sociodemography of gonorrhoea in Leeds, 1989–93', *BMJ*, 314(7096): 1715–18.

Ladson-Billings, G. and Tate, W. (1995) 'Towards a critical race theory of education', *Teachers College Record*, 97(1): 47–68.

Langer, E. (1983) *The Psychology of Control*, Beverly Hills, CA: Sage Publications.

Langer, E. and Rodin, J. (1976) 'The effects of choice and enhanced personal responsibility for the aged: a field experiment in an institutional setting', *Journal of Personality and Social Psychology*, 34: 191–8.

Laub, J. H. and Sampson, R. J. (1993) 'Turning points in the life course: why change matters to the study of crime', *Criminology*, 31: 301–25.

——(2001) *Understanding Desistance from Crime*, Chicago, IL: University of Chicago Press.

Laubscher, L. (2005) 'Toward a (de)constructive psychology of African American men', *Journal of Black Psychology*, 31(2): 111–29.

LeBel, T., Burnet, R., Maruna, S. and Bushway, S. (2008) 'The "chicken and egg" of subjective and social factors in desistance from crime', *European Society of Criminology*, 5(2): 131–59.

Leonardo, Z. (2005) *Critical Pedagogy and Race*, Oxford: Blackwell.

Lewis, S., Raynor, P., Smith, D. and Wardak, A. (2006) *Race and Probation*, Cullompton: Willan.

Liamouttong, P. (2010) *Performing Qualitative Cross-Cultural Research*, Cambridge: Cambridge University Press.

Liebling, A. and Maruna, S. (2005) *The Effects of Imprisonment*, Cullompton: Willan Publishing.

Liebow, E. (1967) *Tally's Corner: A Study of Negro Corner Men*, Lanham, MD: Rowman and Littlefield.

Lipsitz, G. (2006) *The Possessive Investment in Whiteness: How White People Profit from Identity Politics*, Philadelphia, PA: Temple University Press.

Locke, K. (2001) *Grounded Theory in Management Research*, London: Sage.

Lopez, K. A. and Willis, D. G. (2004) 'Descriptive versus interpretive phenomenology: their contributions to nursing knowledge', *Qualitative Health Research*, 14(5): 726–35.

MacMullan, T. (2009) *Habits of Whiteness*, Bloomington, IN: Indiana University Press.

Madison, D. (2005) *Critical Ethnography: Methods, Ethics, and Performance*, London: Sage.

Maguire, M. (1996) *Street Crime*, Aldershot: Dartmouth.

Majors, R. and Billson, J. (1992) *Cool Pose: The Dilemmas of Black Manhood in America*, New York: Touchstone.

Mandikate, P. (2007) 'Culture and psychotherapy', *Prison Service Journal*, 173 : 15–20.

Marable, M. (1993) *Race, Reform, and Rebellion*, Jackson, MS: University of Mississippi.

Marriot, D. (2000) *On Black Men*, Edinburgh: Edinburgh University Press.

Maruna, S. (2001) *Making Good: How Ex-Convicts Reform and Rebuild Their Lives*, Washington, DC: American Psychological Association.

——(2007) *Restorative Reintegration: Harnessing the Power of Redemptive Ritual*, California: ICCA.

——(2010) 'Re-entry as a rite of passage', *Punishment and Society*, 1: 1–26.

Maruna, S. and Farrall, S. (2004) 'Desistance focused criminal justice policy research', *The Howard Journal*, 43(4): 358–67.

Maruna, S. and Immarigeon, R. (2004) *After Crime and Punishment*, Cullompton: Willan Publishing.

Maruna, S., Lebal, T., Mitchell, N. and Naples, M. (2004) 'Pygmalion in the reintegration process: desistance from crime through the looking glass', *Psychology, Crime, and Law*, 10: 271–81.

Maruna, S. and Matravers, M. (2007) 'Criminology and the person', *Theoretical Criminology*, 11(4): 427–42.

Maruna, S. and Roy, K. (2006) 'Amputation or reconstruction? Notes on the concept of "knifing off" and desistance', *Journal of Contemporary Criminal Justice*, 22(2): 1–21.

Maruna, S., Wilson, L. and Curran, K. (2006) 'Why God is often found behind bars: prison conversions and the crisis of self-narrative', *Research in Human Development*, 3(2, 3): 161–84.

Mason, J. (2002) *Qualitative Researching*, London: Sage.

Matthews, R. (2009) 'Beyond "so what?" criminology', *Theoretical Criminology*, 13(3): 341–62.

Matua, A. (2006) *Progressive Black Masculinities*, New York: Routledge.

Matza, D. (1964) *Delinquency and Drift*, New York: John Wiley and Sons Inc.

Mauer, M. (1999) *Race to Incarcerate*, New York: The New Press.

——(2010) 'Justice for all? Challenging racial disparities in the criminal justice system', *Human Rights*, 37(4). Online.

McAdams, D. (1988) *Power, Intimacy, and the Life Story*, London: Guildford Press.

McArthur, L. Z. and Baron, R. (1983) 'Toward an ecological theory of social perception', *Psychological Review*, 90: 215–38.

McCoy, M. (1999) *Black Picket Fences: Privilege and Peril among the Black Middle Class*, Chicago, IL: University of Chicago Press.

McGuire, J. and Priestly, P. (1985) *Offending Behaviour: Skills and Strategies for Going Straight*, London: Batsford.

McNeill, F. (2012) 'Four forms of "offender" rehabilitation: towards an interdisciplinary perspective, *Legal and Criminological Psychology*, 1–19. Online.

Mears, D. P. (2007) 'Towards rational and evidence-based crime policy', *Journal of Criminal Justice*, 35(6): 667–82.

Men's Health Forum (2009) *Challenges and Choices: Improving Health Services to Save Men's Lives*, London: Men's Health Forum.

Mertens, D. (2007) 'Transformative paradigm: mixed methods and social justice', *Journal of Mixed Methods Research*, 1(3): 212–25.

——(2009) *Transformative Evaluation and Research*, New York: Guildford Press.

Merton, R. (1938) 'Social structure and anomie', *American Sociological Review*, 3: 672–82.

Messerschmidt, J. (1993) *Masculinities and Crime*, Lanham, MD: Rowman and Littlefield.

——(1997) *Crime as Structured Action: Gender, Race, Class, and Crime in the Making*, London: Sage.

——(2003) 'Masculinities and crime', in F. T. Cullen and R. Agnew (eds), *Criminological Theory: Past to Present*, Los Angeles: Roxbury, pp. 430–40.

——(2005) *Masculinities and Crime: Beyond a Dualist Criminology*, Los Angeles, CA: Roxbury.

Millen, D. (1997) 'Some methodological and epistemological issues raised by doing feminist research on non-feminist women', *Soc Res Online*, 2(3).

Miller, J. (2008) 'The status of qualitative research in criminology', paper presented at National Science Foundation's Workshop on Interdisciplinary Standards for Systemic Qualitative Research, Harvard University.

Miller, J. and Glassner, B. (2004) 'The "inside" and the "outside": finding realities in interviews', in D. Silverman (ed.), *Qualitative Research: Theory, Method and Practice*, Thousand Oaks, CA: Sage, pp. 125–39.

Mills, C. W. (1959) *The Sociological Imagination*, New York: Oxford University Press.

Milner, R. (2007) 'Race, culture, and researcher positionality: working through dangers seen, unseen, and unforeseen', *Educational Researcher*, 36(7): 388–400.

Milovanovic, D. and Schwartz, M. (1999) *Race, Gender, and Class in Criminology: The Intersections*, New York: Garland.

Miner-Romanoff, K. (2012) 'Interpretive and critical phenomenological crime studies: a model design', *The Qualitative Report*, 17(54): 1–32.

Ministry of Justice (2009) *HM Prison Grendon: Report on a Full Announced Inspection, 2–6 March 2009*, London: Ministry of Justice.

——(2010) *Statistics on Race and the Criminal Justice System*, London: Ministry of Justice.

Morgan, P. D. (1998) *Slave Counterpoint: Black Culture in the Eighteenth-Century*, Chapel Hill, NC: University of North Carolina Press.

Mutua, A. (2006) *Progressive Black Masculinities*, London: Routledge.

Newberry, M. (2010) 'The experiences of Black and Minority Ethnic (BME) prisoners in a therapeutic community prison', in R. Shuker and E. Sullivan (eds) *Grendon and the Emergence of Forensic Therapeutic Communities: Developments in Research and Practice*, Oxford: Wiley-Blackwell.

Newton, M. (2000) 'Ethnic minorities at Grendon: Trends in admission and length of stay', in J. Shine (ed.), *A Compilation of Grendon Research*, Wotton under Edge: PES, HMP Leyhill.

Nurse, A. (2002) *Fatherhood Arrested*, Nashville, TN: Vanderbilt.

Oliver, W. (1989) 'Black males and social problems: prevention through Afrocentric socialization', *Journal of Black Studies*, 20: 15–39.

Olumide, J. (2002) *Raiding the Gene Pool: The Social Construction of Missed Race Identity*, London: Pluto.

Owers, A., Leighton, P., McGory, C., McNeill, F. and Wheatley, P. (2011) *Review of the Northern Ireland Prison Service*, Northern Ireland: PRT.

Parker, L. and Lynn, M. (2002) 'What's race got to do with it? Critical race theory's conflicts with and connections to qualitative research methodology and epistemology', *Qualitative Inquiry*, 8(1): 7–22.

Parker, M. (2007) *Dynamic Security: The Democratic Therapeutic Community in Prison*, London: Jessica Kingsley Publications.

Parker, T. (1970) *The Frying Pan*, London: Hutchinson.

Patel, T. and Tyrer, D. (2011) *Race, Resistance, and Resistance*, London: Sage.

Paternoster, R. and Bushbay, S. (2009) 'Desistance and the "feared self": toward an identity theory of criminal desistance', *The Journal of Criminal Law and Criminology*, 99(4): 1103– 56.

Perea, J. (1997) 'The Black and White binary paradigm of race: exploring the normal science of American racial thought', *California Law Review*, 85: 1213–58.

Perri, 6 and Bellamy, C. (2012) *Principles of Methodology: Research Design in Social Science*, London: Sage.

Pfeifer, T. (2009) 'Deconstructing Cartesian dualisms of Western racialized systems: a study in the colors Black and White', *Journal of Black Studies*, 39: 528–47.

Phillips, C. (2007) 'Ethnicity, identity, and community cohesion in prison', in M. Wetherell, M. Lafleche, and R. Berkeley (eds), *Identity, Ethnic Diversity, and Community Cohesion*, London: Sage.

Phillips, C. and Bowling, B. (2003) 'Racism, ethnicity, and criminology: developing minority perspectives', *British Journal of Criminology*, 43(2): 269–90.

Pietila, A. (2010) *Not in My Neighbourhood*, Chicago: Ivan R Dee.

Pilcher, J. K. (2001) 'Engaging to transform: hearing black women's voices', *International Journal of Qualitative Studies in Education*, 14: 283–303.

Pinkney, A. (1984) *The Myth of Black Progress*, Cambridge: Cambridge University Press.

Pinnock, D. (1997) *Gang Rituals and Rites of Passage*, Cape Town: Africa Sun Press.

Pogrebin, M. (2004b) 'Introduction', in M. Pogrebin (ed.), *A View of the Offender's World: About Criminals*, Belmont, CA: Sage.

Polk, K. (1997) 'Males and honor contest violence', *Homicide Studies*, 3(1): 6–29.

Porter, J. and Washington, R. (1979) 'Black identity and self-esteem: a review of studies of the black self-concept, 1968–78', *Annual Review of Sociology*, 5: 53–74.

Powell, K. (2008) *The Black Male Handbook*, New York: Atria Books.

Proctor, A. (2006) 'Intersections of race, class, gender, and crime: future directions for feminist criminology', *Feminist Criminology*, 1(1); 1 – 27.

Pryce, K. (1979) *Endless Pressure*, London: Penguin.

Quinney, R. (1970) *The Social Reality of Crime*, Toronto: Little, Brown, and Company
——(1971/2000) 'Crime: phenomenon, problem, and subject of study', in R. Quinney (ed.), *Bearing Witness to Crime and Social Justice*, Albany, NY: State University of New York Press, pp. 3–66.

Rapport, M. (2000) 'Combining methodological approaches in research: ethnography and interpretive phenomenology', *Journal of Advanced Nursing*, 31(1): 219–25.

Reno, R. (2002) *Redemptive Change, Atonement and the Christian Cure of the Soul*, Pennsylvania: Trinity Press.

Ribbens, J. and Edwards, R. (1998) *Feminist Dilemmas in Qualitative Research*, London: Sage.

Rich, J. (2009) *Wrong Place, Wrong Time: Trauma and Violence in the Lives of Young Black Men*, Baltimore, MD: Johns Hopkins University Press.

Richeson, M. (2009) 'Sex, drugs, and race to castrate: a black box warning of chemical castration's potential racial side effects', *Harvard Black Letter Law Journal*, 25: 96–131.

Robinson, R. (2005) 'Human agency, negated subjectivity and white structural oppression', *American University Law Review*, 53: 1361–419.

Rodriguez, D. (2008) 'Investing in white innocence: colour blind racism, white privilege, and the new white racist fantasy', in L. Guerrero, *Teaching Race in the 21st Century*, London: Palgrave Macmillan.

Roediger, D. (2008) *How Race Survived US History*, London: New Left Books.

Rose, D. and Clear, T. (1998) 'Incarceration, social capital, and crime: implications for social disorganisation theory', *Criminology*, 36(3): 441–9.

Rossi, P. (1994) 'The war between the Quals and Quants: is a lasting peace possible?' *New Directions for Program Evaluation*, 61: 23–36.

Roy, K. (2006) 'Father stories: a life course examination of paternal identity among low income African American men', *Journal of Family Issues*, 27(1): 31–54.

Russell, K. (2002) 'Development of a Black criminology: the role of the black criminologist', in S. Gabbidon, H. Greene, and V. Young (eds), *African American Classics in Criminology and Criminal Justice*, New York: Sage.

Russsell-Brown, K. (2002) *The Colour of Crime*, New York: New York University Press.

Sabo, D., Kupers, T. and London, W. (2001) *Prison Masculinities*, Philadelphia, PA: Temple University Press.

Saldana, J. (2005) *Ethno-Drama: An Anthology of Reality Theatre*, New York: Rowman and Littlefield.
——(2009) *The Coding Manual for Qualitative Researchers*, London: Sage.

Sale, M. (1997) *The Slumbering Volcano*, Durham, NC: Duke University Press.

Sampson, R. and Laub, J. (1993) *Crime in the Making: Pathways and Turning Points through Life*, Cambridge, MA: Harvard University Press.

Sampson, R. and Wilson, J. (1995) *Toward a Theory of Race, Crime, and Urban Inequality*, Stanford, CA: Stanford University Press.

Sanelowski, M. (2004) 'Qualitative research,' in M. Lewis-Beck, A. Bryman, and T. Lao (eds), *The Sage Encyclopedia of Social Science Research Methods*, London: Sage.

Sawicki, J. (1991) *Disciplining Foucault*, New York: Routledge.

Schlosser, J. (2008) 'Issues in interviewing inmates: navigating the methodological landmines of prison research', *Qualitative Inquiry*, 14(8): 1500–25.

Schneider, C. (2003) 'Integrating critical race theory and postmodernism implications of race, class, and gender', *Critical Criminology*, 12: 87–103.

Scott, J. (1991) 'The evidence of experience', *Critical Inquiry*, 17: 773–9.

Scull, A. (1977) *Decarceration, Community Treatment and the Deviant: A Radical View*, New Jersey: Prentice Hall.

Seibold, C. (2000) 'Qualitative research from a feminist perspective in the postmodern era: methodological, ethical and reflexive concerns', *Nursing Inquiry*, 7: 147–55.

Serin, R. and Lloyd, C. (2009) 'Examining the process of offender change: the transition to crime desistance', *Psychology, Crime and Law*, 15(4): 347–64.

Serrant-Green, L. (2002) 'Black on Black: methodological issues for black researchers working in minority ethnic communities', *Nurse Researcher*, 9(4): 30–44.

——(2004) 'Black Caribbean men, sexual health decisions and silences', unpublished doctoral thesis, Nottingham School of Nursing, University of Nottingham, UK.

——(2010) 'The sound of silence: a framework for researching sensitive issue or marginalised perspectives in health', *Journal of Research in Nursing*, 16(4): 347–60.

Sharkey, P. (2008) 'The intergenerational transmission of context', *AJS*, 113(4): 931–69.

Shaw, C. (1930/1966) *The Jack Roller: A Delinquent Boy's Own Story*, Chicago, IL: University of Chicago Press.

Shaw, C. and McKay, H. (1942) *Juvenile Delinquency and Urban Areas*, Chicago, IL: University of Chicago Press.

Sherlock, J. (2004) *Young Parents: From Custody to Community*, London: Prison Reform Trust.

Sherman, W. L. and Strange, H. (2004) 'Experimental ethnography: the marriage of qualitative and quantitative research', *Annals of the American Academy of Political and Social Sciences*, 595(1): 204–21.

Short, J. (1997) *Poverty, Ethnicity, and Violent Crime*, Boulder, CO: Westview Press.

Shuker, R. and Sullivan, E. (2010) *Grendon and the Emergence of Forensic Therapeutic Communities*, Malden, MA: Wiley-Blackwell.

Siennick, S. E and Osgood, D. W. (2008) 'A review of research on the impact on crime of the transitions to adult roles', in A. M. Liberman (ed.), *The Long View of Crime: A Synthesis of Longtitudinal Research*, New York: Springer, pp. 161–87.

Silva, E. (2005) *Critical Pedagogy and Race*, Oxford: Blackwell.

Silverman, D. (ed.) (2004) *Qualitative Research: Theory, Method and Practice*, Thousand Oaks, CA: Sage.

Smart, U. (2001) *Grendon Tales: Stories from a Therapeutic Community*, Winchester: Waterside Press.

Smith, B., Frazier, D. and Smith, B. (1978) *The Combahee River Collective Statement*, Boston, MA: CRC.

Solorzano, D. G. (1998) 'Critical race theory, race and gender microaggressions, and the experience of Chicana and Chicano scholars', *Qualitative Studies in Education*, 11: 121–36.

Solorzano, D. and Yosso, T. (2002) 'Critical race methodology: counterstorytelling as an analytical framework', *Qualitative Inquiry*, 8(1): 23–44.

Soothill, K., Fitzpatrick, C. and Francis, B. (2009) *Understanding Criminal Careers*, Cullompton: Willan Publishing.

Spalek, B. (2008) *Ethnicity and Crime: A Reader*, Maidenhead: Open University Press.

Spence, L. (2010) 'White space, black space', *The Urbanite*, 68: 43–5.

Stanfield, J. H. and Dennis, R. M. (1993) *Race and Ethnicity in Research Methods*, London: Sage Publications.

Steele, C. M. (1997) 'A threat in the air: How stereotypes shape intellectual identity and performance', *American Psychologist*, 52: 613–29.

Steele, C. M. and Aronson, J. (1995) 'Stereotype threat and the intellectual performance of African Americans', *Journal of Personality and Social Psychology*, 69: 797–811.

Strauss, A. (1987) *Qualitative Analysis for Social Scientists*, Cambridge: Cambridge University Press.

Strauss, A. and Corbin, J. (1997) *Grounded Theory in Practice*, London: Sage.

——(1998) *Basics of Qualitative Research*, London: Sage.

Strauss, A. and Corbin, J. (1998) *Basics of Qualitative Research Techniques and Procedures for Developing Grounded Theory*, 2nd edn, London: Sage.

Sullivan, E. (2007) 'Straight from the horse's mouth', *Prison Service Journal*, 173: 9–14.

Sykes, G. M. and Matza, D. (1957) 'Techniques of neutralisation: a theory of delinquency', *American Sociological Review*, 22: 664–70.

Sykes, G. M. and Messinger, S. L. (1960) 'The inmate social system', in R. A. Cloward (ed.), *Theoretical Studies in Social Organization of the Prison*, New York: Social Science Research Council, pp. 5–19.

Thomas, J. (1993) *Doing Critical Ethnography*, London: Sage.

Tonry, M. (2011) *Punishing Race*, Oxford: Oxford University Press.

Trahan, A. (2011) 'Qualitative research and intersectionality', *Critical Criminology*, 19: 1–14.

Trainor, J. (2002) 'Critical pedagogy's "other": Constructions of whiteness in education for social change', *College Composition and Communication*, 53(4): 631–50.

Trochim, M. W. and Donnelly, J. P. (2007) *The Research Methods Knowledge Base*, 3rd edn, Mason, OH: Thomson Custom.

Turner, H. (1998) *The Structure of Sociological Theory*, Belmont, CA: Wadsworth Publishing Company.

Turner, V. (1969) *The Ritual Process: Structure and Anti-Structure*, New York: De Gruyter.

Turner, V. and Bruner, E. (1986) *The Anthropology of Experience*, Chicago: University of Illinois.

Tyson, L. (2006) *Critical Theory Today*, London: Routledge.

Uggen, C., Manza, J. and Behrens, A. (2004) 'Less than the average citizen: stigma, role transition, and the civic reintegration of convicted felons', in S. Maruna and R. Immarigeon (eds), *After Crime and Punishment: Ex-Offender Reintegration and Desistance from Crime*, Cullompton: Willan Publishing.

Unnever, J. and Gabbidon, S. (2011) *A Theory of African American Offending: Race, Racism, and Crime*, New York: Routledge.

Utsey, S. (1997) 'Racism and the psychological well-being of African American men', *Journal of African American Men*, 3(1): 69–87.

Valdes, F., Culp, J. and Harris, A. (2002) *Crossroads, Directions and a New Critical Race Theory*, Philadelphia, PA: Temple Press.

Van Gennep, A. (1960) *The Rites of Passage*, Chicago, IL: University of Chicago Press.

Wacquant, L. (2002a) 'The curious eclipse of prison ethnography in the age of mass incarceration', *Ethnography*, 3(4): 371–97.

——(2002b) 'Deadly symbiosis: when ghetto and prison meet and mesh', *Punishment and Society*, 3(1): 95–134.

Walker, S., Spohn, C. and DeLone, M. (2004) *The Color of Justice: Race, Ethnicity, and Crime in America*, Belmont, CA: Wadsworth.

Walklate, S. (1995) *Gender and Crime*, London: Prentice Hall.

Walsh, N. (2010) *Baltimore Behind BARS*, Baltimore, MD: Justice Policy Institute.

Waymer, D. (2008) 'A man: an auto-ethnographic analysis of black male identity negotiation', *Qualitative Inquiry*, 14(6): 968–89.

Weaver, B. and McNeill, F. (2010) 'Travelling hopefully: desistance research and probation practice,' in J. Brayford, F. Cowe and J. Deering (eds), Publishing *What Else Works? Creative Work with Offenders*, Cullompton: Willan.

Webber, C. (2007) 'Background, foreground, foresight: the third dimension of cultural criminology', *Crime, Media, and Culture*, 3(2): 139–57.

Weber, L. (2001) *Understanding Race, Class, Gender, and Sexuality: A Conceptual Framework*, Boston, MA: McGraw-Hill.

Weber, L. and Parra-Medina, D. (2003) 'Intersectionality and women's health: charting a path to advances', *Gender Research*, 7: 181–230.

Webster, C. (2007) *Understanding Race and Crime*, Maidenhead: Open University Press.

Webster, L. and Mertova, P. (2007) *Using Narrative Inquiry as a Research Method: An Introduction to Using Critical Event Narrative Analysis in Research on Learning and Teaching*, London: Routledge.

Weems, M. (2003) *Public Education and Imagination-Intellect*, New York: Peter Lang.

Wells-Barnett, I. (1991) *Selected Works of Ida B Wells Barnett*, New York: Oxford University Press.

West, C. (1993) *Race Matters*, Boston, MA: Beacon Press.

——(2004) *Democracy Matters*, Harmondsworth: Penguin.

West, C. and Zimmerman, D. (1987) 'Doing gender', *Gender and Society*, 1(2): 125–51.

Wetherell, M. (1996) *Identities, Groups, and Social Issues*, London: Sage.

White, A. (2008) *Ain't I a Feminist? African American Men Speak out on Fatherhood, Friendship, Forgiveness and Freedom*, Albany, NY: SUNY Press.

White, J. and Cones, J. (1999) *Black Men Emerging*, Chicago, IL: Freeman.

Wideman, D. and Preston, R. (1996) *Soulfires: Young Black Men on Love and Violence*, New York: Penguin Books.

Wideman, J. (1994) *Fatheralong: A Meditation on Fathers and Sons, Race and Society*, New York: Pantheon Books.

Wilkinson, K. (2009) *The Doncaster Desistance Study*, Sheffield: Sheffield Hallam University Press.

Williams, M. and May, T. (1996) *Introduction to the Philosophy of Social Research*, London: UCL Press.

Williams, P. (1997) *Seeing a Colour Blind Future*, London: Virago.

Wilson, A. (1994) *Black on Black Violence*, New York: Afrikan World Info Systems.

Wilson, D. (2003) *Voices of Desistance: An Ethnographic Evaluation of the C-FAR Training Programme*, Birmingham: BCU.

Wilson, D. and Moore, S. (2004) *Playing the Game: The Experiences of Young Black Men in Custody*, Birmingham: Children's Society.

Wilson, J. and Chaddha, A. (2009) 'The role of theory in ethnographic research', *Ethnography*, 10(4): 549–64.

Wilson, W. (1989) *Absent Fathers in the Inner City*, New York: Sage.

——(2009) *More Than Just Race: Being Black and Poor in the Inner City*, New York: W. W Norton.

Winlow, S. (2004) 'Masculinities and crime', *Criminal Justice Matters*, 55(1): 18–19.

——(2008) *Criminal Identities and Consumer Culture*, Cullompton: Willan Publishing.

Winn, M. (2010) 'Our side of the story: moving incarcerated youth voices from the margins to the center', *Race, Ethnicity, and Education*, 13(3): 313–25.

Wright, C., Weekes, D., McLaughlin, A. and Webb, D. (1998) 'Masculinised discourses within education and the construction of Black male identities amongst African Caribbean youth', *British Journal of Sociology of Education*, 19(1): 75–87.

Yosso, T. (2002) 'Towards a critical race curriculum', *Equity and Excellence in Education*, 35(2): 93–101.

Young, J. (2011) *The Criminological Imagination*, Cambridge: Polity Press.

Zamudio, M., Russell, C., Rios, F. and Bridegman, J. (2011) *Critical Race Theory Matters: Education and Ideology*, London: Routledge.

Zhang, S., Roberts, R. and McCollister, K. (2009) *Therapeutic Community in a California Prison*, New York: Sage.

Index

Taylor & Francis

eBooks

FOR LIBRARIES

ORDER YOUR
FREE 30 DAY
INSTITUTIONAL
TRIAL TODAY!

Over 23,000 eBook titles in the Humanities,
Social Sciences, STM and Law from some of the
world's leading imprints.

Choose from a range of subject packages or create your own!

Benefits for
you

▶ Free MARC records

▶ COUNTER-compliant usage statistics

▶ Flexible purchase and pricing options

Benefits
for your
user

▶ Off-site, anytime access via Athens or referring URL

▶ Print or copy pages or chapters

▶ Full content search

▶ Bookmark, highlight and annotate text

▶ Access to thousands of pages of quality research
at the click of a button

For more information, pricing enquiries or to order
a free trial, contact your local online sales team.

UK and Rest of World: **online.sales@tandf.co.uk**

US, Canada and Latin America:
e-reference@taylorandfrancis.com

www.ebooksubscriptions.com

ALPSP Award for
BEST eBOOK
PUBLISHER
2009 Finalist

Taylor & Francis eBooks
Taylor & Francis Group

A flexible and dynamic resource for teaching, learning and research.